INFORMATION SERVICES TO DIVERSE POPULATIONS

Developing Culturally Competent Library Professionals

Nicole A. Cooke

Library and Information Science Text Series

LIBRARIES UNLIMITED™

An Imprint of ABC-CLIO, LLC

Santa Barbara, California • Denver, Colorado

Library of Congress Cataloging-in-Publication Data

Names: Cooke, Nicole A., author.
Title: Information services to diverse populations : developing culturally competent
  library professionals / Nicole A. Cooke.
Description: Santa Barbara, California : Libraries Unlimited, an imprint of
  ABC-CLIO, LLC, [2017] | Series: Library and information science text
  series | Includes bibliographical references and index.
Identifiers: LCCN 2016031669 (print) | LCCN 2016045514 (ebook) | ISBN
  9781440834608 (paperback : acid-free paper) | ISBN 9781440834615 (ebook)
Subjects: LCSH: Libraries and minorities. | Libraries and minorities—United
  States. | Minorities in library science—Recruiting. | Multicultural services
  librarians—Employment. | Libraries and society. | Libraries and
  community. | Cultural competence. | Diversity in the workplace. |
  Social justice. | Library schools—Curricula.
Classification: LCC Z711.8 .C66 2017 (print) | LCC Z711.8 (ebook) |
  DDC 027.6—dc23
LC record available at https://lccn.loc.gov/2016031669

ISBN: 978–1–4408–3460–8
EISBN: 978–1–4408–3461–5

21 20 19 18 17   1 2 3 4 5

This book is also available as an eBook.

Libraries Unlimited
An Imprint of ABC-CLIO, LLC

ABC-CLIO, LLC
130 Cremona Drive, P.O. Box 1911
Santa Barbara, California 93116-1911
www.abc-clio.com

This book is printed on acid-free paper ∞

Manufactured in the United States of America

As with anything I write or accomplish, I dedicate my work to my mother and grandmother who always demanded that I do better in life than they did. They are tough acts to follow, and I never take their love and support for granted.

Recent Titles in
Library and Information Science Text Series

Information Services to Diverse Populations

Contents

Preface

While delivering a talk entitled "Power, Privilege and Positionality: Applying a Critical Lens to LIS Education" at the 2014 American Library Association (ALA) Annual Conference, an audience member asked me: "Diversity is trendy again in libraries and library schools. How do we keep such an important topic from being trendy?" My response to her was threefold:

1. I have been doing this work (working to diversify the field of librarianship) for over 15 years, as a library practitioner, and now as a library faculty member, and this work is not a trend for me, it is a commitment and a career. And we should be encouraging others to make similar commitments.

2. People need to write and present about diversity at professional conferences, often. We need to "slam the conferences"[1] and ensure that issues of diversity and social justice are consistent themes and not just novelty or token topics.

3. We need to have regularly offered classes in diversity and social justice (particularly those taught by full-time faculty) in more than just a handful of ALA-accredited library programs.

This is how we can help ensure that more library and information science (LIS) professionals treat diversity as more than just a trend and actually make diversity a priority and a dedicated career path. In writing this text, I hope to

---

[1]"Slam the conferences" is a reference or head nod to "Slam the Boards!" which is an ongoing initiative in which librarians make a concerted effort to answer questions on online Q&A sites such as Yahoo! Answers and even some social media sites. The idea is to increase the visibility and credibility of librarians among the general public.

contribute to the corpus and discussions the field continues to have about the how/why/what/when/where of diversifying the profession.

I have been fortunate to have the opportunities to teach dedicated courses on diversity, social justice, and race, gender, and sexuality in the information professions (in addition to infusing issues of diversity and cultural competence into other courses that I teach) (Cooke 2014a). In 2013, I developed and introduced a class at my institution (*Information Services to Diverse Populations*, the impetus for this text) because I did not see anything else like it in the curriculum, and I felt strongly that aspiring LIS professionals needed to be taught about cultural awareness, empathy, and community analysis techniques *before* graduating and immersing themselves in a diverse community. On-the-job training is valuable and essential to new professionals, but the LIS curricula around the country should be committed enough to regularly and consistently include diversity and related issues into their plan to produce quality and prepared information professionals, and they should want to stand behind one of the core tenets of the field (American Library Association 2004). It is my great belief that libraries should reflect the communities they serve, and that includes having librarians who belong to said communities. Patrons should be able to come to the library and see themselves in some way in the staff, the collections, and the programs. In order to do this, in part, LIS programs need to recruit and retain more students of color and students from a variety of diverse backgrounds. And part of that process is to have more LIS faculty of color and faculty from diverse backgrounds (Cooke 2014b). *The Virtuous Circle Model*, created by Jaeger and Hill (2007), describes this cycle in great detail; the process of effectively and compassionately serving diverse communities is multifaceted, dynamic, ongoing, and involves the professions at multiple levels.

The *Information Services to Diverse Populations* class, as you will see as you progress through the book, takes a broad look at diversity, not only encompassing racial and ethnic diversity, but also addressing other growing and equally deserving communities such as the blind and differently abled, the homeless, the mentally ill,lesbian, gay, bisexual, trans, and queer (LGBTQ) communities, and more. As part of my commitment to this area of the curriculum, I revised and institutionalized a previously dormant course, *Social Justice in the Information Professions*, and assumed and institutionalized a third class, *Race, Gender, and Sexuality, in the Information Professions* course after previous instructors left the institution. This cadre of courses not only allows more students to see themselves in the curriculum, but also allows students to focus their learning in a way that not only makes them marketable but also conditions and prepares them to serve a wide variety of diverse communities. Classes such as these provide LIS professionals a way to talk the talk *and* walk the walk. Teaching these topics in graduate school is but one way to inspire new professionals to take up this mantle and become advocates for diversity and social justice in their careers—this is but one way to get more people to write about and teach these subjects to others and more people to slam the conferences with innovative programs and ideas.

Addressing diversity and social justice in the training and education of LIS professionals is increasingly important, which is in contrast to the lack of literature in this area. This book is designed to be a comprehensive resource for graduate students, especially those with aspirations of working with diverse populations and LIS practitioners who may not have had a class in school but find themselves working with diverse communities.

This text aims to do the following:

1. Introduce readers (LIS students and those new to this area of study) to contexts and situations that will promote the development of empathy and cultural competence in current and future librarians.
2. Introduce readers to research in the areas of diversity and social justice in librarianship.
3. Introduce readers to potential employment and networking opportunities related to diversity and social justice in librarianship.

The text will assist students in learning more about important areas of librarianship, areas that are underserved, and encourage the development of cultural competence in future librarians. The development of cultural competence will benefit LIS students, librarians and library staff, employers, and the profession at large.

ORGANIZATION OF THE BOOK

This book aims to address theory and practice, beginning with a discussion of diversity, inclusive library services, and cultural competence and then moving into discussions that will hopefully enable you, the reader, to envision how these concepts can be applied in your library practice. Chapters 1 and 2 (Introduction to Diversity, Inclusion, and Information Services and Developing Cultural Competence) discuss the larger landscape of diversity and some of the academic ideas (some from different disciplines and other professions) that shape the context of services to diverse populations. In many ways, the LIS field is still trying to embrace some of these ideas, and while the field has embraced some ideas wholeheartedly (i.e., diversity recruitment), other concepts have generally been ignored (i.e., institutional racism that prevents the retention of said diverse candidates). Included in this section are discussions of concepts that will prepare LIS professionals from any background or population to be caring and competent agents of change and service to diverse populations (i.e., privilege, empathy, and cultural competence). In Chapters 3 and 4 (A Sampling of Diverse Populations and Services to Diverse Populations), the discussions revolve around contexts of inclusive services and spotlight specific diverse populations and user groups that library and other information organizations routinely serve. Serving diverse populations is certainly about ethnic and racial minorities but quickly broadens out to encompass diversity of gender, sexual orientation, socioeconomic status, and physical ability and populations that are incarcerated, homeless, and recently migrated. The list is not comprehensive but instead provides a broad foundation upon which to learn and establish practice in diverse communities. Chapter 4 continues discussing other practical matters and issues that contribute to the ongoing and effective services to diverse communities. These include outreach, collection development, community analysis, community building, evaluation, and recruitment;

all of these issues are dynamic, iterative, and absolutely necessary for the field in the short term and in the long term.

Chapter 5 (Managing Diversity) aims to discuss what happens when outstanding diverse candidates successfully complete LIS graduate programs and enter the workforce. The work of diversifying the field of LIS does not end with recruitment, rather much work needs to be done to retain, promote, and develop people of color, those from diverse groups, and those who have strong inclinations toward continuing this line of work and inquiry. The literature suggests that library and information professionals from diverse groups encounter stereotypes, discrimination, and a lack of opportunity, which can result in these librarians reaching, but not cracking, the proverbial glass ceiling. This can result in attrition and burnout, both of which keep the field from progressing and effectively servicing increasingly diverse communities. The final chapter, Chapter 6 (Becoming New Storytellers: Counter-Storytelling in LIS), concludes the book with a personal reflection, detailing parts of my journey as a minority librarian and LIS educator and the subsequent challenges associated with these roles. The chapter also serves as a call-to-action to readers, challenging you to look at your LIS practice holistically and critically and join the ranks of LIS professionals who serve diverse and marginalized populations and are telling new and wonderful stories about these communities. Three appendices are included at the end of the book to assist and direct those interested in reading more of the related literature and to provide resources and ideas for those using this text in a classroom setting.

With this text and other resources, initiatives, and conferences in the field, it is hoped that the field can move past diversity as being a trend, or taboo subject, and recognize it as an important and required component of LIS curricula and overall strategy for the betterment of the profession.

REFERENCES

American Library Association. 2004. "Core Values of Librarianship." June 29. Accessed February 9, 2016. http://www.ala.org/advocacy/intfreedom/ statementspols/corevalues.

Cooke, Nicole A. 2014a. "Creating Opportunities for Empathy and Cultural Competence in the LIS Curriculum." *SRRT Newsletter* 187. http://libr.org/srrt/ news/srrt187.php#9.

Cooke, Nicole A. 2014b. "The Spectrum Doctoral Fellowship Program: Enhancing the LIS Professoriate." *InterActions: UCLA Journal of Education and Information Studies* 10 (1). http://escholarship.org/uc/item/7vb7v4p8.

Jaeger, Paul T., and Renee E. Franklin Hill. 2007. "The Virtuous Circle: Increasing Diversity in LIS Faculties to Create More Inclusive Library Services and Outreach." *Education Libraries* 30 (1): 20–26.

Acknowledgments

There are three very important women in my life to whom I owe public gratitude.

1. Dr. Betty J. Turock (Mama B) who ushered me out of my doctoral program and into the professoriate with a mandate to leave the library profession better and more diverse than I found it.

2. Dr. Blanche Woolls, my editor and mentor, who chased me around for years to write this book. Her words of encouragement for me and my ability to influence the field through writing cannot be measured.

3. And finally, Dr. Linda C. Smith, who has diligently fostered my development as a scholar and teacher and provided me with the support and latitude necessary to create the course that inspired this book.

I remain grateful to these women for being my champions.

And my sincere thanks to my students at the School of Information Sciences at the University of Illinois, Urbana-Champaign, who have taken the *Information Services to Diverse Populations* class and are making the library world a better place.

Introduction to Diversity, Inclusion, and Information Services

WHY IS DIVERSITY IN LIBRARY AND INFORMATION SCIENCE (LIS) IMPORTANT?

In the first (of eight) tenets of the American Library Association's (ALA) Code of Ethics (2008), it is stated that librarians must "provide the highest level of service to all library users through appropriate and usefully organized resources; equitable service policies; equitable access; and accurate, unbiased, and courteous responses to all requests." Similarly, the ALA's Library Bill of Rights (1996) states, "A person's right to use a library should not be denied or abridged because of origin, age, background, or views." These are the ideas and principles that guide this text—all community members should be privy to equal access and quality resources and services, and as part of that they should have services and resources that meet their specific information needs. Library services are not one-size-fits-all, rather libraries should be as flexible, accommodating, and as diverse as our communities. Diversity is ever present and increasing in our society, and libraries should be able to meet their communities where they are, instead of offering a prepared slate of services and resources deemed suitable for them.

No one or right strategic plan, set of policies, or mission statement is appropriate for all situations or organizations. Developing specialized services and resources for diverse populations is a special endeavor, one that ultimately benefits services to all because it means that the library staff has taken the time and interest to collaborate with and get to know the community; this kind of relationship and trust building is essential to good and efficient service. Tailoring services, resources, and experiences to diverse user groups is also an ethical and legal issue. Librarians are champions of equitable access to materials and information, and particularly when supported by public funds, they have a legal obligation to provide service without discrimination based on class, race, gender, sexuality, religion, or other defining social or physical characteristics.

This book will address a selection of groups whose needs are not always recognized or well defined and not always met. This book will not address the needs of those in the business or technical sector, who would typically be served by special libraries. Instead, the focus is on groups who are defined in terms of socioeconomic, ethnic, or physical characteristics. The specific groups discussed are differentiated on the basis of age. This text looks explicitly at adult learners and seniors (children and young adults are abundantly and sufficiently addressed in other texts, articles, and programs); disabling conditions (physical and developmental disabilities); cultural, social, gender identities and sexual orientation; and language facility (non-English-speaking and the adult illiterate). For each of these groups, defining characteristics are described and suggestions are made on how libraries and staff may best serve these groups.

Within any library service community, there are nontraditional or even invisible groups to consider such as institutionalized populations, specific ethnic or religious groups, and others; and similarly, not every group discussed here may be part of a given library's service population. Unfortunately, this text cannot encompass every potential diverse population libraries serve around the world. In addition to the diverse user groups being introduced in this text, there are so many more diverse groups in existence around the country. Many groups are specific to individual communities, which are further specific to their regional, racial, religious, and cultural makeup of the larger environment. Other groups could include veterans, the Amish, homeschoolers, victims of domestic violence, and many, many more. What do all of these diverse populations have in common? They all require libraries to get to know them personally, and they deserve quality programming, services, and resources that are tailored to their specific information needs.

The intent of this text is to give an overview of issues associated with library resources and services to a sampling of diverse groups. The assumption is that service to any one group is a microcosm of general library service; the same quality service to one group should be extended to all groups, perhaps with some modifications or attention to different foci of needs. Orange and Osborne (2004) argue that librarians need to shift their focus from developing special services for specific user groups (with funds that are limited and may disappear) to sustaining quality services for all user groups. They suggest that libraries reframe the notion of outreach so that it is based on equity rather than on underserved populations per se. If the focus is on certain underserved or "special" populations, these services could be marginalized and are the first to be cut in times of budget crisis. But if the focus is on equitable service delivery, then service to specific populations is part of a larger systemic approach that serves all and has the knowledge and ability to tailor and customize services when necessary. This approach requires more of librarians and library staff—it requires flexibility, cultural competence, openness, and empathy toward the many diverse users that patronize libraries. It is in this spirit that this book is written.

Although public, academic, school, and special libraries may vary in ways resources and services are provided, an equitable and responsive library should be responsive to the heterogeneous society in which it exists; it should be actively involved in creating experiences for the community, with the community's input, and should have culturally and linguistically diverse collections and services. The "IFLA/UNESCO Multicultural Library Manifesto" (2012) states:

> The library staff is the active intermediary between users and resources. Professional education and continuing training focused on services to multicultural communities, cross-cultural communication and sensitivity, anti-discrimination, cultures and languages should be provided. The staff of a multicultural library should reflect the cultural and linguistic characteristic of the community to ensure cultural awareness, reflect the community the library serves, and encourage communication.

To this end, staff in libraries should be willing and able to serve diverse users in these capacities and should be aware of differences that may exist between themselves and the people they are serving. Patrons from diverse groups may have a variety of visible and invisible differences (or perhaps barriers) that could require extra attention, different resources, intercultural understanding, empathy, and so on. Diverse patrons can be perceived as "others" (as they may be perceived in society at large), and that could influence their approach and usage of the library and its services. This hesitancy is above and beyond the library anxiety that many library users (and nonusers) experience. It becomes that much more crucial that the library staff strives to make all patrons feel at ease, and that patrons are welcomed and can be assisted. Library professionals should strive to develop empathy and cultural competence (Elturk 2003; Overall 2009) (see Chapter 2), exhibit patience, encourage patrons, and ensure that patrons are aware of the helping role of the library. And when interfacing with patrons, library professionals should be ready, willing, and able to work with the differing work styles, language barriers, accents, and cultural norms that patrons may possess (e.g., a man of the Muslim faith may be uncomfortable speaking with a female librarian and might be more comfortable speaking with a male colleague) (Brothen and Bennett 2013). These professional attributes benefit all patrons, and particularly those from diverse user groups.

HOW DIVERSE ARE WE?

Librarianship has long been a profession dominated by women, specifically white women. According to the updated edition of the ALA's Diversity Counts document (2012a) (which reported 2009–2010 information derived from the Census Bureau's Census Bureau American Community Survey), white women comprised 72.5 percent of credentialed librarians in the country (down .5 percent from 2000–2001). The updated Diversity Counts report, released in 2012, states that there was an inconsiderable gain in the percentage of racial and ethnic minorities working as credentialed librarians—from 11 percent in 2000 to 12 percent in 2009–2010. Even with numerous programs, initiatives, and conferences specifically designed for and dedicated to recruiting and mentoring outstanding minority candidates (see Appendix 3), there still has only been a 1 percent increase in almost a decade. This is problematic; not only should the field be more diverse, but the field should be more representative of the communities being served by libraries and other information-centered organizations. Additional data reported by the updated Diversity Counts report (2012b) include:

1. Latinos compose 16.3 percent of the population, but just 3.1 percent of credentialed librarians;
2. African Americans compose 12.6 percent of the population, but just 5.1 percent of credentialed librarians;
3. Asian and Pacific Islanders compose 5 percent of the population, but just 2.7 percent of credentialed librarians; and,
4. Native Americans were less than 1 percent of the population and just 0.2 percent of credentialed librarians.

The field continues to not reflect, and perhaps not fully understand, the communities it serves.

THE INTERSECTIONALITY OF DIVERSE USERS

This book highlights several diverse user groups, and it is worth noting the intersections of these groups (see Figure 1.1). Diverse user groups do not exist in silos, rather most users represent multiple diversities (e.g., an African-American homeless veteran is suffering from post-traumatic stress disorder (PTSD) and needs assistance applying for benefits). Recalling that a one-size-fits-all approach to library services is not desirable, learning how to compassionately and competently serve diverse user groups will enable library professionals to serve all users.

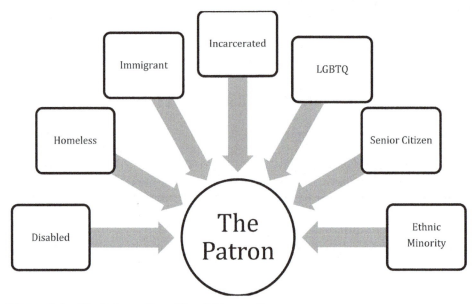

Figure 1.1   The Intersectionality of Diverse Users

Apple (2006, 61–62) aptly states, "Our communities are increasingly plural-istic and intersectional"; yet these community members are often still consid-ered the "other" and not served in the manner in which they deserve, with staff and resources that look like them and represent their experiences and informa-tion needs. Additionally, Campbell (2005, 271) says, "Libraries are organized and structured mainly by middle-class professionals who have absorbed the norms of their profession and class." This can result in feelings of exclusion on the part of diverse individuals and groups and a subsequent unwillingness to use the library and its resources, even if they are vitally needed. No one wants to feel unwanted or embarrassed. Diversity is not a trend, it is an imperative, and services and collections to diverse populations should be at the forefront of the library's priorities.

A BIT OF HISTORY

To further emphasize the need for quality services to diverse populations, a bit of history is presented here. The history of library services to diverse popula-tions is complex and not always positive or flattering. Known for welcoming immigrants (Novotny 2003) from other lands and preparing them for life in the United States, North American libraries and their library associations were also deeply segregated (Gollop 1999; Graham 2001). Du Mont (1986) recounts the early history of blacks in library education and services prior to the Civil War and the subsequent library services that were available to black communities, particularly communities in the South. In a particularly notable portion of her historical treatment, Du Mont relays the stark refusal of many library schools to admit black students in the 1930s.

LIS educator Wayne Wiegand has done significant research in archives and public records about the segregation that existed in libraries in the South (1954–1968) (Wiegand and Wiegand 2014). The records paint a stark and dis-heartening picture of how black youth were disenfranchised from library re-sources. Yet, it also depicts the bravery and activism of black youth who protested, determined that they would gain fair access to the library and infor-mation. LIS educator Cheryl Knott (2016) also addresses library segregation and makes a significant contribution to this discussion by offering a necessary reimagining of American public library history. Knott's work traces the preva-lence and subsequent termination of Jim Crow libraries in the American South. Constrained by Jim Crow laws and other legal issues, in addition to the prejudi-ces of members of the library profession, minorities were referred to branch libraries, where they were provided with inferior service and collections. Graham (2001) similarly details the path of libraries during the Civil Rights era, but even after that particularly difficult period in history, services to diverse populations, minorities in particular, were slow to emerge and somewhat inconsistent. Stern (1991) discusses the development of ethnic and special col-lections in particular libraries and/or regions; this was a start but still indi-cated that services to diverse populations were not mainstream. Even in current times, there is still ample evidence that libraries in less affluent areas still demonstrate informal segregation, based on the amount and quality of services and resources and by virtue of the neighborhood in which they are located (Buddy and Williams 2005; Hall 2007).

This is not to say that some libraries do not excel at embracing their communities and providing quality, yet customized, services. For example, Queens Borough Public Library (part of the New York Public Library) has long been an example of services to patrons for whom English is not their first language; services include English as a second language (ESL) classes and a robust system of job information centers (Berger 2012). The Seattle Public Library has increased their services for their homeless patrons (Ho 2006), and the Ferguson Public Library (Missouri) and the Enoch Pratt Free Library in Baltimore, Maryland, have both been commended for their services to their lower income and minority patrons during community uprisings (in 2014 and 2015, respectively). To be sure, libraries do phenomenal work when it comes to serving their patrons (see also Osborne, 2004), but these accounts should be the rule in library services, not the notable exceptions.

TRANSFORMATIVE LIBRARY SERVICES

In order to improve the profession in regard to diversity, the profession cannot be idealized or romanticized. As LIS educator Lorna Peterson (1999) suggests, the profession must be viewed critically and in context; a holistic and contextual approach is necessary in order to diversify the field in a meaningful and consistent manner. Peterson was explicitly discussing the language used in the profession around diversity. The words "diversity" and "multiculturalism" can become muddied and overgeneralized, ultimately diluting the work and examination that need to be done. Essentially, by celebrating watered-down multicultural efforts, emphasis and momentum are lost on the work that needs to be done around race and other such specific and sensitive issues. To emphasize Peterson's point about language, consider Box 1.1 that lists definitions of commonly used words related to diversity.

Peterson advocates for critique and careful enunciation of diversity problems and proposed solutions. Honma (2005) concurs with Peterson by asking:

> Why is it that scholars and students do not talk openly and honestly about issues of race and LIS? Why does the field have a tendency to tiptoe around discussing race and racism, and instead limit the discourse by using words such as "multiculturalism" and "diversity"? Why is the field so glaringly white yet no one wants to talk about whiteness and white privilege?

Another LIS educator and diversity advocate, Clara Chu (1999, 6), also suggests that a holistic and contextual approach is required in order to work toward transformative library services. Chu says that LIS should be examined through a "socio-political context" with a particular eye toward recognizing the dynamics and dimensions of race, privilege, and the power structure that exist within communities. Chu reminds that information is not neutral or value-free, and equity of access is always a concern. Not everyone in the community, particularly in underrepresented communities, has equal access to information

---

Box 1.1   Definitions

Culture: Customary beliefs, social forms, and material traits of a racial, religious, or social group; a set of shared attitudes, values, goals, and practices that characterizes an institution or organization.

Diversity: State or fact of being diverse; different characteristics and experiences that define individuals.

Globalization: The process of integrating regions via communications and economics.

Multiethnic/multicultural: Existence of, and interest in, many cultures within a society rather than in only a mainstream culture.

Multiculturalism: The policy or practice of giving equal attention or representation to the cultural needs and contributions of all the groups in a society.

American Library Association. "Diversity Standards: Cultural Competency for Academic Libraries (2012)," May 4, 2012, accessed March 5, 2016, http://www .ala.org/acrl/standards/diversity. Document ID: c9831d45-0593-0c14-d1f0 -d428464031f7

---

or the ability to navigate and interpret said information. Librarians need to work toward eradicating "the culture of silence" that exists in many diverse communities and ensuring that all library users have positive and transformative library experiences for patrons, which is described as accessing and using "information transforms one's reality and pushes one towards action for one's self." In order to provide transformative library services, librarians (particularly those of color) "need to collaborate with other librarians who are also working for social justice to advance multicultural librarianship and increase diversity in our professional ranks" (3).

TAKING RISKS AND DEVELOPING EMPATHY

Among the first steps in working toward transformative library services is to offer classes in LIS graduate programs that deal with diversity, social justice, and other such issues. Quite a few articles have discussed the need for diversity to be addressed substantively and consistently in the LIS curricula (Freiband 1992; Honma 2005; Jaeger et al. 2011; McCook 2000; Pawley 2006),but articles and recommendations do not always translate into classes. Such classes are enlightening and informative and will provide a solid foundation on which to build empathy and cultural competence. Classes related to diversity and social justice can sometimes be challenging, as they may introduce new topics that may be considered taboo or sensitive and require a great deal of reflection and the recognition of certain privileges. Students should be willing to respect others' viewpoints, they should be comfortable with being uncomfortable, and they should be willing to take risks in the classroom that will subsequently allow opportunities for growth.

LESSON PLAN

Essential Readings:

Honma, Todd. "Trippin' over the Color Line: The Invisibility of Race in Library and Information Studies." *InterActions: UCLA Journal of Education and Information Studies* 1, no. 2 (2005). https://escholarship.org/uc/item/4nj0w1mp.

Peterson, Lorna. "The Definition of Diversity: Two Views. A More Specific Definition." *Journal of Library Administration* 27, no. 1–2 (1999): 17–26.

Questions to Ask:

1. What diverse populations exist in your community? (This could be the community in which you work or the community in which you live.)
2. How does your library serve these populations?

As will be discussed in a later chapter, in addition to having faculty and curriculum committees deem diversity and related issues as worthy of a dedicated course(s) (or at least a meaningful component of other courses), there is still the matter of having faculty and instructors who are willing and able to teach this content. It is critical to have instructors who themselves are culturally competent and who believe in the necessity of diversity and cultural competence training of the next generations of librarians; this training matters and has been proven in the literature to improve the quality of services to diverse populations (Mestre 2010).

REFERENCES

American Library Association. 1939/1996. "Library Bill of Rights." Accessed March 5, 2016. http://www.ala.org/advocacy/proethics/codeofethics/codeethics.

American Library Association. 1939/2008. "Code of Ethics of the American Library Association." Accessed March 5, 2016. http://www.ala.org/advocacy/proethics/codeofethics/codeethics.

American Library Association. 2012a. "Diversity Counts." ALA Office for Research and Statistics and ALA Office for Diversity. Last modified September 28, 2012. http://www.ala.org/offices/diversity/diversitycounts/divcounts.

American Library Association. 2012b. American Library Association releases new data to update "Diversity Counts" report. ALA Office for Research and Statistics and ALA Office for Diversity. Last modified September 28, 2012. http://www.ala.org/news/2012/09/american-library-association-releases-new-data-update-diversity-counts-report.

Apple, M. W. 2006. *Educating the "Right" Way: Markets, Standards, God, and Inequality.* New York: Routledge.

Berger, Joseph. 2012. "Queens Libraries Speak the Mother Tongue." *The New York Times*, January 2. Accessed January 9, 2016. http://www.nytimes.com/2012/01/03/nyregion/queens-libraries-serve-59-languages.html?_r=0.

Brothen, Erin, and Erika Bennett. 2013. "The Culturally Relevant Reference Interview." In *Library Services for Multicultural Patrons: Strategies to*

Encourage Library Use, edited by Carol Smallwood and Kim Becnel, 297–302. Lanham, MD: Rowman & Littlefield.

Buddy, Juanita Warren, and Merchuria Chase Williams. 2005. "A Dream Deferred: School Libraries and Segregation." *American Libraries* 36 (2): 33–35.

Campbell, Brian. 2005. " 'In' versus 'With' the Community: Using a Community Approach to Public Library Services." *Feliciter* 51: 271–273.

Chu, Clara M. 1999. "Transformative Information Services: Uprooting Race Politics." Speech, Black Caucus of the American Library Association Conference, Las Vegas, July 19–22.

Du Mont, Rosemary Ruhig. 1986. "Race in American Librarianship: Attitudes of the Library Profession." *Journal of Library History* 21 (3): 488–509.

Elturk, Ghada. 2003. "Diversity and Cultural Competency." *Colorado Libraries* 29 (4): 5–7.

Freiband, Susan J. 1992. "Multicultural Issues and Concerns In Library Education." *Journal of Education for Library and Information Science* 33 (4): 287–294.

Gollop, Claudia J. 1999. "Library and Information Science Education: Preparing Librarians for a Multicultural Society." *College & Research Libraries* 60 (4): 385–395.

Graham, Patterson Toby. 2001. "Public Librarians and the Civil Rights Movement: Alabama, 1955–1965." *The Library Quarterly: Information, Community, and Policy* 71 (1): 1–27.

Hall, Tracie D. 2007. "Race and Place: A Personal Account of Unequal Access." *American Libraries* 38 (2): 30–33.

Ho, Vanessa. 2006. "New Library a Haven for Homeless." *The Seattle Post Intelligencer*, November 28. Accessed January 9, 2016. http://www.seattlepi.com /local/article/New-library-a-haven-for-homeless-1221014.php.

Honma, Todd. 2005. "Trippin' over the Color Line: The Invisibility of Race in Library and Information Studies." *InterActions: UCLA Journal of Education and Information Studies* 1 (2). http://escholarship.org/uc/item/4nj0w1mp.

"IFLA/UNESCO Multicultural Library Manifesto: The Multicultural Library— A Gateway to a Cultural Diverse Society in Dialogue." March 5, 2012. Accessed January 10, 2016. http://www.ifla.org/files/assets/library-services-to -multicultural-populations/publications/multicultural_library_manifesto -en.pdf.

Jaeger, Paul T., Mega M. Subramaniam, Cassandra B. Jones, and John Carlo Bertot. 2011. "Diversity and LIS Education: Inclusion and the Age of Information." *Journal of Education for Library and Information Science* 53 (3): 166–183.

Knott, Cheryl. 2016. *Not Free, Not for All: Public Libraries in the Age of Jim Crow.* Amherst, MA: University of Massachusetts Press.

McCook, Kathleen de la Peña. 2000. "Ethnic Diversity in Library and Information Science." *Library Trends* 49 (1): 1–5.

Mestre, Lori S. 2010. "Librarians Working with Diverse Populations: What Impact Does Cultural Competency Training Have on Their Efforts?" *The Journal of Academic Librarianship* 36 (6): 479–488.

Novotny, Eric. 2003. "Library Services to Immigrants: The Debate in the Library Literature, 1900–1920, and a Chicago Case Study." *Reference & User Services Quarterly* 42 (4): 342–352.

Orange, Satia Marshall, and Robin Osborne. 2004. "Introduction." In *From Outreach to Equity: Innovative Models of Library Policy and Practice*, edited by Robin Osborne, xi–xvii. Chicago: American Library Association.

Osborne, Robin, ed. 2004. *From Outreach to Equity: Innovative Models of Library Policy and Practice.* Chicago: American Library Association.

Overall, Patricia Montiel. 2009. "Cultural Competence: A Conceptual Framework for Library and Information Science Professionals." *The Library Quarterly* 79 (2): 175–204.

Pawley, Christine. 2006. "Unequal Legacies: Race and Multiculturalism in the LIS Curriculum." *The Library Quarterly: Information, Community, and Policy* 76 (2): 149–168.

Peterson, Lorna. 1999. "The Definition of Diversity: Two Views. A More Specific Definition." *Journal of Library Administration* 27 (1–2): 17–26.

Stern, Stephen. 1991. "Ethnic Libraries and Librarianship in the United States: Models and Prospects." *Advances in Librarianship* 15: 77–102.

Wiegand, Wayne, and Shirley Wiegand. 2014. "This Hallowed Place: The Desegregation of Public Libraries in the American South, 1954–1968." Lecture, African American Expression in Print and Digital Culture from Center for the History of Print & Digital Culture, Madison, WI, September 18.

Chapter 2

Developing Cultural Competence

WHAT ARE WE DOING IN OUR PRACTICE?

The communities served by libraries are increasingly diverse, diverse in dynamic and nuanced ways. Recent critiques of library and information science (LIS) on social media platforms and in the literatures related to critical pedagogy (Bishop et al. 1999, 2003; Elmborg 2006; Leckie, Given, and Buschman 2010; Olson 1998, 2001; Pawley 2006) and feminist pedagogy (Accardi 2013; Accardi, Drabinski, and Kumbier 2010; Hannigan 1994; Olson 1997) have suggested that LIS graduate programs and professional competencies are wrongly and stubbornly focused on training aspiring librarians and information professionals to serve middle-class and affluent nonminority patrons. Services to these majority and homogeneous populations are centered on technology such as maker spaces in libraries and classes on Microsoft Word and other white-collar applications. What services are being offered to the potentially technologically disadvantaged blue-collar workers who come to the library at night to access email because they have no Internet connection at home? What other diverse populations are our libraries not serving or underserving? (See Chapter 4 for examples.) These deficits in services are not necessarily intentional or the result of malice, rather they are most likely a result of a lack of cultural awareness and insufficient knowledge of the communities being served.

The field of librarianship remains overwhelmingly white and female (American Library Association 2012a, 2012b), and as such, the professional workforce does not adequately mirror the diverse communities being served. It can be a difficult task for a homogeneous majority workforce to serve unfamiliar communities that are increasingly pluralistic and intersectional (Apple 2006, 61), but it needs to be done in a sensitive and authentic way. Vanessa Morris (2007, 10) suggests that librarianship needs a more "humanistic lens" in order to serve "fluidly pluralistic patron communities where citizens possess overlapping cultural identities, and may have interchanging information needs based on those various identities." Morris continues by stating:

Because the profession is basically white and female, it behooves library schools to ensure that students are taught competencies that create librarians that are culturally aware of their own social and cultural privilege as well as aware of the social and cultural realities of the under-privileged. (11)

Therefore, the process of building and maintaining cultural competence is a multistep endeavor. Library professionals must engage in critical self-reflection and *then* become involved in the process of getting to know their communities, by conducting their own research and investigation and by building relationships with community members and talking to them. Cultural competence, as will be described in the following sections, is a nuanced, dynamic, and continuous process. It is a process that requires time and effort but one that yields profound results. Kathleen de la Pena McCook (2000, 165) reminds us that "librarians must be involved in community-building initiatives so that our work is seen as vital to the growing national agenda for civic involvement. This is important because the work we do can be essential in helping communities gain resiliency."

CRITICAL SELF-REFLECTION: A PRECURSOR TO CULTURAL COMPETENCE

A good deal of internal work needs to be done, by the individual and an organization, before the work of becoming culturally competent can begin. This section describes a multistep and critical self-reflection that needs to occur before cultural competence is possible. In order to understand others and learn about them, we must first understand ourselves.

Reflection is a method by which learners critically and thoughtfully contemplate the content they are learning and applying to their lives and repertoires. Author Jennifer Moon (2004, 76) suggests that reflection is a form of personal documentation, the purpose to document "experiences and development" in such a way that will enhance intellectual and emotional growth. Ideally, the practice of reflection will develop LIS professionals as reflective practitioners and provide an additional sense of direction and purpose to the service work being done in libraries. Moon indicates that there are several levels of reflection, including descriptive reflection as in describing an event; dialogic reflection as in stepping back from an event and contemplating the reasons for said event; and critical reflection as in contemplating reasons for events in the "broader social, ethical, moral or historical contexts" (75). It is surmised that librarians willing to engage in critical self-reflection, in advance of getting to know their diverse communities, will experience dialogic, if not critical, reflection.

Librarian and author Troy Swanson (2010) concurs by stating:

Reflective practice describes the inward activity that is performed in an outward fashion during dialogue. One questions oneself, and through the process of understanding one's actions, one is able to develop a "theory of actions." ... In this process, one can become more sensitive to one's own reasons for action, while developing the ability to understand the actions of others. Critical reflective practice allows us to consider our own beliefs of the other with a certain amount of equality. (286)

In this way, critical self-reflection will lead to an outcome—readiness to engage with cultural competence building; but it will also enable an individual to query his or her own value system. In addition to evaluating the pulse of one's own value system, it is important to situate ourselves in regard to our own intersectionality, privilege, and marginality. Only then can the circumstances and scenarios of others be understood and fully appreciated.

Intersectionality

Intersectionality is a feminist sociological theory posited by Kimberlé Crenshaw, a legal scholar who focuses on issues of race and gender. Crenshaw suggests that everyone possesses multiple identities, and these identities comprise a whole and multifaceted person. Each identity is representative of how each person experiences life in society. Each person has different and valid experiences, but the rights certain groups experience may not be equivalent to the rights experienced (or not experienced) by other groups. For example, if examining her own intersectionality, this author would describe herself as: African-American, Christian, a holder of graduate degrees, heterosexual, female, middle-class, able-bodied, young, and an American citizen. Each of these separate and equally significant identities works in tandem to form a larger identity (see Figure 2.1). This identity can become complex if there is dissonance between the identities. In the year 2015, being a member of the Christian faith was an advantage as opposed to being a member of the Muslim faith, as was being heterosexual as

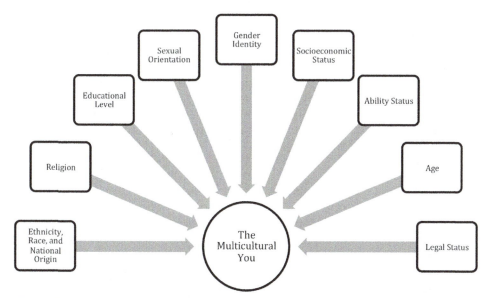

Figure 2.1   Author's rendering, inspired by Paul Gorski's Circles of My Multicultural Self activity (http://www.edchange.org/multicultural/activities/circlesofself.html)

opposed to being a transgendered person, being able-bodied, and a university graduate. These identities work in my favor and afford me certain levels of social privilege. However, being African-American as opposed to being white, and being a female as a opposed to being a male still prove to be a disadvantage in certain circumstances and environments; these nonprivileged identities can serve as conduits to marginality. Intersectionality is complex, but it is what makes humans wonderfully diverse and unique. Crenshaw (1995, 378) states, "Through an awareness of intersectionality, we can better acknowledge and ground the differences among us and negotiate the means by which these differences will find expression in constructing group politics."

Social Privilege

As mentioned in the previous paragraph, social privilege is another sociological concept that suggests that certain identities have advantages not native or common to other groups. Black and Stone (2005) offer this explanation of social privilege:

> First, privilege is a special advantage; it is neither common nor universal. Second, it is granted, not earned or brought into being by one's individual effort or talent. Third, privilege is a right or entitlement that is related to a preferred status or rank. Fourth, privilege is exercised for the benefit of the recipient and to the exclusion or detriment of others. Finally, a privileged status is often outside of the awareness of the person possessing it. (244)

Privilege can be a sensitive and complicated issue, one that can be met with defensiveness and/or guilt. Derald Wing Sue (2001, 795), who has researched extensively in this area, suggests that this type of reaction is common because "issues of race, gender, sexual orientation, and disability seem to touch 'hot buttons' in all of us because they bring to light issues of oppression and the unpleasantness of personal biases." The idea of acknowledging privilege is to raise awareness of those without the same advantages, not to belittle or chastise those who benefit from social privilege(s). As Elturk (2003, 5) simply states:

> We need to recognize and admit that our society suffers from biases, stereotypes, prejudices, racism and institutional racism. It is not something we need to feel guilty about, nor should we be held responsible for the situation as long as we are working to end these injustices.

With this understanding in mind, it becomes easier to recognize and accept the privileges that exist around us. For example, heterosexual individuals, who do not have to be fearful of showing affection to their partner in public, enjoy a privilege. Christian women, who do not have to worry about being physically or verbally accosted for wearing a religious headscarf such as the hijab/burka/niqab for Muslim women, benefit from a privilege. These social privileges are not about the individual, but rather they are part and parcel of an identity-based group to which he or she belongs. They are not earned, nor are they simply dismissed or rejected. Understanding the privileges each group is afforded, and consequently the marginalities of others, facilitates the understanding of and empathy for people and groups different from us.

Social Marginalization

Think of social marginalization as the flip side of a coin, the other side being social privilege. When the privileges of others are unchallenged and those in disadvantaged positions remain so, that is known as social marginalization. Vasas (2005, 194) defines social marginalization as "the process through which individuals or groups are peripheralized on the basis of their identities, associations, experiences, and environments." Marginalization creates vulnerable communities and populations. Social marginalization is also a social justice issue, insomuch as vulnerable populations are subject to systemic inequities, which become worse the longer they are left untreated, and correcting these long-term imbalances becomes very difficult and unsurprisingly devolves into vicious catch-22.

Bring the pieces of intersectionality, social privilege, and social marginalization together, and reflect on how they impact the diverse people patronizing libraries. Consider the homeless patron who may come into your library and think about his or her intersectionality. Not only is he or she homeless, but this person might be a veteran, mentally unstable, a college graduate, a senior citizen, a Latina, Jewish, and/or gay (refer back to Figure 1.1). The possibilities are endless. Is this homeless patron welcome in your library? Does this intersectionality make him or her more or less of a person worthy of service? Does your library offer services and collections diverse and robust enough to accommodate this patron as a whole person? Or can your collection only accommodate one or two of his or her identities? Will this person see him- or herself at your library and want to return?

Librarian, author, and social justice advocate Audre Lorde (1984, 27) once said, "It is not our differences that divide us. It is our inability to recognize, accept, and celebrate those differences." Libraries and their staffs need to be ready, willing, and able to assess themselves in order to be able to accept and celebrate the differences of their patrons. Effective and culturally responsive services require this critical self-reflection and empathy toward diverse populations.

CULTURAL COMPETENCE

Once the self-work has been completed, the work of becoming and staying culturally competent begins. An interdisciplinary concept with roots in the literatures of medicine, nursing, psychiatry, psychotherapy, occupational therapy, clinical psychology, counseling, substance abuse, public health, transplantation, ethnology, student affairs, child and family welfare, law enforcement (Smith 1997, 5), education, and social work, cultural competence requires that practitioners be willing and able to work with and for clients and patrons of diverse backgrounds and cultures. Different than cultural awareness and cultural sensitivity, cultural competence compels us to act and not just be cognizant of people's differences. In the case of library services, librarians should be actively collecting materials representative of the populations being served and then cataloging them accordingly. Librarians should be having programs and designing instruction sessions that will reflect the needs of diverse users. Librarians should be trained and poised to continuously learn about the cultures, customs, behaviors, and information needs of the varied user groups using their libraries.

Being culturally competent is important, because it is not uncommon for members of the public to feel as though their service providers employ oppressive practices, "cannot relate to their life circumstances, are insensitive to their needs, do not accept or respect them, are arrogant and contemptuous, and have little insight as to their own personal biases" (Sue 2001, 801). And for agencies such as libraries that provided free and added value services, if patrons feel they are not welcome or represented in the library, they do not have to patronize us or return for subsequent visits.

As Boyle and Springer (2001, 58) suggest, being culturally competent entails being knowledgeable about "(1) how ethnicity, social class, and oppression contribute to group identity, coping skills, and problems encountered by minority groups, (2) how group factors interact with individual development, and (3) how inequity is upheld in social service systems." The authors' suggestions imply that cultural competence should be happening on three levels: the micro or individual, meso or organizational, and macro or societal.

Cultural competence, while perhaps most important for individuals, is a goal for organizations to strive for as well. It is not unusual to have cognitive dissonance exist when a culturally competent person(s) works for an organization that is not culturally competent or is "monocultural," has a "personal resistance to cultural competence," (Sue 2011, 804), or has "cultural conditioning and biased education" (816). This cognitive dissonance can be difficult, particularly when individuals are working against, or in the absence of, organizational policies, strategic plans and goals, and the like that are not culturally competent or empathetic, but having this competence on the front lines is crucial because that is what the patrons will see and appreciate first. A suggestion for dealing with dissonance between individuals and their organizations is to rely upon and become involved with other like-minded colleagues and professional organizations (see Appendix 3); there are numerous groups, committees, and LIS organizations dedicated to issues of diversity, social justice, and cultural competence that can assist library staff who may need extra support and guidance in this area.

Cultural Competence in the LIS Literature

"Many fields have codified cultural competence. It may be time for librarianship to adopt a similar code" (Press and Diggs-Hobson, 2005, 407). Fortunately, the concept of cultural competence has made its way into the LIS literature. Among the best treatments to date were written by Patricia Montiel Overall (2009) and Ghada Elturk (2003), with Overall taking a scholarly and theoretical approach and Elturk succinctly applying the theory to everyday library practice. Overall (2009, 189–190) defines cultural competence, as it pertains to LIS as:

> Cultural competence is the ability to recognize the significance of culture in one's own life and in the lives of others; and to come to know and respect diverse cultural backgrounds and characteristics through interaction with individuals from diverse linguistic, cultural, and socioeconomic groups; and to fully integrate the culture of diverse groups into services, work, and institutions in order to enhance the lives of both those being served by the library profession and those engaged in service.

Overall notes that the LIS profession has much work to do in this area, and at the time this chapter is being written, this is still the case, particularly as diverse communities are increasingly pluralistic and the professional ranks continue to *not* be as diverse as the communities being served. She also warns against using cultural competence as a buzzword; again, cultural competence is about more than awareness, it is about continued learning and action. Elturk (2003) also explains that being culturally competent requires work, commitment, and practice. There are no golden rules or prescriptive steps to achieving and maintaining cultural competence; rather it is like learning an additional language and working to attain fluency.

Other LIS scholars compliment and extend the work of Overall and Elturk in their suggestions that cultural competence as well as issues of race, diversity, and social justice be taught in LIS graduate programs (Cooke and Sweeney 2017; Cooke, Sweeney, and Noble 2016; Gollop 1999; Honma 2005; Kumasi and Hill 2013; Pawley 2006). Incorporating this content into the LIS graduate programs (see Chapter 5) is but one step toward infusing more cultural competence into the field and into libraries.

Cultural Competence Continuum

Another cultural competence article that deserves special notation is that of Cross et al. (1989)—"Towards a Culturally Competent System of Care"—a discussion rooted in applied health sciences. This article is significant because it presents cultural competence as a continuum and as a process. The steps of continuum include:

1. Cultural destructiveness: racism and attitudes, which actively harm and/or denigrate other cultures;
2. Cultural incapacity: no intent to actively harm, but racism and destructive attitudes remain;
3. Cultural blindness: otherwise known as color blindness, a deliberate lumping together of groups and refusal to acknowledge differences between them;
4. Cultural precompetence: acknowledgment of the differences between groups, but little to no movement toward working with/for diverse groups;

5. Basic cultural competence: increasing acceptance and respect for differences, efforts to engage in self-assessment and research about diverse groups; and

6. Advanced cultural competence: high levels of respect for and knowledge of other cultures, actively working for and with diverse groups.

The continuum is a useful way to think about culture competence development because it implies progression and movement. However, it might be even more useful to think of this development as a cycle, instead of a linear process, as cultural competence does not simply begin and end, it is an ongoing process (see Figure 2.2). Maintaining cultural competence requires consistent work, and if that work is not done, it is possible to move backward on the scale, particularly since diverse communities are dynamic and prone to change. It is also possible to be culturally competent in one culture and not in another. For example, if you are a branch librarian in a large public library system, you might be working in a library that serves a predominantly Chinese population. Becoming knowledgeable of that community, of their culture, rituals, information habits, language capabilities, and the like does not mean that you will remain culturally competent if you are transferred to another branch that serves a community comprised of second generation Nigerian-Americans. Each community is distinct and has its own needs; there are also communities within communities, all of which deserve recognition and special attention in regards to library services and collections.

Press and Diggs-Hobson (2005) build on the notions presented in the continuum and suggest practical steps for becoming culturally competent in libraries, and they also emphasize the consistent work required to maintain competency. This work includes maintaining a professional attitude and engaging in ongoing self-reflections; continuously building new knowledge about the communities being served in regard to library instruction, reference, collection development, and other core functions of library service (Alpi 2001; Helton 2010; Mi 2005); and continually developing and refining skill sets. This includes staff training, proficiency in cross-cultural communication (Mestre 2010), and conducting a community analysis (discussed in the next sections of this chapter). Cultural competence is not just a skill set, but it is a foundational knowledge base that requires us to be critical thinkers and critically conscious (Kumagai and Lypson 2009).

CULTURAL HUMILITY

Perhaps an extension of the aforementioned cultural competence continuum is the concept of cultural humility, also first seen in the applied health sciences literature. Levi (2009, 97) states that cultural humility "goes beyond the concept of cultural competence" and requires practitioners to examine and identify the underlying issues that produce and exacerbate instances of inequality in the diverse communities we serve. Specifically, Levi suggests that practitioners should:

Take responsibility for our interactions with others, by actively listening to those from differing backgrounds while at the same time being

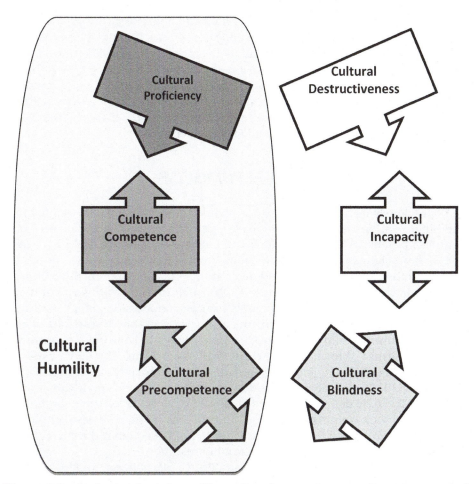

Figure 2.2 Author's adaptation of the cultural competence continuum presented in Cross, T., B. Bazron, K. Dennis, and M. Isaacs. 1989. "Towards a Culturally Competent System of Care." Vol. I. Washington, DC: Georgetown University Child Development Center, Child and Adolescent Service System Program Technical Assistance Center.

attuned to what we are thinking and feeling about other cultures; cultural humility encourages self-reflection and self-awareness. Cultural humility does not have an end point of understanding; it mandates a lifelong commitment. (97)

Isaacson (2014, 251) concurs by suggesting that practitioners should exercise humility and vulnerability in order for patrons to be able to assert their expertise about their own lives and culture. This is certainly applicable to librarians serving diverse publics. Very much like cultural competence, cultural humility is an "ongoing, courageous, and honest process of self-critique and self-awareness" that challenges us to examine our "own patterns of unintentional and intentional racism, classism, and homophobia" (Tervalon and Murray-Garcia 1998, 120). Where cultural humility stretches the idea of cultural competence is in its challenge to recognize the power dynamics and imbalances that exist between service providers and those receiving services. Cultural humility also challenges practitioners to rectify these power imbalances whenever possible, especially in regard to race, ethnicity, class, linguistic ability, and sexual orientation. In this way, services to diverse populations are really a social justice issue. Revisiting Figure 2.2, cultural humility is not a static end goal; rather, it is a dynamic mind-set or orientation that culturally competent practitioners engage within when serving their diverse communities and stakeholders.

COMMUNITY ANALYSIS

As previously mentioned, librarians should make every effort to get to know and build relationships with their diverse patron groups. There is no one-size-fits-all approach to library services and collections. Sarling and Van Tassel (1999, 9) proclaimed, "Information needs become more complex as our society becomes more diverse. . . . It is no longer sufficient to rely on intuitive impressions in designing services." Their 1999 proclamation is just as valid and needed decades later. One way to move past our impressions of a community and thoroughly ascertain what patron groups want in their libraries is to conduct a community analysis. There are many ways to conduct a community analysis—formal, informal, long-term, and short-term. The text *Assessing Information Needs: Managing Transformative Library Services* by Grover, Greer, and Agada (2010) is an excellent guide and provides the steps to do this process well; in order to be done well, libraries should have goals for their community analysis and seek training on various data collection and analysis techniques. If the right information is not collected, or is not collected in the correct way, the community analysis will not yield quality results.

By collecting both quantitative and qualitative information, and ideally both types of information should be sought, librarians will have rich information through which to become more familiar with their communities and be able to use that information to build and improve collections, create programs, and improve services. Quantitative information, such as that derived from the U.S. Census or surveys, can provide an overview of the community, and these data can be compared to nearby or similar communities, on both the local and national levels. Qualitative information, such as that derived from interviews and focus groups, observation, and community meetings, provides rich anecdotal information and puts the quantitative data into context. Qualitative data give a voice to the community and their needs.

Ultimately, this process is about getting to know your community, which can also be achieved through conversation and relationship development. This relationship building can happen inside the library, but it may be most beneficial for librarians to come from behind the desk and get to know people in the community, *in* their own settings and locations. Public librarian Cecilia Feltis describes this as "dating" your community (Jaeger et al. 2015, 161). Feltis describes going to local businesses and centers in her community, personally introducing herself and the library's services.

By taking time out and demonstrating genuine interest in her community members and their needs, she was able to improve her collection and increase the usage of the library by the community. Community analysis is a valuable tool that allows librarians to get to know the individuals, groups, agencies, and lifestyles of a given community (Greer and Hale 1982); it will identify gaps in services and collections and provide the information necessary to innovate in new areas.

CULTURALLY COMPETENT LIBRARY SERVICE—A CALL TO ACTION

In 1999, John Berry issued a call to action in *Library Journal*, urging library professionals to become culturally competent. He stated:

> Cultural competence would allow LIS professionals and libraries to reconstruct themselves. Unfortunately, the history of the profession has shown that cultural competence has rarely blessed our professional practice or even penetrated our professional consciousness. Librarians seldom learn the language, collect the literatures, or understand in any deep way the beliefs, traditions, morals and morés, lifestyles, or aspirations and expectations of the minority cultures in their midst. We reach out to hand them only our culture and heritage, rather than receiving and learning about theirs and respectfully adding them to our collections and personal service. (Berry 1999, 112)

Berry echoes Overall (2009), Elturk (2003), and others by highlighting the importance of prioritizing the cultures of our patrons, instead of assuming that we as professionals know what is best for the community. The community members determine their own needs and the library should be providing opportunities for these patrons to express their experiences and needs, and in turn, the library should be listening and responding.

With open-mindedness and a commitment to cultural competence, a culturally competent library, comprised of culturally competent professionals, will value diversity, be adaptable and able to embrace varying levels and types of diversity, be willing to engage in the continuous acquisition of cultural knowledge, and be led by culturally competent administrators. It will have mechanisms and policies in place in order to infuse diversity and inclusion throughout the organization.

Sandra Rios-Balderrama (2006, 3) reminds us that the development of cultural competence in libraries is critical, and to achieve it we must: "(1) be interested in learning from and with people from other cultures; (2) self-assess our own cultural values and consider how we obtained them; and (3) grow our competency level from awareness to knowledge to experience." Growing our cultural competence is an ongoing process, one that may not always be easy, but is worthwhile and necessary if libraries are to remain at the heart of our communities.

LESSON PLAN

Essential Readings:

Grover, Robert, Roger C. Greer, and John Agada. *Assessing Information Needs: Managing Transformative Library Services.* Santa Barbara, CA: ABC-CLIO, 2010.

Press, Nancy Ottman, and Diggs-Hobson, Mary. "Providing Health Information to Community Members Where They Are: Characteristics of the Culturally Competent Librarian." *Library Trends* 53, no. 3 (2005): 397–410.

Sue, Derald Wing. "Multidimensional Facets of Cultural Competence." *The Counseling Psychologist* 29, no. 6 (2001): 790–821.

Tervalon, Melanie, and Jann Murray-Garcia. "Cultural Humility versus Cultural Competence: A Critical Distinction in Defining Physician Training Outcomes in Multicultural Education." *Journal of Health Care for the Poor and Underserved* 9, no. 2 (1998): 117–125.

Questions to Ask:

1. Where are you on the cultural competence continuum? Where do you aspire to be on the continuum?

2. Where do you think others are on the continuum?

3. What strategies can you/have you developed to work with colleagues and organizations that are not yet culturally competent?

4. What practical things can you do in your organization to better serve patrons from other cultures and enable them to better use your library?

Assignment:

Download and complete the Circles of My Multicultural Self exercise found at this URL: http://www.edchange.org/multicultural/activities/circlesofself.html.

The Circles of My Multicultural Self Exercise (as depicted in Figure 1.1 and Figure 2.1) is a powerful one, one that I use in many of my courses, guest lectures, and training workshops. It is an opportunity to reflect on our individual identities and consider how our own cultures and beliefs are similar to and different from that of the people we serve and work with in libraries. In order to get the most from this exercise, I would encourage you to dig deep and think about who you are beyond cursory labels such as wife, son, teacher, friend, and the like. Instead, I challenge you to think about the core of who you are. For example, what is your gender identity? What is your sexual orientation? What is your socioeconomic status? How do these points of your identity intersect and/or work in opposition of one another? Do you privilege certain identities over others? Why do you do that, and how does it make you feel?

Feel free to add more circles, other shapes, and connectors to the original graphic, and change their sizes to reflect importance, and so forth, as you critically reflect on the various components of your individual identity. Then, contemplate how your multifaceted identity might influence your practice as a culturally competent librarian.

REFERENCES

Accardi, Maria T. 2013. *Feminist Pedagogy for Library Instruction*. Sacramento, CA: Library Juice Press, LLC.

Accardi, Maria T., Emily Drabinski, and Alana Kumbier, eds. 2010. *Critical Library Instruction: Theories and Methods*. Sacramento, CA: Library Juice Press, LLC.

Alpi, Kristine M. 2001. "Multicultural Health Information Seeking: Achieving Cultural Competency in the Library." *Journal of Hospital Librarianship* 1 (1): 51–59.

American Library Association. 2012a. "Diversity Counts." ALA Office for Research and Statistics and ALA Office for Diversity. Last modified September 28, 2012. http://www.ala.org/offices/diversity/diversitycounts/divcounts.

American Library Association. 2012b. American Library Association releases new data to update "Diversity Counts" report. ALA Office for Research and Statistics and ALA Office for Diversity. Last modified September 28, 2012. http://www.ala.org/news/2012/09/american-library-association-releases-new-data-update-diversity-counts-report.

Apple, Michael W. 2006. *Educating the "Right" Way: Markets, Standards, God, and Inequality*. New York: Routledge.

Berry, John. 1999. "Culturally Competent Service." *Library Journal* 124 (14): 112.

Bishop, Ann Peterson, Bharat Mehra, Imani Bazzell, and Cynthia Smith. 2013. "Participatory Action Research and Digital Libraries: Refraining Evaluation." In *Digital Library Use: Social Practice in Design and Evaluation*, edited by Ann Peterson-Kemp, Nancy A. Van House, and Barbara B. Buttenfield, 161–190. Boston, MA: MIT Press.

Bishop, Ann P., Tonyia J. Tidline, Susan Shoemaker, and Pamela Salela. 1999. "Public Libraries and Networked Information Services in Low-Income Communities." *Library and Information Science Research* 21 (3): 361–390.

Black, Linda L., and David Stone. 2005. "Expanding the Definition Of Privilege: The Concept of Social Privilege." *Journal of Multicultural Counseling and Development* 33 (4): 243–255.

Boyle, David P., and Alyson Springer. 2001. "Toward a Cultural Competence Measure for Social Work with Specific Populations." *Journal of Ethnic and Cultural Diversity in Social Work* 9 (3–4): 53–71.

Cooke, Nicole A., and Miriam E. Sweeney, eds. 2017. *Teaching for Justice: Implementing Social Justice in the LIS Classroom*. Sacramento, CA: Library Juice Press.

Cooke, Nicole A., Miriam E. Sweeney, and Safiya U. Noble. 2016. "Social Justice as Topic and Tool: An Attempt to Transform an LIS Curriculum and Culture." *The Library Quarterly: Information, Community, Policy* 86 (1): 107–124.

Crenshaw, Kimberlé. 1995. "Mapping the Margins: Intersectionality, Identity Politics, and Violence against Women of Color." In *Critical Race Theory: The Key Writings that Formed the Movement*, edited by Kimberlé Crenshaw, Neil Gotanda, Gary Peller, and Kendall Thomas, 357–383. New York: New Press.

Cross, T., B. Bazron, K. Dennis, and M. Isaacs. 1989. "Towards a Culturally Competent System of Care." Vol. I. Washington, DC: Georgetown University Child Development Center, Child and Adolescent Service System Program Technical Assistance Center.

Elmborg, James. 2006. "Critical Information Literacy: Implications for Instructional Practice." *The Journal of Academic Librarianship* 32 (2): 192–199.

Elturk, Ghada. 2003. "Diversity and Cultural Competency." *Colorado Libraries* 29 (4, Winter): 5.

Gollop, Claudia J. 1999. "Library and Information Science Education: Preparing Librarians for a Multicultural Society." *College & Research Libraries* 60 (4): 385–395.

Greer, Roger C., and Martha L. Hale. 1982. "The Community Analysis Process." In *Public librarianship: A Reader*, edited by Jane Robbins-Carter, 358–367. Englewood, CO: Libraries Unlimited.

Grover, Robert, Roger C. Greer, and John Agada. 2010. *Assessing Information Needs: Managing Transformative Library Services*. Santa Barbara, CA: ABC-CLIO.

Hannigan, Jane Anne. 1994. "A Feminist Standpoint for Library and Information Science Education." *Journal of Education for Library and Information Science* 35 (4): 297–319.

Helton, Rae. 2010. "Diversity Dispatch: Increasing Diversity Awareness with Cultural Competency." *Kentucky Libraries* 74 (4): 22–24.

Honma, Todd. 2005. "Trippin' over the Color Line: The Invisibility of Race in Library and Information Studies." *InterActions: UCLA Journal of Education and Information Studies* 1 (2). https://escholarship.org/uc/item/4nj0w1mp.

Isaacson, Mary. 2014. "Clarifying Concepts: Cultural Humility or Competency." *Journal of Professional Nursing* 30 (3): 251–258.

Jaeger, Paul T., Nicole A. Cooke, Cecilia Feltis, Michelle Hamiel, Fiona Jardine, and Katie Shilton. 2015. "The Virtuous Circle Revisited: Injecting Diversity, Inclusion, Rights, Justice, and Equity into LIS from Education to Advocacy." *The Library Quarterly: Information, Community, Policy* 85 (2): 150–171.

Kumagai, Arno K., and Monica L. Lypson. 2009. "Beyond Cultural Competence: Critical Consciousness, Social Justice, and Multicultural Education." *Academic Medicine* 84 (6): 782–787.

Kumasi, Kafi D., and Renee F. Hill. 2013. "Examining the Hidden Ideologies within Cultural Competence Discourses among Library and Information Science (LIS) Students: Implications for School Library Pedagogy." *School Libraries Worldwide* 19 (1): 128–139.

Leckie, Gloria J., Lisa M. Given, and John Buschman. 2010. *Critical Theory for Library and Information Science: Exploring the Social from across the Disciplines*. Santa Barbara, CA: ABC-CLIO.

Levi, Amy. 2009. "The Ethics of Nursing Student International Clinical Experiences." *Journal of Obstetric, Gynecologic, and Neonatal Nursing* 38 (1): 94–99.

Lorde, Audre. 1984. *Sister Outsider: Essays and Speeches*. Berkeley, CA: The Crossing Press.

McCook, Kathleen de la Peña. 2000. "Reconnecting Library Education and the Mission of Community." *Library Journal* 125 (14): 164–165.

Mestre, Lori S. 2010. "Librarians Working with Diverse Populations: What Impact Does Cultural Competency Training Have on Their Efforts?" *The Journal of Academic Librarianship* 36 (6): 479–488.

Mi, Misa. 2005. "Cultural Competence for Libraries and Librarians in Health Care Institutions." *Journal of Hospital Librarianship* 5 (2): 15–31.

Moon, J. 2004. *Reflection in Learning and Professional Development*. New York: RoutledgeFalmer.

Morris, Vanessa J. "A Seat at the Table: Seeking Culturally Competent Pedagogy in Librarian Education." Paper presented at the Annual ALISE Conference, Seattle, WA, January 2007. http://www.pages.drexel.edu/~gdc27/final/documents/seatatthetable.pdf.

Olson, Hope A. 1997. "The Feminist and the Emperor's New Clothes: Feminist Deconstruction as a Critical Methodology for Library and Information Studies." *Library and Information Science Research* 19 (2): 181–198.

Olson, Hope A. 1998. "Mapping beyond Dewey's Boundaries: Constructing Classificatory Space for Marginalized Knowledge Domains." *Library Trends* 47 (2): 233–254.

Olson, Hope A. 2001. "The Power to Name: Representation in Library Catalogs." *Signs* 26 (3): 639–668.

Overall, Patricia Montiel. 2009. "Cultural Competence: A Conceptual Framework for Library and Information Science Professionals." *The Library Quarterly* 79 (2): 175–204.

Pawley, Christine. 2006. "Unequal Legacies: Race and Multiculturalism in the LIS Curriculum." *The Library Quarterly: Information, Community, Policy* 76 (2): 149–168.

Rios-Balderrama, Sandra. 2006. "The Role of Cultural Competence in Creating a New Mainstream." *Colorado Libraries* 32 (4): 3.

Sarling, Jo Haight, and Debra S. Van Tassel. 1999. "Community Analysis: Research that Matters to a North-Central Denver Community." *Library and Information Science Research* 21 (1): 7–29.

Smith, Linda S. 1997. "Concept Analysis: Cultural Competence." *Journal of Cultural Diversity* 5 (1): 4–10.

Swanson, Troy. 2010. "Information Is Personal: Critical Information Literacy and Personal Epistemology." In *Critical Library Instruction: Theories and Methods*, edited by Maria T. Accardi, Emily Drabinski, and Alana Kumbier, 265–277. Sacramento, CA: Library Juice Press.

Tervalon, M., and J. Murray-Garcia. 1998. "Cultural Humility versus Cultural Competence: A Critical Distinction in Defining Physician Training Outcomes in Multicultural Education." *Journal of Health Care for the Poor and Underserved* 9 (2): 117–124.

Vasas, Elyssa B. 2005. "Examining the Margins: A Concept Analysis of Marginalization." *Advances in Nursing Science* 28 (3): 194–202.

Chapter 3

A Sampling of Diverse Populations

INTRODUCTION

As has been described in Chapter 1, there are so many populations that can be considered diverse in one or more ways; it would not be feasible to address them all in this text. Instead, a selection of groups whose needs are not always recognized, well defined, or acted upon, will be highlighted. The recommendations and considerations for the highlighted populations are certainly applicable to other groups and communities.

Chapter 4 will specifically discuss specific services to diverse populations, but first a brief discussion of certain diverse groups of patrons and their needs and concerns, implicit or explicit, when interacting with libraries. The populations introduced here include those from diverse racial and ethnic backgrounds; seniors or older adults; those who experience a range of physical or cognitive impairments and mental illnesses; international students and new Americans; the hungry, homeless, and impoverished; the lesbian, gay, bisexual, trans, and queer (LGBTQ) community; and the incarcerated.

RACE, ETHNICITY, AND NATIONAL ORIGIN

The library and information science (LIS) literature has had good discussions about patrons from underrepresented racial and ethnic backgrounds, particularly in regard to their use of academic libraries. Patrons from underrepresented groups have cultural backgrounds that differ significantly from the mainstream or dominant culture; these differences can include food, dress, communication skills, language, religion, and overall worldview. Differences can also encompass their view and usage of libraries. David Alexander (2013, 61) states:

A student's worldview helps shape how students interact with libraries, and students of color typically have a worldview that differs from that of students from the dominant cultural group. In addition, a student's previous experiences with racism and oppression may cause students to view institutions such as a large academic library with suspicion.

This speaks to the importance of having diverse librarians (Zhao 2012) and specialized collections, not only for consumption by the general public but also to most effectively serve the ethnic communities in question. Having this level of cultural competence about a community allows librarians to understand the nuances that exist within communities (Alexander 2013) and appreciate the importance of communities' languages, dialects, oral traditions, and culture and heritage (Taylor and Patterson 2004).

Pertinent examples for this discussion are tribal libraries and Native American communities (Burke 2007; Lloyd 2007) who have distinct technological and infrastructure needs (Dunn 2004; Teixeira 1994). Breu (2003, 256) also suggests that there are issues of trust and feelings that mainstream libraries are not relevant to their needs.

Native peoples tend not to use mainstream libraries. They feel that 'anglo' community libraries are not for them, that these facilities will not contain materials relevant to their lives, their history or their contemporary concerns and, furthermore, that the library neither seeks nor welcomes their presence.

Furthermore, Taylor and Patterson (2004, 2) contend:

Native Americans emphasize an oral tradition, a tradition in which stories can be transitory, changing, and adapted according to circumstances, and contain what mainstream culture sometimes views as fanciful knowledge. These stories are a mixture of personal and community history containing psychological insights and subtle humor, which requires insider information and is intended for small groups of known individuals. This contrasts sharply with knowledge that is rational and scientific, never changing words written hard and fast in books, with a mass audience.

Trust, language barriers, and varying conceptions about what constitutes knowledge are also an issue for other linguistic and ethnic minority communities, for whom English is not a first language and who may subsequently experience lower levels of English proficiency (Adkins and Hussey 2006; Chu 1999).

DISABILITY AND AGE

Older Adults/Seniors

When working with older adults, it is important for librarians to approach each person as an individual who may not share the characteristics or interests commonly associated with the elderly. One should avoid assuming that older adults experience a decline in cognitive ability because many do not. Indeed, unless disease attacks the brain, intellectual capacities can improve with age (Mates 2003). Other assumptions must also be avoided, for example, older adults are not necessarily retired; they may be working full-time, part-time, or they may be underemployed and actively looking for work, and they may need information about government information, housing, insurance, and other financial issues (Wicks 2004). Many grandparents are now raising their own grandchildren and consequently are very involved in technology, gaming, and other activities not readily associated with this age group. These older adults have information needs that do not fit the mold of the "typical" senior citizen.

Seniors may, however, have particular technology and hardware needs as a result of vision or other physical considerations that may result in difficulty with navigation and coordination. In addition to Americans with Disabilities Act (ADA) compliance (Mates 2012) and software, hardware, and design considerations, Xie and Bugg (2009) emphasize the importance of teaching online safety and evaluation skills, given that many seniors may not be prepared for the preponderance of online misinformation and scam artists (Curzon, Wilson, and Whitney 2005). Information access and training in regard to health information (including information about sex and sexual health) is also increasingly pertinent. As baby boomers continue reaching retirement age, they are changing the picture of how senior citizens relate to computers (Chu et al. 2009).

Seniors may be isolated and/or homebound because of their geographic location or mobility status; gerontological training for library staff is advisable (Moore and Young 1985), as is encouragement to come up with creative programming (Lipschultz 2009; McDonough 2013) for those patrons not able to physically come to the library but who may wish to be part of the community. The Reference and User Services Association (RUSA) of the American Library Association (ALA) (2008) issued "Guidelines for Library and Information Services to Older Adults" that provides salient reminders for librarians serving older adults, in person and at a distance.

Older adults are certainly not the only diverse population that has physical impairments or disabilities; disabilities cross through all socioeconomic, ethnic, and otherwise diverse populations. In addition to technology constraints experienced by those who are differently abled (Billingham 2014; Cassner, Maxey-Harris, and Anaya 2011; Comeaux and Schmetzke 2013; Lazar and Jaeger 2011; Miller-Gatenby and Chittenden 2001; Power and LeBeau 2009; Southwell and Slater 2013; Tatomir and Durrance 2010), there is a panoply of physical features that libraries need to consider in order to be compliant with the ADA (http://ada.gov) and provide a welcoming and accessible environment. Librarians need to be especially cognizant of adequate signage, a barrier-free layout that includes clear pathways, wide aisles, accessible shelves, good lighting, and appropriate collections (e.g., captioned videos) (Miller-Gatenby and Chittenden 2001, 316–318). It would also behoove library administrators to train their staff in multimodal methods of service delivery and communication skills and techniques that cater to those with physical or cognitive impairments (322), impairments that can be visible or invisible (e.g., patrons with dyslexia or mental health issues) (Petrie and Swallow 2009).

Mental Illness

Perhaps one of the most prevalent invisible impairments is mental illness, which every library deals with, whether they recognize the symptoms or not. Turner (2004, 12) proposes that it is possible to deal with the unanticipated consequences of the presence of mentally ill (which may include those who are homeless, substance abusers, veterans, domestic abuse victims, children, seniors, and really any other person entering the library) in the library, without compromising professional ethics and principles and without creating overly stringent policies and procedures that attempt to address every conceivable situation. She suggests that libraries consider some overarching themes in their approach to library services: everyone has a right to use the library; staff should be adaptable in their approach when dealing with these diverse populations; and, libraries and their staffs should strive to address problem situations and *not* problem patrons.

The Association of Specialized and Cooperative Library Agencies (ASCLA) reminds library professionals that the mentally ill are no more or less prone to violence than any other member of the population and should not be automatically discriminated against. (See Box 3.1.)

Many people who experience mental illness are properly medicated and pose no threat to those around them.

Box 3.1 Addressing Mental Health Issues in the Library

ASCLA ("People with Mental Health Issues" 2010) makes suggestions for treating the mentally ill with the same respect and tolerance as with other patrons, including:

1. Do not be quick to assume that these patrons are a problem or security risk;
2. Do not assume that mental illness equates to deviant or criminal behavior;
3. Allow extra time and patience for those easily disoriented;
4. Become familiar with the wide range of behaviors associated with mental illness, and encourage other patrons to do the same;
5. Be liberal with the library's signage (which allows patrons to be independent);
6. Do not overempathize in an attempt to relate to the patron; and
7. Establish community partnerships that may be able to provide resources for the mentally ill (e.g., mental health clinics, group homes, homeless shelters, social workers, etc.).

See http://www.ala.org/ascla/ for more information.

As librarians we are not experts in mental health, nor can this be expected of us. However, for our own protection, we must be able to deal effectively with angry, confused or disruptive patrons. Not all angry patrons are mentally ill, nor necessarily irrational, and most mentally ill patrons are not dangerous. (Wollam and Wessel 2003, 17)

With this in mind, Wollam and Wessel (2003) do encourage librarians to become aware of distress signals and the physical characteristics that could indicate an impending situation or problem; such signs include a lack of impulse control, quickly shifting moods, escalating behavior, increased perspiration, clenched fists, darting eyes, and/or yelling (18). Additionally, librarians can work toward de-escalating tense situations by showing empathy and acknowledging distress; reframing requests with different language; allowing the patron to vent verbally; reiterating the desire to assist that patron; assuming a nonaggressive posture and refraining from sudden movements; maintaining a physical distance; not being in an isolated space with the patron; and using a calm voice and matching the patron's breathing (18–19). However, above all, safety for all should be the priority; staff should be mindful about using panic buttons if available, removing themselves from the situation, and requesting assistance from colleagues and authorities when necessary.

Autism Spectrum Disorders

Autism, Asperger's disorder, and pervasive developmental disorder (the three disorders that comprise the autism spectrum) (Coates 2009) are other potentially invisible, and increasingly prevalent, conditions experienced by members of the community. These disorders, which are on the rise (Centers for Disease Control 2014; Goring 2015), are complex neurological conditions that impact an individual's ability to communicate and are accompanied by a wide range of symptoms and behaviors (Whelan 2009). Librarians would benefit from training to learn how to best serve this population and their caregivers; specialized communication skills and techniques, in addition to increased awareness and understanding, would enable libraries to have a more welcoming and flexible environment. Specific suggestions for working with patrons on the spectrum include simplifying language and avoiding jargon; being aware of patrons' learning and communication preferences; and, making allowances for social norms, when patrons behave outside those norms (Halvorson 2006; Whelan 2009). Regarding communication skills and techniques, Halvorson (2006, 21) encourages librarians to be slow with advice or opinions; do not touch the patrons or insist on eye contact; be prepared to spend extra time with them; be clear with guidelines and expectations; do not shame the patrons if they do not or cannot conform to existing rules or norms; and be cognizant of bullying behavior from others directed toward the patrons on the spectrum.

Bress (2013) extends these suggestions by saying the library's physical space should be uncluttered, have quiet areas, be highly visual, and give consideration to lighting (e.g., patrons on the spectrum may have sensitivity to fluorescent lighting). It may be very difficult to have an entire library that consistently fits these parameters, but perhaps there could be a room or smaller space to which a patron can retreat, when overwhelmed or overstimulated. Other suggestions include having a wide range of materials in the collection, dedicated sensory tools and apps (Ennis-Cole and Smith 2011; Klipper 2013; McGrath 2013), dedicated programs and story times (Akin and MacKinney 2004; Barack 2014; D'Orazio 2007; Leon 2011), and onboarding and training dedicated volunteers and mentors (Henry 2010) who can assist with these programs and services.

MIGRATION AND IMMIGRATION: INTERNATIONAL STUDENTS AND NEW AMERICANS

This category of diverse population is multifaceted and includes people who are new to North American culture and may (or may not) be new to the English language. Many international students and New Americans do speak English, which is not their first language, but may still experience difficulties in their new environments, as they try to maintain their culture while simultaneously trying to acclimate to another (Asher, Case, and Zhong 2009). In the literature, academic libraries primarily serve international students, and New Americans are served by public libraries, but there are no hard and fast rules to this. Rather, the needs of these two similar populations and subsequent recommendations for services are applicable in all library settings. These patron groups may still speak in their native tongues at home (Orellana, Dorner, and Pulido 2003) and typically have particular difficulty with jargon, slang, colloquialisms, and conversational English (Asher 2008, 2011). These patrons also have different communication skills and preferences, which often impact their interactions with libraries and librarians (Liu 1993); library anxiety is particularly acute for nonnative English speakers (Jiao and Onwuegbuzie 1997).

Research about the information behaviors of international students has revealed that these users "are accustomed to lecture, recitation, rote memory, and recall, while American students are accustomed to analyzing, synthesizing, critiquing, and expanding" (Macdonald and Sarkodie-Mensah 1988, 426). With a predilection toward print materials, international students are receptive to library instruction sessions and orientation tours, particularly those that are accompanied with print handouts, guides, slides, and visual aids (Greenfield 1986). These students would also prefer to ask questions in their native tongues, but with so many librarians not having the ability to speak other languages, that is unlikely a service most libraries can offer (Ferrer-Vinent 2010; Marcus 2003). When working with international students, library professionals should be consistently checking for comprehension, making eye contact, and taking care to listen closely to the students (Amsberry 2009; Carlyle 2013; Mundava and Gray 2008; Ye 2009). Print communications and visual aids, such as newsletters, web guides, pathfinders, and the like, are also useful and permit international students some autonomy and independence when using the library (Knight, Hight, and Polfer 2010).

The literature suggests that when dealing with New Americans, trust is a key factor as to whether or not they will use the library (Vårheim 2014). Relationship building is an important prerequisite for serving this diverse population. Historically, New Americans have relied on public libraries as a resource for learning about their new communities and as an opportunity for social inclusion (Becvar and Srinivasan 2009; Caidi and Allard 2005; Kennan et al. 2011; Vårheim 2011). In this instance, social inclusion not only encompasses information literacy skills but is also about so much more. Libraries can help New Americans with their everyday-life information-seeking activities.

> Social inclusion requires an ability to develop effective information practices that enable connection to compliance, making available everyday and nuanced information that constitute elements of the information landscape which need to be accessed and understood in order to participate in their adopted community. (Kennan et al. 2011, 191)

Using the New York Public Library as an example, particularly the Queens Public Library that serves New American populations in 59 different languages (Berger 2012), libraries can serve as sites of English language learning (Burke 2007) as well as sites of acclimation and integration. Having appropriate collections and creative programs can facilitate this acclimation and inclusion (Abridged 2009; Adkins and Burns 2013; Al-Qallaf and Mika 2009; Tetteh 2011). In order to be effective, libraries should survey their communities and incorporate these users into the libraries as much as possible (e.g., bring teenagers as pages or volunteers, invite community gatekeepers to serve on boards and committees, etc.) and establish community partnerships (The New York Public Library 2013).

THE HUNGRY, HOMELESS, AND IMPOVERISHED

Libraries have often had questionable relationships with homeless patrons or those otherwise hungry or impoverished. The homeless, in particular, are a diverse user group who are viewed as problematic or bothersome, particularly if they have strong body odor, carry all of their belongings with them, stay in the library during all open hours, or use the public restrooms to bathe. In the early 1990s, a public library and a homeless patron engaged in a series of lawsuits. The library ejected the patron after intense confrontations and complaints from community members who said the homeless man smelled, used the library as a personal lounge, and created an overall uncomfortable environment. The homeless man countered, saying that by ejecting him they were denying him his basic rights to access information (Hanley 1992). This case is oft cited and characterizes the relationships many libraries have had with their homeless patrons.

As mentioned in the earlier section on mental illness, the homeless are often mentally ill, but these two situations are not mutually exclusive. The homeless, like the mentally ill, are not inherently violent or less intelligent than other patrons. The homeless are also an exceptionally intersectional group—there are high proportions of homeless teens (Eyrich-Garg and Rice 2012; Woelfer and Hendry 2011), particularly those who are gay, lesbian, or transsexual/transgender (Winkelstein 2014). Many homeless are veterans who have been unable to find sufficient employment; many homeless are elderly or immigrants, and the homeless span every racial and ethnic group and every age category. In 2013 and 2014, there were two nationally covered news stories that brought this fact to bear, one a five-part *New York Times* article that featured a homeless girl named Dasani and her family (Elliott 2013) and the second, a *Chicago Sun Times* article that revealed one of the players on the world championship little league baseball team was homeless (Sfondeles 2014). These accounts highlight how pervasive homelessness is and that not everyone "looks" or acts homeless.

Homelessness is especially challenging for children, and libraries can serve as a safe haven for them (Pribesh, Gavigan, and Dickinson 2011). Adams (2010, 53) states:

> School, especially the school library, may be the only thing a homeless student can count on as a place that is safe, comfortable, and full of books, magazines, online resources, and more that can bring enjoyment and respite from the daily stresses in his or her life.

Adams (2011) goes on to suggest that librarians not only be mindful of respecting these children's privacy but also be willing to pay them a little more attention, and if possible, maintain a slush fund so that they do not have to pay fines and fees and keep supplies on hand that might make it easier for them to complete their schoolwork and other basic daily tasks. Collections should be relevant to them, perhaps having books that reflect homelessness and poverty so that they can see themselves in a more "normal" light. She says:

> Homelessness can be very confusing for children, and it comes with a lot of misconceptions. We try to untangle that confusion as soon as they arrive: "No, you're not a bum. You don't live in a cardboard box. You don't stink. Mom is not a bad person. She isn't crazy." (53)

In addition to print collections and materials, libraries should be mindful of serving those who are information poor (Armstron, Lord, and Zelter 2000; Britz 2004; Hersberger 2003, 2005, 2013). Information poverty "relates to the availability and accessibility of essential information that people need for development" (Britz and Blignaut 2001, 63). Those who are information poor may be homeless, but that is not always the case; the information poor may not have the knowledge of available resources, and they may not have the ability to use them. Furthermore, the information poor may be those affected by the "the digital divide" (Barber and Wallace 2008; Bertot 2003; Kinney 2010; Mossberger, Tolbert, and Stansbury 2003; Weiss 2012; Yu 2006; Zickuhr and Smith 2012), which means that they may not have the infrastructure, hardware, and financial capabilities to access the Internet in their homes. However, this does not automatically mean that the homeless or impoverished are not technologically savvy or capable; their technological needs may be more sophisticated or complex than anticipated. Their technological needs are about survival and socialization (Berman 2005; Grace 2000; Roberson and Nardi 2010).

To emphasize the point that the homeless and impoverished are no less deserving of quality and dignified services, Holt (2006, 184) states:

> The wrong library question that many public libraries might ask at this point is "What services should my library offer to the poor?" The right question is more complex: How can my library develop and fit its services

into the lives of the poor so they will benefit from what we know how to do? The differentiation is not mere words. The first question is marked by passive "supply-side" thinking about library services, i.e. "If we offer them (i.e. services), they will come." The second question is proactive, involving process (finding out what is needed) and outcomes.

The homeless, impoverished, and information poor are long-standing diverse populations seen in libraries, and there are many professional groups dedicated to improving services and collections for this population (see Box 3.2).

LGBTQ COMMUNITY

This label is debated, as it is not felt that it is inclusive enough of the sexual diversity even *within* this community. Other labels or titles include transsexual, intersexed, nonheterosexual, noncisgender, and the like. This is not to mention that these labels refer to those who are open and public about their sexuality. For the purposes of this brief introduction, LGBTQ will be used to discuss this diverse population served by libraries. In addition to internal diversity, the LGBTQ community is particularly intersectional (Greenblatt 2003), and there is a growing and integral connection among services to this

---

Box 3.2   Resources for Serving the Homeless, Impoverished, and Information Poor

Hunger, Homelessness and Poverty Task Force

Social Responsibilities Round Table of the American Library Association, http://www.hhptf.org

The ALA's Policies for Library Services to the Poor

http://www.ala.org/aboutala/governance/policymanual/updated policymanual/section2/52libsvcsandrespon#B.8.10

Outreach Resources for Services to Poor and Homeless People

The ALA's Office for Diversity, Literacy and Outreach Services http://www.ala.org/advocacy/diversity/outreachtounderserved populations/servicespoor

National Coalition for the Homeless: Fact Sheets and Lesson Plans

http://www.nationalhomeless.org/factsheets/index.html

The Institute for Children, Poverty, and Homelessness (ICPH): Reports and Briefs

http://www.icphusa.org/Publications/Reports/

National Center for Homeless Education: Issues Briefs

http://center.serve.org/nche/briefs.php

National Center for Children in Poverty: Fact Sheets

http://www.nccp.org/publications/fact_sheets.html

community, particularly as it pertains to homeless, mentally ill, or incarcerated LGBTQ individuals. This group is particularly intersectional and encompasses all races/ethnicities, all socioeconomic classes, all religions, all geographic areas, and so on. This group is unfortunately also prone to physical and mental health concerns because of fear of the medical system, and, as a result, there are high rates of suicide (McKay 2011).

Making use of the library can be challenging for LGBTQ patrons because of their own reluctance to ask questions and because of potential homophobic responses from library staff members (Stenback and Schrader 1999). Seborg (2005) suggests that training staff to work with the LGBTQ community be a priority for libraries so that staff can be prepared to create safe spaces, advocate for and secure appropriate and useful collections, and be able to communicate with patrons who may have particularly sensitive information needs. The LGBTQ community has distinct information needs related to coming out, self-discovery, identity, and physical and mental health (Creelman and Harris 1990; Whitt 1993). With this said, the collection should be more than just a collection of resources about HIV and AIDS. LGBTQ young adults also deserve special consideration and need resources that reflect their experiences (see Box 3.3).

An important, and possibly overlooked, option for interacting with this community is to develop and maintain robust virtual services and resources, including finding aids and library guides, in general and those specific to LGBTQ issues that can be displayed in the library and put on the library's website (Thompson 2012). These resources allow patrons to find information privately and independently, qualities that are important to the LGBTQ community. "Owing to fear of stigma and rejection, LGBTQ individuals find the anonymity of online reference safer and easier for asking questions than broaching the subject face to face" (104). Finally, Thompson (2012) suggests libraries train their staff to effectively work with this population and work toward making the libraries a welcoming environment overall, and Gough and Greenblatt (1992) recommend that librarians should stop the assumptions, stereotypes, and biases that are inherent in the larger heterosexist society.

THE INCARCERATED

The incarcerated is another diverse population that is far-reaching across library types. In addition to having a dedicated branch or specialty of librarianship—prison librarianship—that works with individuals who are detained, many libraries will serve the patrons once they are released and trying to reacclimatize into society. Even youth services and teen librarians will be working with detained or formerly detained young adults and should be cognizant of including this patron group into the library and the community (Austin 2012; Bodart 2008; Gilman 2008; Herring 2009; Hockenberry, Sickmund, and Sladky 2015; Puzzanchera 2014; Roos 2012).

Arguably, the need for prison librarians is increasing even if the funding and ability of libraries to serve these patrons inside of prisons and jails is not

Box 3.3   Resources for Serving LGBTQ Youth

LGBTQ youth are often ignored or given the short shrift when it comes to library collections. They are too old for the children's section and might be redirected to the LGBTQ section for adults. They deserve age-appropriate and relevant materials. The following are but a few of the professional works on this topic.

Books:

Alexander, Linda B., and Sarah D. Miselis. "Barriers to GLBTQ Collection Development and Strategies for Overcoming Them." *Young Adult Library Services* 5, no. 3 (2007): 43–49.

Cart, Michael, and Christine A. Jenkins. *The Heart Has Its Reasons: Young Adult Literature with Gay/Lesbian/Queer Content, 1969–2004.* Vol. 18. Lanham, MD: Scarecrow Press, 2006.

Cart, Michael, and Christine A. Jenkins. *Top 250 LGBTQ Books for Teens: Coming Out, Being Out, and the Search for Community.* Chicago: American Library Association, 2015.

Hughes-Hassell, Sandra, Elizabeth Overberg, and Shannon Harris. "Lesbian, Gay, Bisexual, Transgender, and Questioning (LGBTQ)-Themed Literature for Teens: Are School Libraries Providing Adequate Collections?" *School Library Research* 16 (2013). http://www.ala.org/aasl/sites/ala.org.aasl/files/content/aaslpubsand journals/slr/vol16/SLR_LGBTQThemedLiteratureforTeens_V16.pdf.

Wickens, Corrine M. "Codes, Silences, and Homophobia: Challenging Normative Assumptions about Gender and Sexuality in Contemporary LGBTQ Young Adult Literature." *Children's Literature in Education* 42, no. 2 (2011): 148–164.

Web Resources:

Safe in the Stacks: Community Spaces for Homeless LGBTQ Youth

The ALA's Gay, Lesbian, Bisexual, and Transgender Round Table (GLBTRT)

http://www.ala.org/glbtrt/tools/homeless-lgbtq-youth

GLBT Reviews

Book and media reviews from the ALA's GLBTRT

http://www.glbtrt.ala.org/reviews/

Over the Rainbow Books

Book list from the ALA's GLBTRT

http://www.glbtrt.ala.org/overtherainbow/

Stonewall Book Awards

The ALA's GLBTRT

http://www.ala.org/glbtrt/award

(Carson 2014; Lehmann 2011). Maintaining libraries and collections inside the walls of the prison's industrial complex is particularly challenging because of the tensions between librarians and prison administration. Librarians, who promote free and complete access to information, are often in conflict with organizational leadership who want to curtail and censor detainees' access to information for a variety of reasons (i.e., information that is undesirable and/ or may incite problem behavior) (Stearns 2004). Librarians are "encouraged" not to promote controversial materials (Mark 2005, 104) and inadvertently forced to compromise patrons' intellectual freedom and privacy (Conrad 2012), which undoubtedly makes the librarians' task of providing adequate reference, instruction, and other services more difficult. As Jones (2004, 15) stated, "Librarians are paid to provide free access to information; correctional officers are paid to work in an environment where freedom is limited." Mark (2005, 103–104) provides an example of this tension:

Box 3.4   Additional Resources about Prison Librarianship

Books:

Clark, Sheila, and Erica MacCreaigh. *Library Services to the Incarcerated: Applying the Public Library Model in Correctional Facility Libraries.* Westport, CT: Libraries Unlimited, 2006.

Steinberg, Avi. *Running the Books: The Adventures of an Accidental Prison Librarian.* New York: Anchor Books, 2011.

Sweeney, Jennifer. *Literacy: A Way Out for At-risk Youth.* Englewood, CO: ABC-CLIO, 2012.

Vogel, Brenda. *The Prison Library Primer: A Program for the Twenty-First Century.* Lanham, MD: Scarecrow Press, 2009.

Web Resources:

Resolution on Prisoners' Right to Read

The ASCLA of ALA

http://www.ala.org/ascla/asclaissues/prisonrights

Diversity and Outreach Columns: ALA's Office for Diversity, Literacy and Outreach Services

http://olos.ala.org/columns/?cat=6

Directory of State Prison Libraries

A directory of prison libraries is maintained by the Washington State Library

http://wiki.sos.wa.gov/ils/

Library Standards for Adult Correctional Institutions

The ASCLA of ALA

http://www.ala.org/ascla/asclaissues/librarystandards

The librarian reserves the right to make decisions on a case-by-case basis. Most of the censorship of controversial books is enforced for safety reasons. For instance, tattoo art books are allowed but, because of health risks, books on tattooing technique are prohibited. Black and white supremacy books are allowed unless they advocate violence. Neither violent Klu Klux Klan books nor any violent Nation of Islam titles are included in the library collection. Sex offenders had special conditions imposed on their library use by their caseworkers; not reading certain titles can be considered treatment for a sex offender. The librarian did not directly censor reading for sex offenders. Instead, if a book with a picture of children or a book on gay teenagers was requested by a sex offender, the librarian called the caseworker to see if there were any restrictions on that inmate's reading.

In addition to censorship, other complicating issues include high rates of mental illness, substance abuse, recidivism and the subsequent need for and lack of proper mechanisms, resources, and policies to ensure librarian safety.

Despite the aforementioned issues, prison libraries are a vital resource (see Box 3.4); librarians assist patrons with information about addiction, mental health, legal information, and perhaps most importantly, materials for leisure and enjoyment (e.g., street literature/urban fiction is especially popular—see Morris 2012 for more information on this genre). Developing literacy skills and encouraging reluctant readers are also other important functions of the prison

---

LESSON PLAN

Essential Readings:

Alexander, David L. "American Indian Studies, Multiculturalism, and the Academic Library." *College and Research Libraries* 74, no. 1 (2013): 60–68.

Austin, Jeanie. "Critical Issues in Juvenile Detention Libraries." Paper presented at YALSA's Trends Impacting Young Adult Services Event, ALA Midwinter Meeting, Dallas, TX, January 21, 2012. http://www.yalsa.ala.org/jrlya/2012/07/critical-issues-in-juvenile-detention-center-libraries/.

Halvorson, Holly. "Asperger's Syndrome: How the Public Library Can Address These Special Needs." *Children and Libraries* 4, no. 3 (2006): 19–27.

Kinney, Bo. "The Internet, Public Libraries, and the Digital Divide." *Public Library Quarterly* 29, no. 2 (2010): 104–161.

Wollam, K., and B. Wessel. "Recognizing and Effectively Managing Mental Illness in the Library." *Colorado Libraries* 29, no. 4 (2003): 17–20.

Questions to Ask:

1. What are ways to build/maintain trust with the diverse populations you will be serving?

2. If your library serves multiple diverse populations, how do you balance resources to address the needs of all (i.e., so as not to favor one group over another)?

Assignment:

It would be very difficult to list every potential media source or item that could be used as an example in a diversity class. Blog posts, Facebook, Twitter, and other social media platforms are rich with videos, podcasts, and other media clips that can succinctly and powerfully reinforce points and concepts (e.g., cultural competence). Media examples are also great ways to learn about individual libraries and their initiatives, as more and more libraries have gone online in an effort to reach and engage their patrons. In particular, I would recommend the following sources:

- NPR's **Code Switch** segments and podcasts tackle a variety of topics, often highlighting cultural habits and issues. While not specifically related to libraries, they are quick, informative, and can provide a window through which to experience a cultural difference from your own.
   http://www.npr.org/sections/codeswitch/.
- YouTube: Searching for terms like "diversity in libraries" will yield a great number of videos, many from individuals, students, libraries, library schools, researchers, consultants, and the ALA and other professional library organizations.
   https://www.youtube.com.
- **TED: Ideas worth spreading:** There are fewer videos here than on YouTube, but they are longer and are more like mini lectures that often provide a deeper perspective on an issue. A favorite of mine is *The Danger of a Single Story* by Chimamanda Ngozi Adichie (https://www.ted.com/talks/chimamanda_adichie_the_danger_of_a_single_story). There are many talks about diversity, not explicitly about libraries, but certainly applicable to the profession.
   https://www.ted.com.

Locate a podcast or video that discusses diversity (it does not have to be explicitly about library services).

What video/podcast did you select, and what facts/points can you take away that will improve your practice?

librarian (Andersen 2005; Conrad 2012; Ellern and Mason 2013; Guerra 2012; Hill, Pérez, and Irby 2008; Shirley 2003).

REFERENCES

Abridged by the Editor. 2009. "Library Services for Immigrants, an Abridged Version." *Public Library Quarterly* 28 (2): 120–126.

Adams, Helen R. 2010. "Serving Homeless Children in the School Library—Part 1." *School Library Monthly* 27 (3): 52–53.

Adams, Helen R. 2011. "Serving Homeless Children in the School Library—Part 2." *School Library Monthly* 27 (4): 52–53.

Adkins, Denice, and C. Sean Burns. 2013. "Arizona Public Libraries Serving the Spanish-Speaking." *Reference and User Services Quarterly* 53 (1): 60–70.

Adkins, Denice, and Lisa Hussey. 2006. "The Library in the Lives of Latino College Students." *The Library Quarterly: Information, Community, Policy* 76 (4): 456–480.

Akin, Lynn, and Donna MacKinney. 2004. "Autism, Literacy, and Libraries: The 3 Rs = Routine, Repetition, and Redundancy." *Children and Libraries: The Journal of the Association for Library Service to Children* 2 (2): 35–43.

Alexander, David L. 2013. "American Indian Studies, Multiculturalism, and the Academic Library." *College and Research Libraries* 74 (1): 60–68.

Al-Qallaf, Charlene L., and Joseph J. Mika. 2009. "Library and Information Services to the Arabic-Speaking Community: A Survey of Michigan Public Libraries." *Public Library Quarterly* 28 (2): 127–161.

American Library Association. 2008. "Guidelines for Library and Information Services to Older Adults." Chicago: Reference and User Services Association. http://www.ala.org/rusa/resources/guidelines/libraryservices. Accessed March 1, 2016.

Amsberry, Dawn. 2009. "Using Effective Listening Skills with International Patrons." *Reference Services Review* 37 (1): 10–19.

Andersen, Lynn. 2005. "Update on Prison Projects." *Progressive Librarian* 25: 96–99.

Armstrong, Annie L., Catherine Lord, and Judith Zelter. 2000. "Information Needs of Low Income Residents in South King County." *Public Libraries* 39 (6): 330–337.

Asher, Curt. 2011. "The Progressive Past." *Reference and User Services Quarterly* 51 (1): 43–48.

Asher, Curt, and Emerson Case. 2008. "A Generation in Transition." *Reference and User Services Quarterly* 47 (3): 274–279.

Asher, Curt, Emerson Case, and Ying Zhong. 2009. "Serving Generation 1.5: Academic Library Use and Students from Non–English-Speaking Households." *College and Research Libraries* 70 (3): 258–272.

Austin, Jeanie. "Critical Issues in Juvenile Detention Libraries." Paper presented at YALSA's Trends Impacting Young Adult Services Event, ALA Midwinter Meeting, Dallas, TX, January 21, 2012. http://www.yalsa.ala.org/jrlya/2012/07/critical-issues-in-juvenile-detention-center-libraries/.

Barack, Lauren. 2014. "Bridging the Gap." *School Library Journal* 60 (7): 28.

Barber, Peggy, and Linda Wallace. 2008. "Libraries Connect Communities." *American Libraries* 39 (9): 52–55.

Becvar, Katherine, and Ramesh Srinivasan. 2009. "Indigenous Knowledge and Culturally Responsive Methods in Information Research." *The Library Quarterly: Information, Community, Policy* 79 (4): 421–441.

Berger, Joseph. 2012. "Libraries Speak the Mother Tongue." *The New York Times* (New York), January 3, NY Region edition, A18.

Berman, Sanford. 2005. "Classism in the Stacks: Libraries and Poor People." *Counterpoise* 9 (3): 51–55.

Bertot, John Carlo. 2003. "The Multiple Dimensions of the Digital Divide: More Than the Technology 'Haves' and 'Have Nots.'" *Government Information Quarterly* 20 (2): 185–191.

Billingham, Lisa. 2014. "Improving Academic Library Website Accessibility for People with Disabilities." *Library Management* 35 (8/9): 565–581.

Bodart, Joni Richards. 2008. "It's All about the Kids: Presenting Options and Opening Doors." *Young Adult Library Services* 7 (1): 35–38, 45.

Bress, Andrea. 2013. "Making Your School Library More Functional to Individuals with Autism." *Library Media Connection* 32 (1): 46–47.

Breu, Reegan. 2003. "Band and Tribal Libraries: What Mainstream Public Libraries Can Learn from Them." *Feliciter* 5: 254–256.

Britz, Johannes J. 2004. "To Know or Not to Know: A Moral Reflection on Information Poverty." *Journal of Information Science* 30 (3): 192–204.

Britz, Johannes J., and James N. Blignaut. 2001. "Information Poverty and Social Justice." *South African Journal of Library and Information Science* 67 (2): 63–69.

Burke, Susan K. 2007. "The Use of Public Libraries by Native Americans." *The Library Quarterly: Information, Community, Policy* 77 (4): 429–461.

Caidi, Nadia, and Danielle Allard. 2005. "Social Inclusion of Newcomers to Canada: An Information Problem?" *Library and Information Science Research* 27 (3): 302–324.

Carlyle, Cate. 2013. "Practicalities: Serving English as a Second Language Library Users." *Feliciter* 3: 18–20.

Carson, Ann E. 2014. "Prisoners in 2013." Bureau of Justice Statistics Prisoners in 2012—Advance Counts. Accessed February 12, 2016. http://www.bjs.gov/content/pub/press/p13pr.cfm.

Cassner, Mary, Charlene Maxey-Harris, and Toni Anaya. 2011. "Differently Able: A Review of Academic Library Websites for People with Disabilities." *Behavioral and Social Sciences Librarian* 30 (1): 33–51.

Centers for Disease Control. 2014. "CDC Estimates 1 in 68 Children Has Been Identified with Autism Spectrum Disorder." U.S. Department of Health and Human Services. Last modified March 27, 2014. http://www.cdc.gov/media/releases/2014/p0327-autism-spectrum-disorder.html.

Chu, Adeline, Jeffrey Huber, Beth Mastel-Smith, and Sandra Cesario. 2009. " 'Partnering with Seniors for Better Health': Computer Use and Internet Health Information Retrieval among Older Adults in a Low Socioeconomic Community." *Journal of the Medical Library Association* 97 (1): 12–20.

Chu, Clara M. 1999. "Literacy Practices of Linguistic Minorities: Sociolinguistic Issues and Implications for Literacy Services." *The Library Quarterly* 69 (3): 339–359.

Coates, Heather. 2009. "Autism Spectrum Disorders: Wading through the Controversies on the Web." *Medical Reference Services Quarterly* 28 (3): 259–267.

Comeaux, Dave, and Axel Schmetzke. 2013. "Accessibility of Academic Library Web Sites in North America: Current Status and Trends (2002–2012)." *Library Hi Tech* 31 (1): 8–33.

Conrad, Suzanna. 2012. "Collection Development and Circulation Policies in Prison Libraries: An Exploratory Survey of Librarians in US Correctional Institutions." *The Library Quarterly: Information, Community, Policy* 82 (4): 407–427.

Creelman, Janet, and Roma M. Harris. 1990. "Coming Out: The Information Needs of Lesbians." *Collection Building* 10 (3–4): 37–41.

Curzon, Paul, Judy Wilson, and Gill Whitney. 2005. "Successful Strategies of Older People for Finding Information." *Interacting with Computers* 17 (6): 660–671.

D'Orazio, Antonette K. 2007. "Small Steps, Big Results." *Children and Libraries: The Journal of the Association for Library Service to Children* 5 (3): 21–23.

Dunn, Kendise E. 2004. "Tribal Libraries." *Rural Libraries* 24 (2): 95–110.

Ellern, Gillian D., and Karen Mason. 2013. "Library Services to Inmates in the Rural County Jails of Western North Carolina." *North Carolina Libraries* 71 (1): 15–22.

Elliott, Andrea. 2013. "Invisible Child." *The New York Times* (New York), December 9, online edition. http://www.nytimes.com/projects/2013/invisible-child/. Accessed March 1, 2016.

Ennis-Cole, Demetria, and Daniella Smith. 2011. "Assistive Technology and Autism: Expanding the Technology Leadership Role of the School Librarian." *School Libraries Worldwide* 17 (2): 86–98.

Eyrich-Garg, Karin M., and Eric Rice. 2012. "Cyber Behavior of Homeless Adolescents and Adults." In *Encyclopedia of Cyber Behavior*, edited by Yan, Zheng, 284–291. Hershey, PA: IGI Global.

Ferrer-Vinent, Ignacio J. 2010. "For English, Press 1: International Students' Language Preference at the Reference Desk." *The Reference Librarian* 51 (3): 189–201.

Gilman, Isaac. 2008. "Beyond Books: Restorative Librarianship in Juvenile Detention Centers." *Public Libraries* 47 (1): 59–66.

Goring, Lisa. 2015. "10 Years of Progress: What We've Learned about Autism." Autism Speaks. Last modified February 23, 2016. Last accessed date September 18, 2016. https://www.autismspeaks.org/news/news-item/10-years-progress-what-we039ve-learned-about-autism.

Gough, Cal, and Ellen Greenblatt. 1992. "Services to Gay and Lesbian Patrons: Examining the Myths." *Library Journal* 117 (1): 59–63.

Grace, P. 2000. "No Place to Go (except the Public Library)." *American Libraries* 31 (5): 53–55.

Greenblatt, Ellen. 2003. "Lesbian, Gay, Bisexual, Transgender Library users: Overcoming the Myths." *Colorado Libraries* 29 (4): 21–25.

Greenfield, Louise. 1986. "Educating the World: Training Library Staff to Communicate Effectively with International Students." *Journal of Academic Librarianship* 12 (4): 227–231.

Guerra, Stephanie F. 2012. "Using Urban Fiction to Engage At-Risk and Incarcerated Youths in Literacy Instruction." *Journal of Adolescent and Adult Literacy* 55 (5): 385–394.

Halvorson, Holly. 2006. "Asperger's Syndrome: How the Public Library Can Address These Special Needs." *Children and Libraries* 4 (3): 19–27.

Hanley, Robert. 1992. "Library Wins in Homeless-Man Case." *The New York Times* (New York), March 25, online archives edition. http://www.nytimes.com/1992/03/25/nyregion/library-wins-in-homeless-man-case.html. Accessed March 1, 2016.

Henry, Spring Lea. 2010. "Hidden Gems: Teens with Autism in the Library." *Voice of Youth Advocates* 33 (3): 208–211.

Herring, Deidra N. 2009. "The Ohio Department of Youth Services Juvenile Prison Library System." *Behavioral and Social Sciences Librarian* 28 (4): 148–165.

Hersberger, Julia A. 2013. "Are the Economically Poor Information Poor? Does the Digital Divide Affect the Homeless and Access to Information?" *Proceedings of the Annual Conference of CAIS:* 45–63.

Hersberger, Julie. 2003. "Are the Economically Poor Information Poor? Does the Digital Divide Affect the Homeless and Access to Information?" *Canadian Journal of Information and Library Science* 27 (3): 45–64.

Hersberger, Julie. 2005. "The Homeless and Information Needs and Services." *Reference and User Services Quarterly* 44 (3): 199–202.

Hill, Marc Lamont, Biany Pérez, and Decoteau J. Irby. 2008. "Street Fiction: What Is It and What Does It Mean for English Teachers?" *English Journal* 97 (3): 76–81.

Hockenberry, Sarah, Melissa Sickmund, and Anthony Sladky. 2015. "Juvenile Residential Facility Census, 2012: Selected Findings." Washington, DC: Office of Juvenile Justice and Delinquency Prevention. Accessed February 14, 2015. http://www.ojjdp.gov/pubs/247207.pdf.

Holt, Glen E. 2006. "Fitting Library Services into the Lives of the Poor." *The Bottom Line: Managing Library Finances* 19 (4): 184.

Jiao, Qun G., and Anthony J. Onwuegbuzie. 1997. "Antecedents of Library Anxiety." *The Library Quarterly: Information, Community, Policy* 67 (4): 372–389.

Jones, Patrick. 2004. "Reaching out to Young Adults in Jail." *Young Adult Library Services* 3 (1): 16–19.

Kennan, Mary Anne, Annemaree Lloyd, Asim Qayyum, and Kim Thompson. 2011. "Settling In: The Relationship between Information and Social Inclusion." *Australian Academic and Research Libraries* 42 (3): 191–210.

Kinney, Bo. 2010. "The Internet, Public Libraries, and the Digital Divide." *Public Library Quarterly* 29 (2): 104–161.

Klipper, Barbara. 2013. "Apps and Autism: Tools to Serve Children with Special Needs." *American Libraries.* www.americanlibrariesmagazine.org/article/apps-and-autism. Accessed April 1, 2016.

Knight, Lorrie, Maryann Hight, and Lisa Polfer. 2010. "Rethinking the Library for the International Student Community." *Reference Services Review* 38 (4): 581–605.

Lazar, Jonathan, and Paul T. Jaeger. 2011. "Reducing Barriers to Online Access for People with Disabilities." *Issues in Science and Technology* 17 (2): 68–82.

Lehmann, Vibeke. 2011. "Challenges and Accomplishments in U.S. Prison Libraries." *The Library Quarterly. Information, Community, Policy* 59 (3): 490–508.

Leon, Annie. 2011. "Beyond Barriers: Creating Storytimes for Families of Children with ASD." *Children and Libraries* 11 (3): 12–14.

Lloyd, Monique. 2007. "The Underrepresented Native American Student: Diversity in Library Science." *Library Student Journal* 2: 1–7.

Lipschultz, Dale. 2009. "Gaming@ Your Library." *American Libraries* 40 (1/2): 40–43.

Liu, Ziming. 1993. "Difficulties and Characteristics of Students from Developing Countries in Using American Libraries." *College and Research Libraries* 54 (1): 25–31.

Macdonald, Gina, and Elizabeth Sarkodie-Mensah. 1988. "ESL Students and American Libraries." *College and Research Libraries* 49 (5): 426.

Marcus, Sandra. 2003. "Multilingualism at the Reference Desk: Keeping Students Connected." *College and Research Libraries News* 64 (5): 322–323.

Mark, Amy E. 2005. "Libraries without Walls: An Internship at Oshkosh Correctional Institution Library." *Behavioral and Social Sciences Librarian* 23 (2): 97–111.

Mates, Barbara T. 2003. *5-Star Programming and Services for Your 55+ Library Customers.* Chicago, IL: American Library Association.

Mates, Barbara T. 2012. "Chapter 1: Information Power to All Patrons." *Library Technology Reports* 48 (7): 7–13.

McDonough, Shannon K. 2013. "Lifetime Arts." *Public Libraries* 52 (3): 29–35.

McGrath, Renee. 2013. "Autism? There's an App for That." *Young Adult Library Services* 11 (2): 20–24.

McKay, Becky. 2011. "Lesbian, Gay, Bisexual, and Transgender Health Issues, Disparities, and Information Resources." *Medical Reference Services Quarterly* 30 (4): 393–401.

Miller-Gatenby, Katherine J., and Michele Chittenden. 2001. "Reference Services for All: How to Support Reference Service to Clients with Disabilities." *The Reference Librarian* 33 (69–70): 313–326.

Moore, Bessie Boehm, and Christina Carr Young. 1985. "Library/Information Services and the Nation's Elderly." *Journal of the American Society for Information Science* 36 (6): 364–368.

Morris, Vanessa Irvin. 2012. *The Readers' Advisory Guide to Street Literature.* Chicago: American Library Association.

Mossberger, Karen, Caroline J. Tolbert, and Mary Stansbury. 2003. *Virtual Inequality: Beyond the Digital Divide.* Washington, DC: Georgetown University Press.

Mundava, Maud C., and LaVerne Gray. 2008. "Meeting Them Where They Are: Marketing to International Student Populations in US Academic Libraries." *Technical Services Quarterly* 25 (3): 35–48.

The New York Public Library. 2013. "New York City Celebrates Immigrant Heritage Week." Last modified April 17, 2013. http://www.nypl.org/help/community-outreach/immigrant-heritage-week.

Orellana, Marjorie Faulstich, Lisa Dorner, and Lucila Pulido. 2003. "Accessing Assets: Immigrant Youth's Work as Family Translators or 'Para-Phrasers.'" *Social Problems* 50 (4): 505–524.

"People with Mental Health Issues: What You Need to Know Library Accessibility Tip Sheet 7." 2010. Chicago: Association of Specialized and Cooperative Library Agencies, a division of the American Library Association.

Petrie, H., C. Power, and D. Swallow. 2009. "Students with Disabilities in Higher Education: Challenges and Tactile Solutions." *Art Libraries Journal* 34 (2): 35–40.

Power, Rebecca, and Chris LeBeau. 2009. "How Well Do Academic Library Web Sites Address the Needs of Database Users with Visual Disabilities?" *The Reference Librarian* 50 (1): 55–72.

Pribesh, Shana, Karen Gavigan, and Gail Dickinson. 2011. "The Access Gap: Poverty and Characteristics of School Library Media Centers." *The Library Quarterly: Information, Community, Policy* 81 (2): 143–160.

Puzzanchera, Charles. 2014. "Juvenile Arrests 2012." Office of Juvenile Justice and Delinquency Prevention, Washington, DC. Accessed February 14, 2015. http://www.ojjdp.gov/pubs/248513.pdf

Roberson, Jahmeilah, and Bonnie Nardi. 2010. "Survival Needs and Social Inclusion: Technology Use among the Homeless." In *Proceedings of the 2010 ACM Conference on Computer Supported Cooperative Work,* 445–448. New York: ACM Press.

Roos, Barbara. 2012. "Beyond the Bars: Serving Teens in Lockdown." *Young Adult Library Services* 10 (2): 12–14.

Seborg, Liesl. 2005. "Sharing the Stories of the Gay, Lesbian, Bisexual and Transgendered Community: Providing Library Service to the GLBT Patron." *Pacific Northwest Library Association (PNLA) Quarterly* 70 (1): 15–17.

Sfondeles, Tina. 2014. "Family of Little League Champ without a Home Base of Their Own." *Chicago Sun Times* (Chicago), August 28, 2014, online edition. http://www.suntimes.com/news/metro/29504225-418/family-of-little-league-champ-without-a-home-base-of-their-own.html#.VI38h4fyBYc. Accessed April 1, 2016.

Shirley, Glennor L. 2003. "Correctional Libraries, Library Standards, and Diversity." *Journal of Correctional Education* 54 (2): 70–74.

Southwell, Kristina L., and Jacquelyn Slater. 2013. "An Evaluation of Finding Aid Accessibility for Screen Readers." *Information Technology and Libraries* 32 (3): 34–46.

Stearns, Robert M. 2004. "The Prison Library: An Issue for Corrections, or a Correct Solution for Its Issues?" *Behavioral and Social Sciences Librarian* 23 (1): 49–80.

Stenback, Tanis L., and Alvin M. Schrader. 1999. "Venturing from the Closet: A Qualitative Study of the Information Needs of Lesbians." *Public Library Quarterly* 17 (3): 37–50.

Tatomir, Jennifer, and Joan C. Durrance. 2010. "Overcoming the Information Gap: Measuring the Accessibility of Library Databases to Adaptive Technology Users." *Library Hi Tech* 28 (4): 577–594.

Taylor, Rhonda Harris, and Lotsee Patterson. 2004. "Native American Resources: A Model for Collection Development." *The Acquisitions Librarian* 16 (31–32): 41–54.

Teixeira, Lauren. 1994. "Magic of Community: The Telecommunications Revolution and Native American Heritage." *Wilson Library Bulletin* 69 (1): 34–37.

Tetteh, Bridget. 2011. "Serving African Immigrants in Colorado Public Libraries." *Colorado Libraries* 35 (4): 1–4.

Thompson, Kelly J. 2012. "Where's the 'T'?: Improving Library Service to Community Members Who Are Transgender-Identified.", *B Sides (University of Iowa SLIS Journal)*, 22: 1–17. https://works.bepress.com/kelly_thompson/2. Accessed April 1, 2016.

Turner, Anne M. 2004. *It Comes with the Territory: Handling Problem Situations in Libraries*. Revised. Jefferson, MD: McFarland.

Vårheim, Andreas. 2011. "Gracious Space: Library Programming Strategies towards Immigrants as Tools in the Creation of Social Capital." *Library and Information Science Research* 33 (1): 12–18.

Vårheim, Andreas. 2014. "Trust in Libraries and Trust in Most People: Social Capital Creation in the Public Library." *The Library Quarterly* 84 (3): 258–277.

Weiss, Robert J. 2012. "Libraries and the Digital Divide." *Journal of the Library Administration and Management Section* 8 (2): 25–47.

Whelan, Debra Lau. 2009. "The Equal Opportunity Disorder: Autism Is on the Rise, and It Can Affect Any Family. Here's What You Need to Know." *School Library Journal* 55 (8): 30–34.

Wicks, Don A. 2004. "Older Adults and Their Information Seeking." *Behavioral and Social Sciences Librarian* 22 (2): 1–26.

Winkelstein, Julie Ann. 2014. "Public Libraries: Creating Safe Spaces for Homeless LGBTQ Youth." *IFLA 2014 Conference Proceedings*, Lyon, France, August 8, 1–8.

Woelfer, Jill Palzkill, and David G. Hendry. 2011. "Homeless Young People and Living with Personal Digital Artifacts." In *Proceedings of the SIGCHI Conference on Human Factors in Computing Systems*, 1697–1706. New York: ACM Press.

Wollam, K., and B. Wessel. 2003. "Recognizing and Effectively Managing Mental Illness in the Library." *Colorado Libraries* 29 (4): 17–20.

Xie, Bo, and Julie M. Bugg. 2009. "Public Library Computer Training for Older Adults to Access High-Quality Internet Health Information." *Library and Information Science Research* 31 (3): 155–162.

Ye, Yunshan. 2009. "New Thoughts on Library Outreach to International Students." *Reference Services Review* 37 (1): 7–9.

Yu, Liangzhi. 2006. "Understanding Information Inequality: Making Sense of the Literature of the Information and Digital Divides." *Journal of Librarianship and Information Science* 38 (4): 229–252.

Zhao, Lisa. 2012. "Organizational Action Increases the Visibility of Chinese American Librarians." *Chinese Librarianship: An International Electronic Journal* 34: 12–19.

Zickuhr, Kathryn, and Aaron Smith. 2012. "Digital Differences." Pew Internet and American Life Project. Accessed September 18, 2016. http://www.pewinternet.org/2012/04/13/digital-differences/.

Chapter 4

Services to Diverse Populations

INTRODUCTION

According to the 2013 "Library Services in the Digital Age" survey, conducted by Pew Internet and American Life Project, public libraries served 96.4 percent of the total U.S. population, offered 3.75 million programs, and 80 percent of respondents said that reference librarians and reference services are a "very important" part of library services (in conjunction with borrowing books and using public computers) (Zickuhr, Lee, and Purcell 2013). Additionally, the 2012 Institute of Museum and Library Services (IMLS) "Public Libraries Survey" indicates that U.S. public libraries answered 284.3 million reference questions (Swan et al. 2014). Despite proclamations and news reports to the contrary, the public is still very much using their libraries. This represents a lot of opportunity for libraries, of all types, to provide services to their constituents (members of diverse populations and in general).

This chapter highlights some of the services that libraries offer and discusses how they can be offered with diverse user groups in mind. A good portion of the chapter is dedicated to reference services, because the literature is very specific when it comes to reference services to diverse populations. The literature is less specific and prolific when it comes to other, equally important, but perhaps behind the scenes services such as collection development and marketing to diverse populations. Recalling that a "one-size-fits-all" approach to library services is not desirable, learning how to compassionately and competently serve diverse user groups will enable library professionals to serve all *users*. An important introductory idea that library staff should become familiar with is that many patrons from diverse backgrounds may not even understand how North American libraries work. The way libraries operate in this country (open stacks, public computers and copy machines, asking for help at a large desk, etc.) may be different, strange, unwelcome, or even false models of education and service (Liu 1995). As individuals, their information-seeking behavior is affected by "different cultural experiences, language, level of literacy, socioeconomic status, education, level of acculturation and value system" (124).

Janes and Meltzer (1990) suggest that library professionals be trained so that they will be able to address the needs of diverse users and individualize or adapt services as necessary. The authors suggest that invisible barriers and implicit assumptions could impact services to these users, even unintentionally. For example, library staff could assume that their experiences, habits, and communication styles in libraries are the same for everyone and that there is little chance that they would be misunderstood. This homogeneity exists not only among the staff but is also often a larger issue of organizational culture. If the organization is not welcoming or understanding of patrons who are marginalized or somehow exist outside the norm of the accepted culture, these potential users will not frequent the library, no matter how wonderful the programs or extensive the collection (Elteto, Jackson, and Lim 2008). Cuesta (2004) advises that staff training cover three types of techniques: techniques for engaging the community, techniques for effective communication with a diverse customer base, and techniques for analyzing the library from the community's perspective. Training could include cultural awareness and sensitivity training, cultural knowledge, and linguistic competence to help staff convey information in a manner that is easily understood by diverse audiences. Cuesta states, "Everything and anything the library does communicates a message to the community" and staff should be aware of this and willing to plan accordingly (113).

Training could also teach staff how to conduct a community analysis, which would provide rich insight into the communities being served (Giesecke and McNeil 2001; Goodman 2011; Grover, Greer, and Agada 2010; Japzon and Gong 2005; LaFlamme 2007; McDonald 2014) and their information behaviors (Liu 1995).

Community analysis can be a mixture of formal and informal techniques that allow the library to get a comprehensive view of its community's needs and habits. This insight can elucidate best practices in library services and also provides an optimal opportunity to engage with communities to inform and improve the library's services. It is very easy to think the library in which we work is doing a good job because it offers particular services or programs. But how did those services come to be? Were they community information or librarian informed? Librarians have a habit of offering services they think are best, assuming "that the user populations would have the same interests and the same information needs as the librarians, or, through education and reading, those populations would eventually come to share the librarians' interests and needs" (McCleer 2013, 264). Instead of this approach, McCleer (2013, 265) suggests:

> Libraries must respond to the cultural and ethnic changes in the demographics of their communities by developing cultural awareness and strengthening cultural understanding. Librarians and researchers can foster increased cultural awareness and understanding in the process of community assessment through awareness and inclusion of diverse community members throughout the entire process.

The cultural wealth and capital of the diverse communities the library seeks to serve should be given the utmost consideration when planning services

---

Box 4.1 The Power of the Community Gatekeeper

As a [committee] group, we decided to talk with one of the gatekeepers from the Vietnamese community. We knew where to go because we had many Vietnamese co-workers (and some of them were on the committee) and they let us know the key people to meet. When we got to the meeting with the gatekeeper, she greeted us warmly. Once we all sat down, she got real (in a wonderfully badass way but it definitely scared some of my fellow committee members). She told us that this was the umpteenth time that SPL had asked to work with the Vietnamese community in order to "serve them." She said that they were tired of being surveyed and probed only to have nothing happen. She asked what was different about this time.

I told her the difference was the people sitting before her. We really did want to make a difference in their community and serve them better. We showed her the process we were going to follow and showed her what we had done for the Spanish speaking community earlier in the year. This seemed to help and she proceeded to tell us how she could help. She was able to get a focus group session set up for us. We were able to ask them our survey questions and were able to get a rich idea of what they wanted to see in their local library. We also were able to have one of our Vietnamese shelvers set up a table in the branch with the highest amount of Vietnamese patrons.

She [the gatekeeper] spoke to them and asked them to fill out the survey (which had been translated into Vietnamese). We found that they wanted Vietnamese newspapers, books (with specific subject areas preferred), magazines, films, and programming in the local branch. This was not surprising. They pretty much just wanted the same kinds of services that English speakers received.

—Cass Mabbott, former public librarian
(email message to the author, May 12, 2015).
Printed with permission.

(Yosso 2005). As part of this cultural capital and wealth, Metoyer-Duran (1993) and Agada (1999) mention the key role of gatekeepers (Agada 1999; Metoyer-Duran 1993); gatekeepers are community elders or leaders who possess a great deal of community knowledge (written, oral, and linguistic) and community influence. These gatekeepers can make the difference between getting to know a community or not, and they can critically influence whether or not their community members buy into the library and its services (see Box 4.1 for an example). As described in Box 4.1, libraries should be purposeful and ready to act when approaching a community and its gatekeepers; having a community experience survey fatigue and feel like the library is using them is a difficult position to overcome.

Many professional standards encourage uniform service to diverse populations and provide suggestions on how to achieve these goals (see Box 4.2). Lists of competencies, while useful guideposts, can at times be overwhelming and put pressure on library staff, particularly those without cultural competence

Box 4.2   Competencies, Standards, and Guidelines Related to Diverse Populations

Code of Ethics of the American Library Association

American Library Association's Office for Intellectual Freedom

http://www.ala.org/advocacy/proethics/codeofethics/codeethics

Diversity Standards: Cultural Competency for Academic Libraries (2012)

Association of College and Research Libraries

http://www.ala.org/acrl/standards/diversity

Guidelines for the Development and Promotion of Multilingual Collections and Services

American Library Association's Reference and User Services Association

http://www.ala.org/rusa/resources/guidelines/guidemultilingual

Guidelines for Library Services to Older Adults

American Library Association's Reference and User Services Association

http://www.ala.org/rusa/resources/guidelines/libraryservices

Guidelines for Library Services to Spanish-Speaking Library Users

American Library Association's Reference and User Services Association

http://www.ala.org/rusa/resources/guidelines/guidespanish

Prisoners' Right to Read (American Library Association)

http://www.ifmanual.org/prisoners

Professional Codes of Ethics for Librarians

The International Federation of Library Associations and Institutions (IFLA)

http://www.ifla.org/faife/professional-codes-of-ethics-for-librarians

Professional Ethics

American Library Association's Committee on Professional Ethics (COPE)

http://www.ala.org/advocacy/proethics

Other Standards/Documents

Alter, Rachel, Linda Walling, Susan Beck, Kathleen Garland, Ardis Hanson, and Walter Metz. *Guidelines for Library Services for People with Mental Illnesses*. Chicago: Association of Specialized and Cooperative Library Agencies, American Library Association, 2007.

Association of Specialized and Cooperative Library Agencies. *Guidelines for Library Services for People with Mental Retardation*. Chicago: Association of Specialized and Cooperative Library Agencies, 1999.

Association of Specialized and Cooperative Library Agencies. *Revised Standards and Guidelines of Service for the Library of Congress Network of Libraries for the Blind and Physically Handicapped*. Chicago: Association of Specialized and Cooperative Library Agencies, 2011.

Bayley, Linda. *Jail Library Service: A Guide for Librarians and Administrators.* Chicago: Association of Specialized and Cooperative Library Agencies, 1981.

Goddard, Martha L., ed. *Guidelines for Library and Information Services for the American Deaf Community.* Association of Specialized Cooperative Library Agencies, 1996.

Lehmann, Vibeke, and Joanne Locke. *Guidelines for Library Services to Prisoners. IFLA Professional Reports, No. 92.* The Hague, Netherlands: International Federation of Library Associations and Institutions, PO Box 95312, 2509 CH, 2005.

or those who have not been adequately trained. Standards, competencies, and guidelines can also be problematic in the sense that they could actually further facilitate marginalization and allow nonprogressive organizations to say "of course we serve diverse communities, we adhere to points #1–#5 on the standards list." Standards should not be used in isolation, rather they should be used in conjunction with community analysis, cultural competence, and other strategies to best serve diverse communities.

Ultimately, the information needs of minorities do not differ primarily because of race, ethnicity, or other diverse characteristics. However, because of an individual's life situation that may include factors associated with race or ethnicity, such as cultural experiences, language, literacy, recent arrival in the United States, socioeconomic status, education, and most generally, levels of acculturation, these patrons may require different services or considerations (Carlson 1990). Hall (1991) discusses the notion of *affectivity*, which is "the more intangible qualities of personal rapport and empathy," and is just as important as familiarity with specific cultural experiences and sensitivity to diversity. So, although it is useful to know that people of color may regard professional distance as "a sign of rudeness or contempt" (322), it is the specific *relationship* between librarian and user that builds an effective interaction, more so than a well-intentioned, albeit blanket "politically correct" or culturally competent, approach.

REFERENCE SERVICES

Service desks are often the public face of the library and represent the bulk of interactions patrons have with librarians and library staff. Interactions at the reference desk can be particularly challenging or rewarding, depending on the nature of the question, how the question is asked, if the necessary resources are available, and how information is communicated between the librarian and the patron. Reference service is both an art and a science and requires training and practice. Specifically, Fitzgibbons (1983, 5–6) suggested that an equitable and responsive reference service model for diverse populations should aim to include these components:

1. Assessing the problems a member of a diverse group experiences when trying to access information and services provided by the library

2. Conducting research that includes contact with associations and service providers about how to improve services for diverse categories of users (and how to attract nonusers)

3. Planning how to adapt the reference interview, collection development, and delivery of service

4. Training staff to work with users with special needs or cultural differences

5. Implementing periodic evaluation of reference services to members of diverse groups

The Reference Interview

Fundamentally, how the professional librarian conducts the reference interview is no different with diverse users than it is with other users (Saunders and Jordan 2013) and should pose no special challenges to a professionally trained librarian (Leonard 1993). It may require additional understanding, conversation, and resources, but these are components that would benefit any reference interaction. The librarian should treat all people and queries with respect and seriousness. However, with diverse users, it is especially important to anticipate some timidity and a possible reticence toward public institutions and asking for assistance. It is crucial to be aware of and to understand both cultural and individual differences. For example, the terms "Latino" (a reference to Latin America) and "Hispanic" (derived from Hispania, the Latin name for the Iberian Peninsula) hardly describe the huge variety of cultural traditions represented. Although most Hispanics come from Mexico, many are from Puerto Rico, the Dominican Republic, Cuba, and countries in Central and South America. Each cultural group has its own traditions, value systems, and social classes. Hispanics may be of any race and also include the indigenous peoples whose native language is something other than Spanish. Within this array of cultural identities, it is *individuals* with unique needs and questions who come to reference desks for help.

It is also important not to make assumptions regarding what diverse users know about libraries (DiMartino and Zoe 2000; Sarkodie-Mensah 2000). Gilton (1994) suggests that culture shock or clash can occur when diverse users are new to library use, not unlike the clash or discomfort that may occur when anyone visits a foreign land or engages in an unfamiliar environment. This can occur in addition to any library anxiety many users experience when using the library. "Five aspects of culture can lead to culture shock or clash: verbal communication; nonverbal communication; orientation modes, or the use of time and space; social value patterns, which include written and unwritten rules of social behavior; and intellectual modes, which include learning styles valued by the culture" (55). All of these are applicable to library use and reference interactions. Stereotype threat is another serious, and perhaps underrecognized phenomenon, that could sour reference interactions (see Box 4.3). False assumptions exist on both sides of the desk; librarians may make assumptions or hold beliefs about a group that is different from them, even if implicitly. And patrons may be making the very same assumptions about the librarians they are approaching (or not) from afar. These explicit and implicit assumptions can affect communication and ultimately determine the outcome of the reference transaction.

In addition to culture shock, library anxiety, and stereotype threat, diverse users may not understand the concept of call numbers, be able to decipher commonly used library terms, or know how to distinguish between printed first names and surnames. In answering reference questions, slang should be avoided and the use of materials explained and demonstrated, giving users the opportunity to observe and then to imitate. Whenever possible, the librarian should escort a new library user through to the end of the process, such as locating a book or a magazine on the shelf. It is easy to mistake nods and smiles as signifying comprehension. This pitfall can be avoided by asking questions that allow users to communicate more precisely what they do or do not understand. It is very easy to misunderstand body language, eye contact (or lack thereof), attempts at humor, and other common communication habits (Strong 2001). The librarian must abandon assumptions and concentrate on the intent of the user's question. After a question is answered, follow-up is especially important and is vital to proper closure of the interview. The same care and consideration extended to diverse users in a physical library setting should be extended to diverse users seeking reference assistance virtually (Shachaf and Horowitz 2007).

Box 4.3   Avoiding the Reference Desk: Stereotype Threat

African-American student, Keisha has hesitantly entered her library because she needs help on her assignment. However, she has had previous interactions with the white librarians that were unhelpful and left her without the information she needed. These interactions also made Keisha feel like she was dumb and not asking the right questions. She has decided to try again, even though she's not confident this interaction will be any better. As she entered, she saw the librarians and thought: "And, as usual, they are all Caucasian," so that Keisha questioned whether she should bring her topic on black Americans to one of them. Would they understand what she was doing and would they really be able to help her? Would they think her questions were elementary and not worthy of a graduate student?

If you were the librarian in line to help Keisha, how would you work with her?

Katopol, Patricia F. "Management 2.0: Stereotype Threat." *Library Leadership and Management* 28, no. 3 (2014), accessed March 1, 2016, https://journals.tdl.org/llm/index.php/llm/article/viewFile/7074/6293.

Reference Services to Persons with Physical and Cognitive Impairments

Among the specific populations for whom librarians need to develop a full range of reference services are individuals with physical and mental disabilities; this includes those with visual impairments (Davies 2007), hearing impairments (Day 2000; Saar and Arthur-Okor 2013), and various mobility impairments (some of which could be invisible to an observer). In 1990, the Americans with Disabilities Act (ADA) was signed into law, representing "a milestone in America's commitment to full and equal opportunity for all its citizens" (U.S. Equal Employment Opportunity Commission 1992). Title II of the ADA governs public services for disabled individuals. It states, "Library services must be provided in a manner that allows *each* eligible user with a disability to equally benefit from the local library" (Gunde 1992). A particular service for persons with disabilities can be denied only if a library can prove that it would incur an undue burden if it were required to offer the service. However, thinking in terms of "requirements" masks a simple reality. As Lenn (1996, 14) observes, it "is important to remember that the purpose of legislation for the disabled is not to create special rights but equal rights."

Developments in adaptive technology have transformed many dreams into realities, such as speech recognition systems, screen enlargement software, and computerized Braille embossers. But lack of funding for high technology should not inhibit service to disabled users. Many aspects of ADA compliance are not technology-intensive and serve the able-bodied population as well. A magnifying glass and an adjustable piece of furniture are two such examples. Other solutions involve forethought more than cost. If a workstation is set up on a push-button adjustable-height table with an adjustable keyboard tray, with a keyboard that has large-type black-on-white keys, and with two pointing devices such as a conventional mouse and a trackball, the workstation will meet the needs of wheelchair users and people who have computer-related repetitive strain injuries or carpal tunnel syndrome as well as other dexterity disabilities (Goddard 2004). Imrie (2004, 282–283) advocates principles of universal design, in which products, environments, and communication systems are designed for the broadest spectrum of users. He stresses that social, attitudinal, and political shifts must first take place so that design principles and technical adaptations take place within an ethos of inclusiveness. By following this advice, libraries simultaneously meet the needs of able-bodied users as well as disabled clientele. Both legally and ethically, librarians should evaluate the reference services they offer from the perspective of the user with a disability. This is a challenging task, given that there are numerous disabling conditions, and in any community served, the incidence of any one disabling condition may be relatively low.

Persons who have developmental disabilities fall into a wider variety of categories than generally assumed. Developmental disabilities include broad categories such as learning disabilities, intellectual disabilities, and attention-deficit/hyperactivity disorder. Characteristics that are often common to these disabilities are difficulties with language, communication, perception, and cognition. Some individuals may also experience problems with emotional and social development.

Because of the potential for confusion and misunderstanding, the term "developmentally disabled" should be defined whenever it is used. Obviously, with such a variety of characteristics, reference needs will vary, and librarians need to plan accordingly. Reference librarians can adapt services to meet their needs. Reference interview sessions will need to be short and focused. Rephrasing or repetition may be necessary, and listening creatively will facilitate communication. The most successful materials are those that have large print, brief texts, and uncluttered pictures. Although children's materials often prove to be good reference tools, mentally disabled adults have the full range of adult concerns, such as vocation, social relationships, sexuality, money management, and parenting; thus, they frequently need to go beyond the resources of a children's reference collection. The adult reference collection can include titles from among the increasing number of materials available for the adult new reader. Because the mentally impaired user may be slow in processing information, it is important to have useful reference materials that circulate or to have space so that the materials may be used for extended periods of time in the library.

Another category of mental disability is mental illness, which is included in the ADA's definition of disability. With the deinstitutionalization of large numbers of seriously mentally ill individuals, without the provision of sufficient community resources to accommodate them, many have become marginalized in our society and even homeless. Libraries have seen an influx of these displaced people in their reference and reading rooms, and, unfortunately, these patrons are often regarded negatively. While libraries are not social service agencies, there are ways libraries can assist these patrons in helpful and respectful ways

Reference Services to the Homeless and Impoverished

Interacting with the homeless, or mentally ill, in a compassionate yet effective manner, can be assisted with training. Many feel that serving these diverse populations is the domain of social workers, and, indeed, there is much overlap between librarianship and social work. Additionally, there are library systems that employ social workers and public health nurses to work *with* library staff and these diverse users (American Library Association 2012; Blank 2014; Jenkins 2014; Knight 2010; Nemec-Loise 2014; Shafer 2014). However, this can be considered a luxury that most libraries will not have. But librarians, with proper training, can be effective as providers of information and referral services. Library staff can assist homeless patrons with their financial, physical, family, work, emotional, substance abuse, and mental health issues by referring them to appropriate resources and by being empathic human beings (Anderson, Simpson, and Fisher 2012).

To this end, Gehner (2010) suggests that library professionals get out of the library and get to know this diverse user group in such a way that enable them to look beyond appearance to understand deprivation and the causes (and not the symptoms) of poverty and homelessness. This deeper understanding of circumstances can assist in the removal of barriers that socially exclude certain groups. Library staff need to "understand that charity is not dignity; dignity is inclusion" (45). Other suggestions for providing reference services to the homeless and impoverished include delivering services at times and places that may be more convenient to these users, focus on services to homeless and poor families, and publicize these initiatives (Holt 2006). Willett and Broadley (2011) even propose that libraries should evaluate their policies, particularly those in place that require proof of residency to acquire a library card; for the homeless, this may not be possible. Are there other alternatives or temporary memberships available? Winkelstein (2014) concurs and suggests that staff be trained specifically to work with members of this community, create partnerships with the surrounding community, and create a glossary of terms to be used in conjunction with other appropriate resources. Overall, the goal should be to create a safe and welcoming environment.

Reference Services to International Students and New Americans

America is proverbially known as a "melting pot," and, as such, libraries are very familiar with international and immigrant patrons. In particular, these diverse users often come to the United States with little, or no, proficiency in the English language. Known as English as a second language (ESL), English for speakers of other languages (ESOL), English as an additional language (EAL), or English as a foreign language (EFL) learners, these populations are frequent library users and perhaps have the hardest time receiving information because they cannot communicate with library staff.

Academic librarians are particularly familiar with international students studying at their colleges and universities. Successful scholars in their native tongues, a lack of English mastery, and different cultural norms may inhibit them while studying in the United States. Studies also suggest that international students have limited knowledge of libraries in an American context, including the idea of female librarians (Carder, Pracht, and Willingham 1997) and may not understand that the reference desk and librarians are there to assist and should be consulted for information (Dunbar 1986; Lewis 1969). As such, these patrons may be less likely to ask for assistance at an American library reference desk without outreach and training (Ganster 2011; Ishimura and Bartlett 2014; Knight, Hight, and Polfer 2010; Pyati 2003). Anxious about possible communication failures, international students are less likely to seek in-person assistance; instead, they rely on the Internet and friends for information (Helms 1995).

Libraries, especially public libraries, have a long history of welcoming and serving immigrant, or New American, populations (Shen 2013; Wang 2012). According to the New York Public Library (NYPL), one of the largest and most diverse library systems in the United States, 40 million people living in the United States are immigrants, approximately 13 percent of the population.

And 23 percent of that population lives below the poverty line, and many live in large cities and urban areas (New York Public Library 2013). New Americans are information poor, and consequently, this diverse user group often relies on the library for access to the Internet and computers and other basic information necessary for everyday life. Additionally, New Americans can require the library's assistance with learning English (ESL classes), basic education (General Educational Development [GED] or equivalent courses), and information about citizenship. The library is also a prime source of community, health, employment, and legal information:

> When providing reference service to ESL students, it is crucial that librarians remain open-minded, patient, and persistent. Keep in mind that these students come from a variety of backgrounds and cultures. They may have little experience with libraries and librarians, or they may be perfectly comfortable in this setting. They may view the services offered in the library as privileges or as rights. They may speak or write perfect English or struggle with grammar or vocabulary. Of course, they may fall somewhere in the middle of all these extremes, and it is the librarian's responsibility to assess and meet their research needs appropriately. (Walker and Click 2011, 23)

For both international and New American users, who may experience barriers due to language, it is helpful if library staff speak simply, meaning speak at a easily understandable pace and avoid slang, colloquialisms, or library jargon (Walker and Click 2011, 20–23). Such barriers can cause self-consciousness and prevent patrons from asking for assistance. Pyati (2003) suggests libraries have extra outreach for these diverse patrons, including special resources on the libraries' websites. Other low stakes accommodations and actions libraries can make include having dedicated web pages and tutorials, having specialized instructions and orientations in other languages (Knight et al. 2010), having foreign language materials in the reference and circulating collections, creating multilingual signage and handouts, and gesturing and pointing (gesturing and pointing are often perceived as rude but can actually be helpful when there is a language barrier). Other investments, which require more time and financial commitment, involve hiring bilingual library staff and creating multilingual online catalogs (Berger 2012).

Reference Services to the Incarcerated

Library services to the incarcerated or detained are important and often overlooked, in part because of the diverse population being served, the libraries' locations, and a lack of resources and staff. Prison libraries are often referenced as a social justice issue but can support curriculum, hobbies and recreational reading, legal endeavors, and overall learning and improvement for those utilizing library services (Clark and MacCreaigh 2006). Prison libraries also provide information about treatment programs (e.g., substance abuse and anger management) and their in-house work duties and can serve as a much-needed space of quiet and a sense of normalcy for the detained (Lehmann 2011). A marginalized population that overlaps with the mentally ill, homeless, lesbian, gay, bisexual, trans, and queer (LGBTQ), young adult, minority, and other diverse populations, the incarcerated particularly benefit from library services as the information gained can aid in rehabilitation, which in turn can aid in their release, reentry, rehabilitation, and avoidance of recidivism (Morris 2013). And once released, libraries can also assist with the development of employment skills and computer skills. An exemplar is the Denver Public Library that works with the formerly detained and supports them in three areas: "job search skills and readiness, computer and Internet skills, and library awareness and understanding" (120). The library trains their staff to work with this diverse population in such a way as to diffuse shame and build confidence in patrons.

Prison libraries often lack dedicated staff, some manned with part-time staff or volunteers, or mobile librarians who enter the facility on an ad hoc basis (Rubin and House 1983). Other services are supported by volunteer organizations that do readers' advisory or answer basic reference questions off-site and through postal mail. Reference services can be particularly challenging in this setting. Dixen and Thorson (2001) state that reference can be abbreviated and sporadic, depending on the librarian's schedule and the availability of resources. Reference interactions could last between 5 and 10 minutes and could happen as infrequently as once a month. This makes the reference interview vitally important, and supplemental reference, via forms in the mail, is often necessary. Clark and MacCreaigh (2006, 194) speak to the range of questions that occur, from both male and female inmates, many of whom have trust (and alternately attachment) issues. The authors state that libraries are fulfilling basic information needs for these patrons, information that aids in informed decision making about their criminal charges, their children and families, and their legal counsel. They caution library professionals providing reference assistance by stating, "While librarians cannot and should not answer any of these questions, we believe that we are duty-bound to provide our patrons with the research tools they need to answer the questions for themselves" (51).

These circumstances are even more challenging when trying to assist with legal information and research. The authors continue by discussing the need for compassion, flexibility, respect, and confidentiality while working with this population, which ranges greatly when it comes to backgrounds, communication skills, and educational levels.

> Along with a sense of fairness, other qualities are required of all librarians who deal with the public: flexibility, high tolerance, good communication skills, awareness of cultural issues and lack of bias toward any group, emotional maturity, and a sense of humor. These skills are even more necessary for a prison librarian because of the extreme circumstances and pressured context surrounding the patrons who come to her. And often, the limited communication skills of some prisoners bring a special challenge, making the reference interview especially important. (51)

Ready reference, readers' advisory, and legal information are especially important to this population. Glennor Shirley cautions about material that is deemed dangerous, in that it could unduly incite inmates who are violent, sex offenders, or who have psychological issues. To that end, prison libraries experience censorship of materials, further limiting the librarian's reach and abilities (Shirley 2003). Librarians who work within prisons or detention centers, or those who work in public libraries, can aid members of this community by forging relationships "with community partners, especially with halfway houses, government agencies, correctional facilities, and other organizations that provide services to felons" (Morris 2013, 120). Partnerships are especially important for this user group in order to maintain its progress and help the group reenter society.

Reference Services to the LGBTQ Community

Another growing population of diverse users is the LGBTQ/questioning individuals (Greenblatt 2010; Howard 2010; McKay 2011; Taylor 2002; Thompson 2012). Austin (2012) writes specifically about LGBTQ youth, a group with high rates of juvenile detention, and this is a fast growing area of service and research in the field of librarianship. The entire LGBTQ population is vulnerable, especially its youth. "For gay and lesbian youth, the public library can be a key resource for information about emerging and often-confusing sexual feelings. A good reference librarian can mean the difference between the youth fleeing the library or considering the library a helpful refuge" (Curry 2005, 65). LGBTQ youth are at-risk and afraid, and these feelings are no different in a library setting. The library can be a "chilly" and potentially unwelcoming environment for out youth or those considering coming out (Mehra and Braquet 2011). Curry and other authors focus on LGBTQ youth, but the best practices that apply to serving them in a library setting apply to the entire LGBTQ community. Curry also discusses the implicit biases that may impact library professionals when serving patrons from the LGBTQ community. The suggestion is that even if librarians at the reference desk do not outright refuse to serve these patrons or interact with them in a purposefully rude way, their demeanor and body language can indicate discomfort, hostility, or even judgment. Such nonverbal communication can deter or stifle reference interviews and interactions. Body language, and subsequently search strategies (or lack thereof), and a lack of a concluding statement or follow-up can convey a lack of objectivity and hesitancy to help LGBTQ patrons. Curry (2005) posits that even when librarians have personal relationships with a gay or lesbian friend, colleague, or family member, that does not always translate to their work behind the reference desk. Residual feelings or biases toward this group of patrons:

> are rooted so deeply that they survive even the lectures on professional ethics that most librarians experience while obtaining their degrees. As a result, a librarian may retain an antagonism or quiet indifference that is revealed in inadequate collection management of gay and lesbian materials, a transgression that is impersonal and often hidden. But does this antagonism or indifference manifest itself in a more direct way: in the reference interview? (Curry 2005, 66).

A failed reference encounter can be compounded when the library's collection and/or public catalog are not current or representative of the community or even exclude the LGBTQ community and its needs and interests. Gough and Greenblatt (1992, 61) refer to this as "systemic bibliographic invisibility," when a library's collection lacks appropriate materials because they do not fit in with existing collection and classification schemes.

Curry's study (2005) found that the best librarians were welcoming, "personal but not nosy," conducted a good reference interview, portrayed a level of comfort when using the words "gay" and "lesbian," found appropriate resources, worked with the patron as opposed to telling them what to do, and referred the patron when more information was required (Curry 2005, 72). In general, when working with LGBTQ youth or adults, librarians should: appear interested in the question; appear comfortable with LGBTQ topics; maintain eye contact; demonstrate a relaxed body posture; give their full attention to the patron; maintain confidentiality by being discrete; and make the patron feel at ease during the interaction (73).

Reference Services for Older Adults

Librarians should be cognizant of the particular learning needs of adult learners (Cooke 2010), and this holds true for older adults who frequent the library. Indeed, older adults may have additional special needs that require accommodation and unassuming services from the library. According to the census, the term "elderly" refers to adults who are 65 years of age or older. This is one of the fastest growing segments of our population, constituting 12.9 percent of the population in 2010 (U.S. Census Bureau 2012, Table 9); this percentage is projected to rise to 20.2 percent by 2050. Librarians should be adapting reference services to meet the needs of this growing population whose needs will be coming to the forefront in the next 25 years (Decker 2010). It is also anticipated that because of improved health care, older adults will be more active. At the same time, a longer life means that more people live with physical and mental ailments.

Good reference service for elderly individuals includes all the basic components of good reference service for the general adult population, with particular attention to the individual needs of elderly users. In its guidelines for library service to older adults, the Reference and User Services Association (RUSA) of the American Library Association (ALA) exhorts libraries to provide a full slate of integrated library services to the elderly. The ALA's Office for Diversity, Literacy and Outreach Services provides suggestions for serving older adults that include having large print materials and magnifying equipment; having comfortable and supportive seating; having accessible shelving (so as to eliminate excessive bending or reaching for materials); having relevant information in a central location (e.g., agency brochures and flyers); and taking care that the physical building is conducive and accessible (e.g., bathrooms, elevators, and checkout stations should have support rails, computer stations should be ADA compliant, and computers might have cordless mouse devices for those suffering from arthritis) (Perry 2014; Reference and User Services Association 2008).

Reference librarians need to avoid stereotyping or patronizing older users and should develop effective communication skills so as to encourage them to ask questions and to ensure that each answer is fully understood by the user.

Some older adults, for example, have had limited exposure to computers and may experience more computer anxiety than younger library users. Whereas the library was once a friendly, welcoming physical place for recreation and leisure, it now feels intimidating and impersonal. Special online catalog instruction sessions (or word processing classes, or workshops dedicated to email, Internet searching, and social media) tailored for older individuals will create a comfortable atmosphere where users can ask questions and experience self-paced practice and one-on-one coaching.

To provide reference service to older adults, it may be necessary to offer remote delivery of materials and services. Certainly, the most common form of remote delivery of reference service to seniors is by telephone. In libraries, where in-person reference service is busy and takes precedence over answering questions over the telephone, special provisions must be made to serve the homebound and the institutionalized elderly. The general rule of serving walk-in users before answering the telephone is logical but may make it difficult for the older adult to access the library. It may be necessary to set up a special telephone service for elderly or disabled persons who cannot easily get to the library. Also, it may be possible to take reference service to elderly individuals by including reference materials in the bookmobile collection when making stops at retirement homes, assisted living facilities, nursing homes, or senior citizen centers or by providing chat and email reference service to these agencies. Training bookmobile staff in basic reference service and teaching care-facility staff to assist with online reference services would ensure that questions could be answered in a timely and predictable fashion.

It is important to communicate to older adults the reference services that are available to them and to make them feel welcome. The library can effectively market services of particular interest to older persons through library brochures, specific informational programs held in the library, and outside agencies. Reference librarians should cultivate communications with other service agencies in the community; often, specialists in services to the elderly can provide training for library staff in working with the elderly and make appropriate referrals to the library if interagency cooperation is practiced. Careful assessment of what use older citizens make of a library may reveal a need to publicize existing reference services or a way to adapt services to meet the needs and capacities of older adults. The library should not be a place where older adults encounter ageism, rather a place that encourages and facilitates lifelong learning and healthy, independent living (Van Fleet 1995). In order to achieve this kind of atmosphere, Van Fleet suggests that librarians serving older adults need patience, they should be sensitive to unspoken needs, and they need to be flexible when implementing service (e.g., in the event of diminishments in vision, hearing, or mobility) (152–154).

INSTRUCTION TO DIVERSE POPULATIONS

Much like reference services, instruction to diverse populations (also referred to as bibliographic instruction or information literacy instruction) involves direct interaction with members of diverse communities and requires many of the same considerations and accommodations, particularly when dealing with communities that do not have the same perceptions and understanding of libraries and those with differing language abilities. Dorner and Gorman (2008), who studied English as a Second Language services in libraries, explain this point by stating,

> Understanding the culture, values, beliefs, and practices that ESL students bring from their home countries and exhibit in the composition classroom can help librarians create programs that help define library services and help to bridge the gap between services provided by the librarian and the ESL composition instructor. (p. 12)

Instruction needs are also quite variable depending on library type – academic libraries focus on teaching patrons how to navigate and use scholarly information, while public libraries may primarily address computer literacy, word processing, Internet navigation and other such topics. What these settings do have in common is their services to adults, and as such librarians should be cognizant of andragogy (Cooke 2010), which is very simply pedagogy for adults. Adult learners have different attention spans, time constraints, information needs, and information processing from that of children and young adults. Adults, and other members of diverse communities, may also experience culture shock and library anxiety more acutely than younger patrons.

Gilton (2005) discusses culture shock and says that those from different cultures and international patrons are among those most prone to discomfort and uncertainty when using libraries. Among the many groups that can experience culture shock are the physically and mentally impaired, LGBTQ patrons, at-risk students, graduate students, distance education students, and senior citizens. Librarians should be aware of the contexts, educational philosophies, learning styles, and multiple intelligences of the diverse populations in their communities and be flexible in how and where they provide instructional services. Instruction may need to be conducted one-on-one (as opposed to in-groups); it may occur in person, over the phone, or over the Internet. Instruction may also be asynchronous in the form of videos or educational modules that can be independently accessed online by patrons. Ultimately, instruction services require relationship building, and librarians need to make additional efforts to build rapport with their communities and really learn about their information and instructional needs and bridge or build gaps in understanding when necessary (Martin et al. 2012).

COLLECTIONS DEVELOPMENT AND CATALOGING FOR DIVERSE POPULATIONS

If reference services and programming are the public faces of the library, collection development could be considered the heart of library services, since it is the collections that community members come in to use and check out. It is also through collections that the library could make its most significant contribution to diversity, by acquiring materials that accurately represent the cultures and languages of the community (see Box 4.4). Librarians and staff must educate themselves and become familiar with the wide assortment of diverse materials that could be useful in libraries. Griswold Blandy (1994, 122–123) states, "We need to become more aware of the limits of our own cultural box and the varieties of other boxes."

In addition to materials in other languages, there are many print and non-print sources that are representative of diverse and underrepresented cultures; these materials are often more expensive and harder to acquire if they are not available through mainstream vendors. While these tasks are easier said than done, especially with ever-shrinking budgets, efforts toward inclusive collection development (and the professional development education and training that would facilitate these efforts) should be made nonetheless. Such intentions and efforts should also be institutionalized and included in library policies and strategic plans. Scarborough (1991) concurs and warns that if libraries do not secure diverse collections, libraries could lose or offend patrons. "Unless things change, libraries risk leaving potential patrons disillusioned by a lack of relevant materials and services" (44). To this end, Cecilia Feltis (Jaeger et al. 2015), a public library director in Fairfield, New Jersey, discusses the need to "date" her town in order to find out who they were and what they wanted to see at their library. Serving a culturally Italian American town, particularly when she herself is not Italian, required that she acquire comprehensive knowledge of the community. Previously, the community did not patronize the library frequently because the library did not have relevant resources of interest (including Italian language materials). Feltis states:

Box 4.4   Why We Need Diverse Books

While this text does not address services to children or young adults, it really should be noted that there have been great and successful efforts to diversify children's and young adult literature. The efforts, initiatives, and literature are definitely applicable to the need for diversifying *all* literature and for securing and maintaining diverse collections in libraries.

Alexander, Linda B., and Sarah D. Miselis. "Barriers to GLBTQ Collection Development and Strategies for Overcoming Them." *Young Adult Library Services* 5, no. 3 (2007): 43–49.

Hughes-Hassell, Sandra, and Ernie J. Cox. "Inside Board Books: Representations of People of Color." *The Library Quarterly* 80, no. 3 (2010): 211–230.

Kurz, Robin F. "Missing Faces, Beautiful Places: The Lack of Diversity in South Carolina Picture Book Award Nominees." *New Review of Children's Literature and Librarianship* 18, no. 2 (2012): 128–145.

Myers, Christopher, "The Apartheid of Children's Literature," *New York Times, Sunday Review*, March 15, 2014.

Myers, Walter Dean. "Where Are the People of Color in Children's Books?" *New York Times, Sunday Review*, March 15, 2014.

"We Need Diverse Books | Official Site of the #WeNeedDiverseBooks Campaign," We Need Diverse Books, April 1, 2014, accessed January 16, 2015, http://weneeddiversebooks.org.

> Conducting some research, as one would for a potential date, helps librarians decide what type of programs to have. Some Internet search options to query are the history of the town, current leaders, cultural makeup, demographics, and size of the population. Once one has those details, it is important to get out of the library and go to where the patrons are. Take flyers to hair salons, go to local restaurants and introduce yourself, go to the municipal office and make sure they know that the library is there as a partner to help the community. (161)

Once Feltis successfully dated her community and established key partnerships in the community, the results were successful and rewarding; the library has become a key component in the life of this diverse user group.

Also worth considering is the diversity of the *types* of diverse literature available for collections. Comic books (Upson and Hall 2013), graphic novels, zines (Gisony and Freedman 2006; Herrada 1995), and media objects often depict and represent diverse communities and should be incorporated into collections, and these materials typically appeal to multiple diverse populations. Libraries must embrace the nontraditional materials that users want to see and use.

The collection development and cataloging processes also display the acute need for diverse and bi/multilingual library professionals, those who can seek out alternative and foreign language materials that are not always available from mainstream vendors.

> Selecting, ordering, cataloging, and providing access to non-English materials reach beyond the boundaries of departments responsible for the individual tasks. Assignments require different levels of language proficiency ranging from bibliographic proficiency to the near-native proficiency of the educated speaker. The highest level of language proficiency is used at the earliest and latest point of technical services (i.e., ordering and cataloging), and the rest requires only bibliographic proficiency or none at all. Because international vendor experiences vary country-by-country, strong cooperation is critical between the partners in the acquisition process. (Ward 2011, 86).

In addition to language skills, collection development and cataloging for diverse populations require library staff who are culturally adept, critical thinkers, and members of the communities for which the library is collecting. There are several scholars in this area who are writing extensively about these issues, making the claim that the proper and extensive cataloging is a social justice issue, in addition to being as issue of access. Library and information science (LIS) educator Hope Olson (1998, 2000, 2001) and librarian and activist Sandford Berman (2008) are considered pioneers in this area of research. Olson says that cataloging is a mechanism by which the "meanings of documents are constructed and enunciated for library users," often by members of dominant systems and cultures (Olson 2000, 53). As a consequence, the Library of Congress Subject Headings, the Dewey Decimal System, and other classification systems unintentionally exclude, marginalize, and distort information belonging to other cultures (typically belonging to members of diverse populations) because they are not culturally relevant or responsive (60). For this

---

Box 4.5   An Example of More Inclusive Cataloging

Imagine a book about our quarterback that also discussed his struggles with racism in the NFL. A cataloger might assign QUARTER-BACKING (FOOTBALL), because it is about football, rather than RACISM-UNITED STATES about racism in America. The book would then be visible to sports researchers, and less so to researchers studying racism in America. The range of options is enormous; a cataloger might also choose RACISM IN SPORTS (204)

Drabinski, Emily. 2008. "Teaching the Radical Catalog." In *Radical Cataloging: Essays at the Front,* edited by K.R. Roberto, 198–205. Jefferson, NC: McFarland.

---

reason, Berman and others have called for radical cataloging, which calls for librarians to recognize the systems in which they live and work and make efforts to expand cataloging schema to be inclusive of the diverse communities being served. Billey, Drabinski, and Roberto (2014) and Drabinski (2013) have continued this line of inquiry using the LGBTQ community as an example of a group that is under- and misrepresented in library classification systems. Specifically, Drabinski (2013) issues a call for critical cataloging (see Box 4.5) and states that "hegemonic library classification structures and controlled vocabularies dialogically engage the catalog as a complex and biased text" (95). Librarians, in all types of libraries, need to be cognizant of these issues and sensitive to the challenges of making information relevant to diverse communities actually available to these communities.

LIBRARIES, SOCIAL WORK, AND DIVERSE POPULATIONS

An increasing number of media news items detail the presence of social workers in libraries (see Box 4.6). Certainly, the two service professions have much in common, and because libraries are often physically prominent in communities, it makes sense that they would be desirable placements for social workers. Social workers (and some public health nurses) have been placed in libraries (full-time and part-time) to work with the homeless, but social workers provide so much more than services to the homeless, who often overlap with the mentally ill, veteran, and LGBTQ young adult populations. Also consider the at-risk children, battered women (Dunne 2002; Harris 1988; Harris et al. 2001), victims of natural disasters, the formerly incarcerated, the socioculturally marginalized, the unemployed, and the chronically or terminally ill, all of whom frequent libraries and could benefit from direct assistance and direction to community resources. Personal crises are not static and are always present somewhere in the community. Librarians are faced with more tasks, fewer resources, and sometime extreme conditions (see Box 4.7), and they do not always have the time to dedicate or the expertise to work with these diverse populations in this capacity, and social workers can fulfill this service need.

Box 4.6　Social Workers in the Library

Public Libraries Add Social Workers and Social Programs

The New Social Worker: The Social Work Careers Magazine
http://www.socialworker.com/feature-articles/practice/public
-libraries-add-social-workers-and-social-programs/

Library Social Worker Helps Homeless Seeking Quiet Refuge

PBS NewsHour
http://www.pbs.org/newshour/bb/library-social-worker-helps
-homeless-seeking-quiet-refuge/

From Nurses to Social Workers, See How Public Libraries Are Serving the Homeless

PBS NewsHour
http://www.pbs.org/newshour/rundown/see-libraries-across
-country-serving-homeless/

Nation's First Library Social Worker Helps Give Hope to the Homeless

The California Report
http://audio.californiareport.org/archive/R201404111630/d

A Little Extra Help—Why Public Libraries Need Social Workers

Public Libraries Online (Public Library Association)
http://publiclibrariesonline.org/2014/09/a-little-extra-help-why
-public-libraries-need-social-workers/

D.C. Adds a Social Worker to Library System to Work with Homeless Patrons

The Washington Post
http://www.washingtonpost.com/local/dc-adds-a-social-worker-to
-library-system-to-work-with-homeless-patrons/2014/08/26/
2d80200c-2c96-11e4-be9e-60cc44c01e7f_story.html

Urban Libraries Become De Facto Homeless Shelters

NPR
http://www.npr.org/2014/04/23/306102523/san-francisco-library
-hires-social-worker-to-help-homeless-patrons

However, there is a tension that exists here, one that consists of boundaries and funding. There is no doubt that many librarians serve as de facto social workers, just as libraries often serve as de facto shelters. But should they serve in this capacity? Do librarians want social workers in their spaces to provide information referrals (long considered to be a library responsibility)? And if social workers are indeed a feasible option, who will pay for them? Is it the responsibility of the library or of the local social services agency? As Cathcart (2008) stated, the line between social work and librarianship is a blurry one.

Certainly, librarians are not providing therapy or case management, and their involvement may often stop at asking a disruptive person to leave

---

Box 4.7   Radical Hospitality

During community uprisings in Ferguson, Missouri (2014), and in Baltimore, Maryland (2015), the libraries were praised for staying open and reaching out to their residents when schools were closed and neighboring buildings were on fire. Observers have deemed the libraries' actions as radical hospitality, which has been described as a practice of putting extraordinary effort and emphasis on making people feel welcome and breaking down barriers that keep people from ongoing participation. This is achieved through consistent community effort and strives to include everyone and exclude no one.

Is this kind of service really radical, or is this just what libraries do/have always done?

(Homan and Pratt 2011).

---

or calling the police. Nevertheless, it's another example of libraries providing a service (say, de facto shelter) that isn't part of their explicit mission, and a case where increased communication, collaboration, and (in some cases) training with social service agencies might be called for. (89)

Westbrook (2015, 6) follows up on Cathcart's line of thought and states that there is a "delicate balance between the librarian's customized information service and the social worker's case management triage, librarians must understand the situated information needs of their in-crisis patrons." However, ultimately Westbrook feels that experienced librarians recognize and possess boundaries and "quickly recognize the difference between casual and intense questions" (6), one that should go to a librarian and another that should be handled by a social worker. It is an emerging and complex issue but one that is ripe for collaborations and community partnerships (Luo et al. 2012).

MARKETING AND OUTREACH TO DIVERSE POPULATIONS

Once libraries have established policies, services, and collections that are inclusive and responsive to diverse communities, perhaps the last, but certainly not the least, activities in which to engage are marketing and outreach. What good are stellar resources and services if the community is not aware of them? Marketing and outreach take on a variety of forms, can target specific services (e.g., the marketing of virtual reference services [Bailey-Hainer 2014]) or resources, or can address the community at larger or smaller subcommunities. Academic library marketing tends to be more insular because it often serves a singularly located community and promotes resources that are limited in applicability and availability; however, the literature urges librarians from all kinds of libraries to come out from behind their service desks to meet people where they are, particularly when they are members of diverse populations

(Aguilar and Keating 2009; Gibbons 2013; Love 2009; Mundava and Gray 2008; Puente, Gray, and Agnew 2009).

The first step to the marketing process is assessing community needs and interests. A particular method of acquiring this information is market segmentation, which is defined as "the process of identifying the salient distinctive characteristics among consumers or patrons and using these distinctions as the basis for differentiated promotions, communications, advertising, and other marketing strategies" (Futterman and Michaelson 2012, 141). Market segmentation (Futterman 2008; Lee 2004) is very much the same process as community analysis (see Chapter 2), with the specific goal of developing a marketing plan.

Love (2009) and Mundava and Gray (2008) provide suggestions on how academic librarians can expand their reach and networks on their campuses. For example, some libraries dedicate personnel to marketing and outreach, and these are the librarians who serve as area/department liaisons, work specifically to establish partnerships and collaborations, and whose job is to promote resources and services to diverse constituents. Personnel dedicated to marketing, outreach, and services to diverse populations are a luxury, and such positions are few and far between. However, all librarians and library staff can play a part in marketing and outreach efforts.

Mundava and Gray (2008) also give suggestions on marketing to international students, but the suggestions are applicable to all kinds of libraries. The process begins with developing a marketing plan; this plan should have measurable goals, be in line with the library's mission, and can benefit from input from across the library. A marketing plan should also include a plan of action, mechanisms of information dissemination, and activities such as open houses, programming, and distribution of targeted advertising and materials. The plan should also include a feedback loop and opportunities for retooling and relaunching.

Like the collection development plan, the marketing plan should incorporate various media, too. Print resources are valuable, but marketing efforts should extend to blogs (Decker and Tomlinson 2014), social media, videos, and other online platforms. Online outreach allows for short and timely content; it promotes anonymous feedback (if anonymous feedback is desired and/or useful); such outlets can have a low enough curve technology-wise that multiple staff in the library can participate in marketing efforts. Marketing could also include billboards, word of mouth, and making physical visits to speak with community members in salons, barbershops, bakeries, and other establishments (as earlier described by Cecilia Feltis). Marketing and outreach are additional tools that the librarian can employ to build and sustain relationships with their diverse communities.

EVALUATION AND ASSESSMENT OF SERVICES FOR DIVERSE POPULATIONS

Much like the process of becoming culturally competent (see Chapter 2), the implementation of services for diverse populations is a dynamic and ongoing process. An important part of this process is the evaluation and refinement of these services. Are the new materials purchased for a particular group being used and checked out? Where these new materials marketed well? Has staff training in racial microaggressions resulted in better attitudes and fewer patron complaints? Has that training improved the overall climate and culture of the library? It is important to note if efforts have been successful or unsuccessful; it is part of the growth process the library goes through in order to be the best service providers possible. Additionally, it is important to seek feedback from the library's target communities—have their perceptions of the library changed? Are community partners seeking the library out, or are they more willing to collaborate with the library on initiatives for shared diverse populations? Similar to the techniques of conducting a community analysis (see Chapter 2), there are many ways to solicit external feedback (quantitative and qualitative), so long as the feedback loop is active and ongoing.

A specific technique that can be used to evaluate and assess a library's diversity efforts is to conduct a climate assessment, which will indicate the health of an organization's culture (Royse, Conner, and Miller 2006; Smith 2008). In addition to documenting the diversity of the library's staff (see Chapter 5 for a discussion on diversity hiring), a climate assessment will document the organization's implicit and explicit commitment to diversity. Is diversity evident in the library's strategic plans, vision, mission statement, policies, services, collections, and programs? Is the commitment to diversity evident and public (e.g., prominently displayed on the library's website and in print materials)? Or are the commitments to diversity expressed orally, informally, and/or when there is a sensitive discussion? Smith (2008) states:

> An organization's culture consists of the values and norms established by the institution as well as personal attitudes, behaviors, and experiences that employees themselves bring to the job. In order to sustain and maximize the benefits of a diverse workforce, evaluation of the work environment for barriers to access and full participation in the life of the institution must be an integral part of the institution's overall strategic plan. To achieve diversity in substance as well as in form, libraries have to open their arms to all perspectives and experiences. That requires competency in matters of cultural pluralism that are not intuitive and must be learned, like any other essential skill.

A culturally conscious organization is the goal, one that fosters an environment of honesty, innovation, and inclusivity at all levels.

CONCLUSION

Many components are involved with the promotion of the library to diverse populations. In addition to quality and relevant programs and collections, libraries should hire diverse staff (including those with language skills), should tap diverse community members to serve on the library's board, and collaborations and partnerships with other community agencies should be established (Gavier and Scobey 2001).

Services and collections should be offered to all members of the community regardless of their circumstances or identifying characteristics. Library staff should acknowledge that programs, collections, and services *do* need to be adapted, or at least assessed, with respect to the needs and abilities of particular groups. Librarians and staff need to identify the diverse user groups within their community that might face obstacles to free and full access to information. It should be stressed that such community assessment needs go beyond simply polling or observing current users of library materials or services. If impediments such as physical or communication barriers exist, members of a group affected by these barriers often are nonusers of the library and thus are invisible to the librarian who only observes the behavior of the user group. Community analysis efforts must extend beyond the walls of the library.

Once groups are identified, librarians need to create plans for services, programs, and collection development that will meet the special needs in question. Plans would include determining the adaptations needed by each group, assessing the library's ability to meet identified needs, and establishing priorities for actions to be taken by the library. Partnerships with other agencies, including local ones and regional or national organizations, can assist in the community analysis process. The library should have policies and procedures, including staff training, which enhance access to full library services. Librarians should work diligently with patrons of diverse user groups without judgment or assumptions; instead, empathy and openness should guide all interactions and library services in general. Finally, librarians should plan regular evaluation of services and facilities for targeted groups so that they can keep up with or even anticipate changes in the needs of their diverse users.

In order to plan services, assemble collections, and develop interaction and engagement skills appropriate to the various groups in their community of users, library staff must begin with an understanding of the diverse groups that constitute their community.

LESSON PLAN

Essential Readings:

If you are interested in conducting a community analysis, you should definitely read:

Grover, Robert, Roger C. Greer, and John Agada. *Assessing Information Needs: Managing Transformative Library Services.* Santa Barbara, CA: ABC-CLIO, 2010.

If you are interested in instruction services, you should definitely read:

Jacobson, Trudi E., and Helene C. Williams, eds. *Teaching the New Library to Today's Users: Reaching International, Minority, Senior Citizens, Gay/Lesbian, First Generation, At-Risk, Graduate and Returning Students, and Distance Learners.* New York: Neal Schuman Pub, 2000.

If you are interested in library marketing, you should definitely read:

Dempsey, Kathy. *The Accidental Library Marketer.* New York: Information Today, 2009.

Other Key Works:

Balderrama, Sandra Rios. "This Trend Called Diversity." *Library Trends* 49, no. 1 (2000): 194–214.

Maloney, Michelle M. "Cultivating Community, Promoting Inclusivity: Collections as Fulcrum for Targeted Outreach." *New Library World* 113, no. 5/6 (2012): 281–289.

Smith, Paula M. "Culturally Conscious Organizations: A Conceptual Framework." *portal: Libraries and the Academy* 8, no. 2 (2008): 141–155.

Questions to Ask:

1. What diverse population(s) do you identify with? What services would you like to see at your library to meet your needs?

2. Looking up a shelter address, finding the right bus route to reach the shelter, and inviting additional questions—is that considered social work or reference work?

Assignment:

Locate an article from a LIS trade publication (such as *Library Journal, School Library Journal, American Libraries, Public Libraries Online, College & Research Libraries News*) that discusses service(s) to a diverse population. What ideas can you implement in your library?

Some examples:

- Barack, L., "LGBTQ and You: How to Support Your Students," *School Library Journal*, May 1, 2014, retrieved from http://www.slj.com/2014/05/diversity/lgbtq-you-how-to-support-your-students/.

- Hudson-Ward, A. "Diversity and Inclusion Online Resources for Education." *College and Research Libraries News* 75, no. 6 (2014, June): 336–345. http://crln.acrl.org/content/75/6/336.full.

- Cottrell, M., "Libraries Create Gender-Neutral Bathrooms," *American Libraries*, October 30, 2015, retrieved from https://americanlibraries magazine.org/2015/10/30/libraries-gender-neutral-bathrooms/.

Another resource of note is Pinterest—https://www.pinterest.com.
Pinterest is a social bookmarking site that allows the user to create and follow boards of interest. Users "pin" items of interest from the Internet; anything with a picture (or a video) can be saved. Pinterest can be a valuable source for course resources, housing links, videos, and images of interest. A class board can also be interactive if students are encouraged to curate the board. The board that I use for my diversity and social justice courses can be found here: https://www.pinterest.com/nicolecooke/diversity-and-social-justice/.

REFERENCES

Agada, John. 1999. "Inner-City Gatekeepers: An Exploratory Survey of Their Information Use Environment." *JASIS* 50 (1): 74–85.

Aguilar, Paulita, and Kathleen Keating. 2009. "Satellite Outreach Services Program to Under-Represented Students: Being in Their Space, Not on MySpace." *The Reference Librarian* 50 (1): 14–28.

American Library Association. 2012. "Extending Our Reach: Reducing Homelessness through Library Engagement." Last modified October 8, 2012. http://www.ala.org/offices/extending-our-reach-reducing-homelessness-through-library-engagement-6.

Anderson, Keith A., Chaniqua D. Simpson, and Lynette G. Fisher. 2012. "The Ability of Public Library Staff to Help Homeless People in the United States: Exploring Relationships, Roles and Potential." *Journal of Poverty and Social Justice* 20 (2): 177–190.

Austin, Jeanie. "Critical Issues in Juvenile Detention Libraries." Paper presented at YALSA's Trends Impacting Young Adult Services Event, ALA Midwinter Meeting, Dallas, TX, January 21, 2012. http://www.yalsa.ala.org/jrlya/2012/07/critical-issues-in-juvenile-detention-center-libraries/.

Bailey-Hainer, Brenda. 2014. "Marketing Virtual Reference Services: The AskColorado Experience." *OLA Quarterly* 10 (2): 12–17.

Berger, Joseph. 2012. "Libraries Speak the Mother Tongue." *The New York Times* (New York), January 3, 2012, NY Region edition, A18.

Berman, Sanford. 2008. *Radical Cataloging: Essays at the Front.* Edited by Keller R. Roberto. Jefferson, NC: McFarland.

Billey, Amber, Emily Drabinski, and K. R. Roberto. 2014. "What's Gender Got to Do with It? A Critique of RDA 9.7." *Cataloging and Classification Quarterly* 52 (4): 412–421.

Blank, Barbara Trainin. 2014. "Public Libraries Add Social Workers and Social Programs." *The New Social Worker*, October 2, 2014. http://www.socialworker.com/feature-articles/practice/public-libraries-add-social-workers-and-social-programs/. Accessed March 1, 2016.

Carder, Linda, Carl Pracht, and Robert Willingham. "Reaching the Whole Population: Adaptive Techniques for Reaching Students Who Fall Through the Cracks." *Programs That Work*: Papers and sessions material presented at the Twenty-Fourth National LOEX Library Instruction Conference, May 16–18, 1996, Ann Arbor, MI: Learning Resources and Technologies, 1997, 67–75.

Carlson, David B. 1990. "Adrift in a Sea of Change: California's Public Libraries Struggle to Meet the Information Needs of Multicultural Communities." Sacramento, CA: California State Library Foundation, Center for Policy Development.

Cathcart, Rachael. 2008. "Librarian or Social Worker: Time to Look at the Blurring Line?" *The Reference Librarian* 49 (1): 89.

Clark, Sheila, and Erica MacCreaigh. 2006. *Library Services to the Incarcerated: Applying the Public Library Model in Correctional Facility Libraries.* Santa Barbara, CA: Libraries Unlimited.

Cooke, Nicole A. 2010. "Becoming an Andragogical Librarian: Using Library Instruction as a Tool to Combat Library Anxiety and Empower Adult Learners." *New Review of Academic Librarianship* 16 (2): 208–227.

Cuesta, Yolanda J. Cuesta. 2004. "Developing Outreach Skills in Library Staff." In *From Outreach to Equity: Innovative Models of Library Policy and Practice,* edited by Robin Osborne, 112–115. Chicago: American Library Association.

Curry, Ann. 2005. "If I Ask, Will They Answer? Evaluating Public Library Reference Service to Gay and Lesbian Youth." *Reference and User Services Quarterly* 45 (1): 65–75.

Davies, J. Eric. 2007. "An Overview of International Research into the Library and Information Needs of Visually Impaired People." *Library Trends* 55 (4): 785–795.

Day, John Michael, ed. 2000. *Guidelines for Library Services to Deaf People.* The Hague, Netherlands: IFLA Headquarters.

Decker, Emy Nelson. 2010. "Baby Boomers and the United States Public Library System." *Library Hi Tech* 28 (4): 605–616.

Decker, Emy Nelson, and Monya D. Tomlinson. 2014. "Using Blogs in the Library to Reach Diverse and Non-Traditional Student Groups." *Journal of Library Innovation* 5 (2): 60–70.

DiMartino, Diane, and Lucinda R. Zoe. 2000. "International Students and the Library: New Tools, New Users, and New Instruction." In *Teaching the New Library to Today's Users: Reaching International, Minority, Senior Citizens, Gay/Lesbian, First Generation College, At-Risk, Graduate and Returning Students and Distance Learners,* edited by Trudi E. Jacobson and Helene C. Williams, 17–43. New York: Neal Schuman.

Dixen, Rebecca, and Stephanie Thorson. 2001. "How Librarians Serve People in Prison." *Computers in Libraries* 21 (9): 48–53.

Dorner, Dan, and G. E. Gorman. 2008. "Indigenous Knowledge and the Role of Information Literacy Education." In *World Library and Information Congress Proceedings: 74th IFLA General Conference and Council,* August 10–14, Quebec, Canada, 10–14. http://archive.ifla.org/IV/ifla74/papers/090 -Dorner-en.pdf. Accessed April 1, 2016.

Drabinski, Emily. 2013. "Queering the Catalog: Queer Theory and the Politics of Correction." *The Library Quarterly* 83 (2): 94–111.

Dunbar, H. Minnie. "Bibliographic Instruction for Freshman Students at Florida International University." National Conference on the Freshman Year Experience, Columbia, SC: University of South Carolina, February 18, 1986, 1–8.

Dunne, Jennifer E. 2002. "Information Seeking and Use by Battered Women: A 'Person-In-Progressive-Situations' Approach." *Library and Information Science Research* 24 (4): 343–355.

Elteto, Sharon, Rose M. Jackson, and Adriene Lim. 2008. "Is the Library a 'Welcoming Space'?: An Urban Academic Library and Diverse Student Experiences." *portal: Libraries and the Academy* 8 (3): 325–337.

Fitzgibbons, Shirley A. 1983. "Reference and Information Services for Children and Young Adults: Definition, Services, and Issues." *The Reference Librarian* 2 (7–8): 1–30.

Futterman, Marc. 2008. "Finding the Underserved." *Library Journal* 133 (17): 42–45.

Futterman, Marc, and Judy Michaelson. 2012. "Data Rules: How Mapping Technology Drives Better Customer Service." *Public Library Quarterly* 31 (2): 141–152.

Ganster, Ligaya. 2011. "Reaching Out to International Students: A Focus-Group Approach to Developing Web Resources and Services." *College and Undergraduate Libraries* 18 (4): 368–384.

Gavier, Maria J., and Sara E. Scobey. 2001. "Enhancing and Promoting Library Services to Attract Diverse Populations." *Colorado Libraries* 27 (4): 12–15.

Gehner, John. 2010. "Libraries, Low-Income People, and Social Exclusion." *Public Library Quarterly* 29 (1): 39–47.

Gibbons, Susan. 2013. "Techniques to Understand the Changing Needs of Library Users." *IFLA Journal* 39 (2): 162–167.

Giesecke, Joan, and Beth McNeil. 2001. "Core Competencies for Libraries and Library Staff." In *Staff Development: A Practical Guide*, edited by Elizabeth Fuseler, Terry Dahlin, and Deborah A. Carver, Chapter 10. Chicago: American Library Association.

Gilton, Donna L. 1994. "A World of Difference: Preparing for Information Literacy Instruction for Diverse Groups." *Multicultural Review* 3 (3): 54–62.

Gilton, Donna L. 2005. "Culture Shock in the Library: Implications for Information Literacy Instruction." *Research Strategies* 20 (4): 424–432.

Gisonny, Karen, and Jenna Freedman. 2006. "Zines in Libraries: How, What and Why?" *Collection Building* 25 (1): 26–30.

Goddard, Marti. 2004. "Adaptive Technology, Access through Technology: Marti Goddard Shows How to Use Technology to Help Meet the Needs of People with Disabilities." *Library Journal* 23 (2): 2–7.

Goodman, Valeda Dent. 2011. "Applying Ethnographic Research Methods in Library and Information Settings." *Libri* 61 (1): 1–11.

Gough, Cal, and Ellen Greenblatt. 1992. "Services to Gay and Lesbian Patrons: Examining the Myths." *Library Journal* 117 (1): 59–63.

Greenblatt, Ellen, ed. 2010. *Serving LGBTIQ Library and Archives Users: Essays on Outreach, Service, Collections and Access*. Jefferson, NC: McFarland.

Griswold Blandy, Susan. 1994. "What to Do until the Expert Comes: Dealing with Demands for Multicultural, International Information Now." *The Reference Librarian* 21 (45–46): 119–135.

Grover, Robert, Roger C. Greer, and John Agada. 2010. *Assessing Information Needs: Managing Transformative Library Services*. Santa Barbara, CA: ABC-CLIO.

Gunde, Michael G. 1992. "Working with the Americans with Disabilities Act, Part III." *Library Journal* 117 (21): 90–91.

Hall, Patrick Andrew. 1991. "The Role of Affectivity in Instructing People of Color: Some Implications for Bibliographic Instruction." *Library Trends* 39 (3): 316–326.

Harris, Roma M. 1988. "The Information Needs of Battered Women." *Reference Quarterly* 28 (1): 62–70.

Harris, Roma, Judy Stickney, Carolyn Grasley, Gail Hutchinson, Lorraine Greaves, and Terry Boyd. 2001. "Searching for Help and Information: Abused Women Speak Out." *Library and Information Science Research* 23 (2): 123–141.

Helms, Cynthia Mae. 1995. "Reading Out to the International Students through Bibliographic Instruction." *The Reference Librarian* 24 (51/52): 295–307.

Herrada, Julie. 1995. "Zines in Libraries: A Culture Preserved." *Serials Review* 21 (2): 79–88.

Holt, Glen E. 2006. "Fitting Library Services into the Lives of the Poor." *The Bottom Line: Managing Library Finances* 19 (4): 179–186.

Homan, Daniel, and Lonni Collins Pratt. 2011. *Radical Hospitality: Benedict's Way of Love*. Brewster, MA: Paraclete Press.

Howard, Jessica L. 2010. "Library Resources and Services for Bisexuals." In *Serving LGBTIQ Library and Archives Users: Essays on Outreach, Service, Collections and Access*, edited by Ellen Greenblatt, 7–12. Jefferson, NC: McFarland.

Imrie, Rob. 2004. "From Universal to Inclusive Design in the Built Environment." In *Disabling Barriers—Enabling Environments*, 2nd ed., edited by John Swain, Sally French, Colin Barnes, and Carol Thomas, 279–284. London: Sage.

Ishimura, Yusuke, and Joan C. Bartlett. 2014. "Are Librarians Equipped to Teach International Students? A Survey of Current Practices and Recommendations for Training." *The Journal of Academic Librarianship* 40 (3–4): 313–321.

Jaeger, Paul T., Nicole A. Cooke, Cecilia Feltis, Michelle Hamiel, Fiona Jardine, and Katie Shilton. 2015. "The Virtuous Circle Revisited: Injecting Diversity, Inclusion, Rights, Justice, and Equity into LIS from Education to Advocacy." *The Library Quarterly* 85 (2): 150–171.

Janes, Phoebe, and Ellen Meltzer. 1990. "Origins and Attitudes: Training Reference Librarians for a Pluralistic World." *The Reference Librarian* 13 (30): 145–155.

Japzon, Andrea C., and Hongmian Gong. 2005. "A Neighborhood Analysis of Public Library Use in New York City." *The Library Quarterly* 75 (4): 446–463.

Jenkins, Mark. 2014. "D.C. Adds a Social Worker to Library System to Work with Homeless Patrons." *The Washington Post* (Washington, DC), August 27, 2014, online edition. http://www.washingtonpost.com/local/dc-adds-a -social-worker-to-library-system-to-work-with-homeless-patrons/2014/08/ 26/2d80200c-2c96-11e4-be9e-60cc44c01e7f_story.html. Accessed March 1, 2016.

Knight, Heather. 2010. "Library Adds Social Worker to Assist Homeless." *San Francisco Chronicle* (San Francisco), January 11, 2010, online edition, SFGate. http://www.sfgate.com/bayarea/article/Library-adds-social-worker-to -assist-homeless-3275950.php. Accessed March 1, 2016.

Knight, Lorrie, Maryann Hight, and Lisa Polfer. 2010. "Rethinking the Library for the International Student Community." *Reference Services Review* 38 (4): 581–605.

LaFlamme, Marcel AQ. 2007. "Towards a Progressive Discourse on Community Needs Assessment: Perspectives from Collaborative Ethnography and Action Research." *Progressive Librarian* 29: 55–62.

Lee, Deborah. 2004. "Marketing 101-Market Research: Market Segmentation and Libraries." *Library Administration and Management* 18 (1): 47–48.

Lehmann, Vibeke. 2011. "Challenges and Accomplishments in US Prison Libraries." *Library Trends* 59 (3): 490–508.

Lenn, Kathy. 1996. "Library Services to Disabled Students: Outreach and Education." *The Reference Librarian* 25 (53): 13–25.

Leonard, Gillian D. 1993. "Multiculturalism and Library Services." *The Acquisitions Librarian* 5 (9–10): 3–19.

Lewis, Mary Genevieve. 1969. "Library Orientation for Asian College Students." *College and Research Libraries* 30 (3): 267–272.

Liu, Mengxiong. 1995. "Ethnicity and Information Seeking." *The Reference Librarian* 23 (49–50): 123–134.

Love, Emily. 2009. "A Simple Step: Integrating Library Reference and Instruction into Previously Established Academic Programs for Minority Students." *The Reference Librarian* 50 (1): 4–13.

Luo, Lili, Deborah Estreicher, Peter A. Lee, Cyndy Thomas, and Glenn Thomas. 2012. "Social Workers in the Library: An Innovative Approach to Address Library Patrons' Social Service Needs." *Qualitative and Quantitative Methods in Libraries (QQML)* 1: 73–82.

Martin, Julia A., Kathleen M. Reaume, Elaine M. Reeves, and Ryan D. Wright. 2012. "Relationship Building with Students and Instructors of ESL: Bridging the Gap for Library Instruction and Services." *Reference Services Review* 40 (3): 352–367.

McCleer, Adriana. 2013. "Knowing Communities: A Review of Community Assessment Literature." *Public Library Quarterly* 32 (3): 263–274.

McDonald, Martha J. 2014. "Structural Approaches to Community Analysis." *Indiana Libraries* 1 (2): 51–59.

McKay, Becky. 2011. "Lesbian, Gay, Bisexual, and Transgender Health Issues, Disparities, and Information Resources." *Medical Reference Services Quarterly* 30 (4): 394.

Mehra, Bharat, and Donna Braquet. 2011. "Progressive LGBTQ Reference: Coming Out in the 21st Century." *Reference Services Review* 39 (3): 401–422.

Metoyer-Duran, Cheryl. 1993. "The Information and Referral Process in Culturally Diverse Communities." *Reference Quarterly* 22 (3): 359–371.

Morris, Jen. 2013. "Free to Learn: Helping Ex-Offenders with Reentry." *Public Library Quarterly* 32 (2): 119–123.

Mundava, Maud C., and LaVerne Gray. 2008. "Meeting Them Where They Are: Marketing to International Student Populations in US Academic Libraries." *Technical Services Quarterly* 25 (3): 35–48.

Nemec-Loise, Jenna. 2014. "A Little Extra Help—Why Public Libraries Need Social Workers." *Public Libraries Online*, September 23, 2014. http://publiclibraries online.org/2014/09/a-little-extra-help-why-public-libraries-need-social -workers/. Accessed March 1, 2016.

The New York Public Library. 2013. "New York City Celebrates Immigrant Heritage Week." Last modified April 17, 2013. http://www.nypl.org/help/community -outreach/immigrant-heritage-week.

Olson, Hope A. 1998. "Mapping beyond Dewey's Boundaries: Constructing Classificatory Space for Marginalized Knowledge Domains." *Library Trends* 47 (2): 233–254.

Olson, Hope A. 2000. "Difference, Culture and Change: The Untapped Potential of LCSH." *Cataloging and Classification Quarterly* 29 (1–2): 53–71.

Olson, Hope A. 2001. "The Power to Name: Representation In Library Catalogs." *Signs* 26 (3): 639–668.

Perry, Claudia A. 2014. "Information Services to Older Adults: Initial Findings from a Survey of Suburban Libraries." *The Library Quarterly* 84 (3): 348–386.

Puente, Mark A., LaVerne Gray, and Shantel Agnew. 2009. "The Expanding Library Wall: Outreach to the University of Tennessee's Multicultural/International Student Population." *Reference Services Review* 37 (1): 30–43.

Pyati, Ajit. 2003. "Limited English Proficient Users and the Need for Improved Reference Services." *Reference Services Review* 31 (3): 264–271.

Reference and User Services Association. 2008. *Guidelines for Library and Information Services to Older Adults.* Chicago: American Library Association, revised 1999, approved 2008.http://www.ala.org/ala/mgrps/divs/rusa/resources/ guidelines/libraryservices.cfm.

Royse, Molly, Tiffani Conner, and Tamara Miller. 2006. "Charting a Course for Diversity: An Experience in Climate Assessment." *portal: Libraries and the Academy* 6 (1): 23–45.

Rubin, Rhea Joyce, and Connie House. 1983. "Library Service in US Jails: Issues, Questions, Trends." *Library Journal* 108 (3): 173–177.

Saar, Michael, and Helena Arthur-Okor. 2013. "Reference Services for the Deaf and Hard of Hearing." *Reference Services Review* 41 (3): 434–452.

Sarkodie-Mensah, Kwasi. 2000. "The International Student on Campus." In *Teaching the New Library to Today's Users: Reaching International, Minority, Senior Citizens, Gay/Lesbian, First Generation College, At-Risk, Graduate and Returning Students and Distance Learners,* edited by Trudi E. Jacobson and Helene C. Williams, 3–16. New York: Neal Schuman.

Saunders, Laura, and Mary Jordan. 2013. "Significantly Different?" *Reference and User Services Quarterly* 52 (3): 216–223.

Scarborough, Katharine. 1991. "Collections for the Emerging Majority." *Library Journal* 116 (11): 44–47.

Shachaf, Pnina, and Sarah Horowitz. 2007. "Are Virtual Reference Services Color Blind?" *Library and Information Science Research* 28 (4): 501–520.

Shafer, Scott. 2014. "Urban Libraries Become De Facto Homeless Shelters." *NPR News around the Nation.* Podcast audio. April 23, 2014. http://www.npr.org/2014/04/23/306102523/san-francisco-library-hires-social-worker-to-help-homeless-patrons.

Shen, Lan. 2013. "Out of Information Poverty: Library Services for Urban Marginalized Immigrants." *Urban Library Journal* 19 (1): 1–12.

Shirley, Glennor L. 2003. "Correctional Libraries, Library Standards, and Diversity." *Journal of Correctional Education* 54 (2): 70–74.

Smith, Paula M. 2008. "Culturally Conscious Organizations: A Conceptual Framework." *portal: Libraries and the Academy* 8 (2): 141–155.

Strong, Gary E. 2001. "Teaching Adult Literacy in a Multicultural Environment." In *Literacy and Libraries: Learning from Case Studies*, edited by GraceAnne A. DeCandido, 110–115. Chicago: Office for Literacy and Outreach Services, American Library Association.

Swan, D. W., J. Grimes, T. Owens, K. Miller, J. Arroyo, T. Craig, S. Dorinski, M. Freeman, N. Isaac, P. O'Shea, R. Padgett, and P. Schilling. 2014. "Public Libraries in the United States Survey: Fiscal Year 2012 (IMLS-2015–PLS -01)." Washington, DC: Institute of Museum and Library Services.

Taylor, Jami Kathleen. 2002. Targeting the Information Needs of Transgender Individuals. *Current Studies in Librarianship* 26 (1/2): 85–109.

Thompson, Kelly J. 2012. "Where's the 'T'?: Improving Library Service to Community Members Who Are Transgender-Identified." *B Sides.* http://ir.uiowa.edu/bsides.

Upson, Matt, and C. Michael Hall. 2013. "Comic Book Guy in the Classroom: The Educational Power and Potential of Graphic Storytelling in Library Instruction." *Kansas Library Association College and University Libraries Section Proceedings* 3 (1): 28–38.

U.S. Census Bureau. 2012. *Statistical Abstract of the United States.* Table 9. Washington, DC: U.S. Government Printing Office.

U.S. Equal Employment Opportunity Commission and the U.S. Department of Justice. 1992. *Americans with Disabilities Act Handbook.* Washington, DC: Government Printing Office.

Van Fleet, Connie. 1995. "A Matter of Focus: Reference Services for Older Adults." *The Reference Librarian* 23 (49–50): 147–164.

Walker, Claire, and Amanda Click. 2011. "Meeting the Reference Expectations of ESL Students: The Challenges of Culture." *College and Research Libraries News* 72 (1): 20–23.

Wang, Hong. 2012. "Immigration in America: Library Services and Information Resources." *Reference Services Review* 40 (3): 480–511.

Ward, Judit H. 2011. "Acquisitions Globalized: The Foreign Language Acquisitions Experience in a Research Library." *Library Resources and Technical Services* 53 (2): 86–93.

Westbrook, Lynn. 2015. " 'I'm Not a Social Worker': An Information Service Model for Working with Patrons in Crisis." *The Library Quarterly* 85 (1): 6–25.

Willett, Peter, and Rebecca Broadley. 2011. "Effective Public Library Outreach to Homeless People." *Library Review* 60 (8): 658–670.

Winkelstein, Julie Ann. 2014. "Public Libraries: Creating Safe Spaces for Homeless LGBTQ Youth." *IFLA 2014 Lyon*, August 8, 2014, 1–8.

Yosso, Tara J. 2005. "Whose Culture Has Capital? A Critical Race Theory Discussion of Community Cultural Wealth." *Race Ethnicity and Education* 8 (1): 69–91.

Zickuhr, Kathryn, Lee Rainie, and Kristen Purcell. 2013. "Library Services in the Digital Age." *Pew Internet Libraries*. January 21. Accessed February 12, 2015. http://libraries.pewinternet.org/2013/01/22/library-services/.

Chapter 5

Managing Diversity

Diversity in librarianship is a multipronged endeavor that entails not only recruiting diverse librarians and library staff to work with diverse populations, but also managing this diverse workforce in such a way that it flourishes and these librarians are retained in the field. Working with patrons is only *part* of the job, and librarians of color need to feel valued and welcome in the profession, or they may leave for more hospitable positions in other fields. In a field that is predominantly comprised of white women (American Library Association 2012a, 2012b), there is a lot of room for error when it comes to having a culturally competent profession that welcomes, celebrates, and understands diversity.

Diversity in libraries should not be a trend, and librarians and staff of color should be more than tokens or "window dressing" (Balderrama 2000, 195). This is not always an easy proposition, particularly for communities and libraries not used to diversity *behind* the service desks. Diverse organizations need strong and committed leadership and policies to ensure that bureaucracy is not a barrier to organizational transformation and the development of a diverse and inclusive workplace. This type of workplace allows staff to "speak one's truth," be comfortable in the library, to have some level of trust with colleagues, and have the freedom to be themselves. Librarians of color have expressed frustration in the library workplace, feeling that their authenticity, credibility, and knowledge are challenged, and their experiences are not valued in less diverse organizations and communities. Some librarians of color claim how ironic it is to be hired to serve their ethnic respective communities, yet are told that they act "too ethnic on the job" (199). Patricia Tarin seconds this perception by stating:

> Minorities, even if their education is equal to that of whites, don't come with the same cultural attitudes, language, social connections, and ways of doing things as whites do; thus they don't have the same cultural advantage. They may do things a little bit differently. (St. Lifer and Nelson 1997, 44)

Another cog in this wheel is the reaction of the patrons to librarians of color; while not unusual, librarians of color are not plentiful enough that their presence as library professionals is normalized and not a novelty. In a blunt, but necessary, article in *Library Journal*, authors St. Lifer and Nelson (1997) definitively state that race does matter in libraries. In the article, an African-American male children's librarian, who also has dreadlocks, was profiled.

> Khafre Abif is in his twenties, black, over six feet tall, and wears a ring in his nose and his hair in dreadlocks. Not exactly the type one would expect to find splayed on the canary-colored rug of a public library reading Goodnight Moon to a gaggle of three and four year olds. Or so he's been told. … Teresa Neely, a colleague and former classmate of Abif's … is less diplomatic. "Black men scare a lot of people based on what they read and hear in the media, and for some that's their only exposure to a person of color. As a tall man with dreadlocks, maybe they think he's a Rastafarian, and they associate a lifestyle with a certain look. He could be selling drugs or smoking reefer." (St. Lifer and Nelson 1997, 42)

The *Library Journal* profile was written in 1997, and some readers may argue that the difficulties described in the pages is now passé; however, in 2016, when this text is being written, there are many librarians of color who will relate to the aforementioned passage and be able to relay their own experiences with implicit and explicit bias, microaggressions, and overt racism in the library world. Again, libraries are microcosms of larger society, and if racism exists in the world, it surely exists in the library.

Sampson (1999, 94) concurs by discussing the difficulties libraries may face when trying to embrace diversity, civility, and equality. Sampson states that diversity in organizations should be approached holistically and consistently.

> Diversity will remain cosmetic if not addressed holistically and systematically. … By excluding the intellectual diversity of ethnically diverse peoples in the design of technological access and content, sustainable and adaptable infrastructures, proactive and creative organizations, ongoing performance and procedure improvements, relevant programming and collections, and new models of leadership, diversity strategies will remain "toothless" and even arrogant. (Sampson 1999, 105–106)

Diversity in library personnel is important, and having diversity as an organizational priority and as part of the library's climate and culture benefits the library as a whole, finding its way into collections, services, and programming (Winston 2010, 62).

MINORITY LIBRARIANS ON THE JOB

Library and information science (LIS) can be a challenging profession and environment for librarians of color; LIS has a long history of tension and separatist tendencies when it comes to librarians of color coming into and advancing in the profession. Libraries are representative of the larger society, for good and for bad; as the country continues to struggle with race, racism, privilege, and issues of social justice and human rights, so do the library profession and other service professions such as social work and medicine. What is important is that history is transparent and not glossed over, or excluded, when teaching and researching library history.

Rosemary Du Mont (1986) paints a troubling portrait of race in American librarianship. In her account, she details 1936 correspondence sent to black librarians in which they were encouraged to attend the annual American Library Association conference. Black librarians would be able to attend "most" meetings and sessions but would be ushered to segregated seating; they would not be able to have meals at the conference, nor would they be allowed to stay at the conference hotels because they were white only. Du Mont (1986, 488) states:

> This incident remains significant when attempting to assess the histori-cal position of the library profession on the question of integration of southern public library facilities and the education of black librarians for public library service. There is little doubt that public library serv-ices to blacks and the education of black librarians have been acknowl-edged concerns of the profession. Yet, the constricted nature of that concern (as reflected in the 1936 conference situation) is also readily apparent.

Du Mont (1986, 491) continued her discussion by recounting the history of the Hampton Library School, which was established in 1925 for the purpose of sep-arately training "Negro" librarians. An example of the "legalized segregation in the south"—the Hampton Library School—served a great purpose as many other library programs would not, or could not depending on geography, admit students of color. Some programs were clear in their own prejudice, stating that it would be "far better to send students to Hampton rather than urge them to come to other institutions where their presence is a distinct embarrassment" (492).

A significant division existed in the library education and professionalization of librarians of color, and, subsequently, there were fissures and blatant omissions in services provided to blacks and other communities of color.

Microaggressions

Fortunately, segregation is not the societal scourge it once was; however, minority groups still face discrimination, a form of which is known as microag-gressions. Microaggressions are "brief, everyday exchanges that send denigrat-ing messages to people of color because they belong to a racial minority group" (Sue et al. 2007, 273). Microaggressions can be subtle and hard to con-front and correct, but they are nonetheless damaging and discouraging. Derald Wing Sue, who has written extensively about microaggressions, and his coau-thors describe the categories and nuances of microaggressions; they include microassaults: "an explicit racial derogation characterized primarily by a verbal or nonverbal attack meant to hurt the intended victim through name-calling, avoidant behavior, or purposeful discriminatory actions"; microinsults:

"communications that convey rudeness and insensitivity and demean a person's racial heritage or identity"; and microinvalidations: "communications that exclude, negate, or nullify the psychological thoughts, feelings, or experiential reality of a person of color" (274). So when minorities are told "You are so articulate" or are mistaken for a service worker instead of a professional librarian, they experience microaggressions (276–277). This author has encountered both of these examples on multiple occasions while working as a librarian and college professor.

The recognition of microaggressions in LIS has become more prevalent, and librarians of color are speaking up more and more. A study by Jaena Alabi (2015) documents microaggressions in academic libraries. Alabi concurs that microaggressions are draining and hard to defend against. Even when a person of color determines that a microaggression has occurred, she may be trapped in a no-win situation. If she responds, she will expend energy educating someone who may respond defensively; if she does not respond, she may feel anger and guilt at herself or internalize the microaggression. Research on the experiences of students and faculty of color reports that being inundated with these negative messages as well as the energy required to respond to racial microaggressions leads to minority students and faculty experiencing self-doubt, frustration, isolation, anxiety, anger, and fatigue (48).

Alabi's research suggests that nonminority librarians do not recognize the microaggressions being experienced by their colleagues of color. This is confirmed by websites such as *Microaggressions in Librarianship* (http://lismicroaggressions.tumblr.com),[1] which is run by librarians of color and described as "a space for those working in libraries, archives, and information fields to share their experiences with microaggressions." An accompanying LIS microaggressions zine is published on a regular basis. Reading the examples on the site, which are submitted by the site's readers, are heartbreaking, enraging, discouraging, and indicative of how much work is yet to be done in the profession.

Librarians' Stereotypes

Librarians' stereotypes are firmly engrained in society, with many people envisioning librarians as older bespectacled white women who wear pearls, fashion their hair into tight buns, and favor no-nonsense cardigan sweaters in order to "shhhh" people (Attebury 2010; Peresie and Alexander 2005; Radford and Radford 1997); these perceptions of librarians date back to at least 1949, when it was first discussed in *American Libraries* magazine (Manley 2007). Alternatively, the stereotype of a young sexpot librarian is also common, and, occasionally, a "cool" pop culture librarian makes his or her way into the mainstream consciousness: Niles, the librarian from *Buffy the Vampire Slayer* or

---

[1]The *Microaggressions in Librarianship* site was "inspired by recent grassroots social media movements, such as The Microaggressions Project, and I, Too, Am Harvard; this space aims to identify, acknowledge, and overcome the microaggressions that continue to exist in our profession and that are the real, lived experiences of LIS professionals from marginalized communities today."

Mary from the movie *Party Girl* (Poulin 2008; Radford and Radford 2003; Shaffer and Casey 2012).

Now add to the mix librarians of color who do not fit existing stereotypes and, in fact, defy them. Unfortunately, librarians of color still stick out and do not always receive the warmest reception from patrons or even other library staff. These less than positive reactions may be a partial result of stereotype threat.

Stereotype threat affects both employees and employers and essentially is the result of societal stereotypes and prejudices making their way into the workplace. Common stereotype threats include older employees have bad memories and are not capable of working; women are not good in science and math and therefore should not hold positions that require such skills (such jobs should be given to Asians); and African-Americans are intellectually inferior and combative and therefore difficult to work with. Stereotype threats can be offensive and upsetting, and perhaps more often than not, it is just frustrating and tiring for librarians of color to be consistently questioned and doubted. An anecdote from a young African-American male library assistant detailed his work in a branch library that serves a heavily Polish immigrant population. Stereotype threat, and maybe sheer prejudice, keeps the Polish patrons from allowing him to assist them. Instead, they approach the reference desk at which he is stationed, say they cannot speak English, and ask for one of his white colleagues. This young library assistant then overhears the Polish patrons speaking English with the white librarians. This type of treatment is fatiguing and can make even the most enthusiastic librarians question their place in the library and in the profession. Roberson and Kulik (2007, 26) concur that stereotype threat can have negative effects on librarians of color. They state:

> The fear of being seen and judged according to a negative stereotype about their group, and the concern that they might do something that would inadvertently confirm the negative stereotype. These individuals are experiencing "stereotype threat." Stereotype threat describes the psychological experience of a person who, while engaged in a task, is aware of a stereotype about his or her identity group suggesting that he or she will not perform well on that task.

Because LIS is still dominated by white females, stereotype threat can also impact library patrons (i.e., patrons of color) who for various reasons feel unwelcome and/or uncomfortable in the library (see Chapter 4's discussion on stereotype threat for an example).

THE VIRTUOUS CIRCLE OF RECRUITMENT AND RETENTION IN LIS

In an article in *Education Libraries*, Paul Jaeger and Renee Franklin (2007) propose the virtuous circle of LIS recruitment. The circle, or cycle, suggests that increased numbers of minorities teaching in LIS graduate programs will shape and transform the LIS graduate curricula (see the next section in this chapter),

Table 5.1 Diverse Student Enrollment in ALA-Accredited LIS Programs—Fall 2014

Ethnicity and Race	Number of Students Enrolled
Hispanic of any race	971
American Indian or Alaska Native	112
Asian	474
Black or African-American	632
Native Hawaiian or Pacific Islander	28
White	9,102
Two or more races	232
International	450
Race or ethnicity unknown	1,543

which in turn will impact the next generations of minority librarians, who will then effectively and competently serve the diverse communities that patronize libraries. Finally, it is hoped that by seeing librarians of color in the community, more students of color will realize librarianship as a viable and rewarding career path. Not only should LIS be more diverse, but the field should be more representative of the communities being served by libraries and other information centered organizations (see Chapter 1 for a discussion of the racial and ethnic diversity within the professional librarian workforce).

Similarly, the Association of Library and Information Science Educators' (ALISE) statistical report of 2015 indicates that in 2014, American Library Association (ALA)-accredited LIS graduate programs are lacking in terms of enrolling and graduating students of color (see Tables 5.1 and 5.2) (Albertson 2016, Table II-4-c-2-ALA and Table II-3-c-2-ALA).

Table 5.2 Masters Degrees Awarded by Ethnicity and Race, 2013–2014

Ethnicity and Race	Number of Degrees Awarded
Hispanic of any race	346
American Indian or Alaska Native	48
Asian	239
Black or African-American	268
Native Hawaiian or Pacific Islander	10
White	4,327
Two or more races	86
International	170
Race or ethnicity unknown	957

The aforementioned numbers of diverse students can stand to be improved. Josey (1993) and Kim and Sin (2006) offer specific suggestions as to how graduate programs can recruit more and retain more students of color. A common theme in the literature is that of support. It is not enough to provide students with funding, rather programs need to facilitate opportunities for socialization, provide opportunities for advising and career development, and assist students with work opportunities. Kim and Sin (2006) go a step further and suggest that programs have diversity in their faculty, highlight their alumni of color, have a diverse curriculum, and demonstrate relationships with ethnic associations.

The need for a diverse LIS workforce remains acute. Ann Knight Randall (1988, 12) stated:

> While there are geographical differences in population growth rates among the racial and ethnic groups, the pattern of an emerging multicultural society increasingly minority in character, especially in urban areas, is apparent. The need is great for a larger number of minority teachers, librarians, and other professionals to reflect the changing demographic makeup of our society.

Almost 30 years later, the field continues to have this same conversation. Hollis (1996, 150) concurs by stating:

> Multiculturalism has been discussed in the literature ad nauseam, yet the reality is slow in coming. Women in general, and White women in particular, can no longer stand back and blame male administrators for the lack of minority gains in the profession. It appears that the old male paradigm has been joined by a new female paradigm, and thus far there is nothing new to show for it. This is disheartening.

The literature suggests courses of action that can assist in the diversification of the profession; paramount among them are changes in hiring practices and foci on retention efforts. Joan Howland (1999) was explicit in her assertion that library managers hire candidates who are in their "own image," which in LIS means that white women and men are most likely to secure jobs and advance into management positions; hence, the cycle continues. Howland says that "there is a rarely acknowledged dark underside to librarianship that is colored by racism and a preference for conformity rather than individualism" (5). This conformity, or homogeneity, encompasses ethnicity, race, religion, class, gender, and other specific aspects of culture. Professionals who enter the field and fall outside of this prescription are subject to challenges and discomfort if they do not or cannot assimilate into the dominant culture. Novices or outsiders are faced with "the not so subtle mandate to buy into the system" and "not color outside the lines" (6). Howland rightly posits that this scenario causes psychological stress and is ultimately detrimental to both the candidate and the organization.

> The bottom line is that it simply is neither logical nor good business practice to recruit and hire librarians from diverse backgrounds, only to expect them to assimilate and become mirrors of the generations of librarians

which have preceded them. Such expectations lead to a cycle that fails both the recruit and the institution. Strategies must be developed to assure retention and maximum professional development. (6–7)

Alire (2001, 98) suggests that the only way to rectify this problem is to have more library leaders of color who are culturally competent and "can create an environment where no one is disadvantaged or preferred because of race, ethnicity, creed, gender, sexual orientation, et cetera"; presumably, this type of environment would be more conducive to the hiring and caring for librarians from diverse and underrepresented backgrounds. While the profession had and has some exceptional leaders of color, people of color in leadership and management positions have not yet reached critical mass. Alire also discusses the particular challenges that leaders of color face; they have to prove themselves in a majority white environment and counteract stereotypes, all the while recruiting, mentoring, and leading other librarians of color. This is a tall and tiring order to be sure.

The second way to increase and maintain diversity in the profession is to focus on retention. It is one very important thing to financially support students of color as they progress through LIS graduate programs; it is entirely another thing to get them professional positions and foster environments that will enable them to keep those positions and successfully remain in their organizations. Elements of a retention plan include mentoring and providing opportunities for advancement and professional development. Acree et al. (2001, 46) emphasize the importance of professional development opportunities, particularly for minority librarians. Continuing education provides an avenue for skill development and networking, both of which can assist librarians in moving beyond entry-level positions. Cooke (2012, 2013a) suggests that professional development is flexible and can be achieved in group settings and as individuals. Professional development can be formal or informal, and if the librarian is really motivated to create his or her personal learning network, the results can be rewarding and motivating (see the end of this chapter for more extensive discussion of professional development).

Another aspect of retention planning is mentoring. Bonnette (2004) and Echavarria and Wertheimer (1997) posit that mentoring is especially important for librarians of color and suggest that it is in the best interest of the profession to support minority librarians whenever and however possible.

> People of color need to be trained in the library and information profession, not to serve only their own communities but to serve all communities. Librarians of color are crucial to the provision of services in communities where knowledge of the language, the values, and the cultural heritage of the growing racial and ethnic minority communities is imperative. (Knowles and Jolivet, as quoted in Echavarria and Wertheimer 1997, 49)

Neely and Peterson (2007) point out that mentoring, while crucial to the recruitment, retention, and advancement of librarians of color, is fairly nuanced. Effective mentoring can take many forms, and one or a combination of efforts may be called for depending on the organization and the librarians in question. Mentoring options include shadowing leaders; cross-training; nominations for awards and other opportunities; promotions beyond entry-level positions; establishing leadership programs; and providing research opportunities and funding. Mentoring is part of the way the profession can support librarians of color and make sure they "feel that they are wanted and they are at home" within their organizations (Josey 1993, 308).

DIVERSITY ON THE LIS FACULTY AND IN THE LIS CURRICULA

The field of LIS has been making slow progress toward diversifying the profession; however, the curricula in graduate programs have been even slower to reflect issues of diversity and social justice. The call to critically examine LIS (Bishop et al. 1999, 2003; Boast 2011; Gilliland 2011; Jimerson 2006; Lonetree 2006; Olson 1998, 2001; Patterson 2000; Pawley 2006) and diversify librarianship and its graduate curricula (Adkins and Espinal 2004; Chu 1999; Gollop 1999; Honma 2005; Josey 1993, 1994; Josey and Abdullahi 2002; Kim and Sin 2006, 2008; Lance 2005; Morris 2007; Neely and Peterson 2007; Peterson 1995, 1996, 1999; Subramaniam and Jaeger 2010; Totten 1977, 2000; Turock 2003; Wheeler 2005; Winston 1998, 2001) are ongoing discussions that represent entrenched, cyclical, and recalcitrant problems in the field (see also Box 5.1 for books related to this topic).

Box 5.1   The Unfinished Business of Recruiting and Retaining Librarians and Faculty of Color

Several books have been written about the status of librarians and faculty of color in LIS. For more information and case studies, please check out the following:

Jackson, Andrew P., Julius Jefferson Jr., and Akilah S. Nosakhere, eds. *The 21st-Century Black Librarian in America: Issues and Challenges.* Lanham, MD: Scarecrow Press, 2012.

Josey, E. J., ed. *The Black Librarian in America.* Lanham, MD: Scarecrow Press, 1970.

Josey, E. J., ed. *The Black Librarian in America Revisited.* Lanham, MD: Scarecrow Press, 1994.

Josey, E. J., and Ann Allen Shockley, eds. *Handbook of Black Librarianship.* Santa Barbara, CA: Libraries Unlimited, Inc., 1977.

Josey, E. J., and Marva DeLoach, eds. *Handbook of Black Librarianship* (2nd Edition). Lanham, MD: Scarecrow Press, 2000.

Lee, Deborah, and Mahalakshmi Kumaran, eds. *Aboriginal and Visible Minority Librarians: Oral Histories from Canada.* Lanham, MD: Rowman & Littlefield Publishers, 2014.

Wheeler, Maurice B., ed. *Unfinished Business: Race, Equity, and Diversity in Library and Information Science Education.* Lanham, MD: Scarecrow Press, 2005.

DIVERSITY WITHIN THE LIS RANKS

LIS graduate students have few opportunities to engage with issues of race, gender, class, privilege, and the like before they graduate and enter the field. This is in part a result of two things: programs are wedded to a slate of "traditional" and "core" courses, like reference, cataloging, and management, which while valuable and should absolutely be offered, the slate may not leave time and opportunity to take electives that may be deemed out of scope; faculties do not always have professors of color and/or instructors who are both willing and able to teach courses about race, gender, class, and the like. According to statistics compiled by ALISE (Albertson 2016, Table I-17), of 959 faculty members teaching in ALA-accredited programs across the United States and Canada, 21 were Hispanics of any race, 2 were American Indians or Alaska Natives, 120 were Asians, 42 were blacks or African-Americans, 2 were Native Hawaiians or Pacific Islanders, and 6 were identified as being multiracial. LIS education needs more and consistent representation from scholars of color (see Box 5.2 for a special *Library Journal* column written by this author on the topic). Library educators E. J. Josey (1993) and Kathleen de la Pena McCook and Kate Lippincott (1997) wrote about this same state of affairs in the 1990s. Josey (1993, 306) lamented:

> In order to have a program of cultural diversity in our library and information science programs, it is important that faculty of color be recruited and urged to participate fully in the school's program of research, service, and teaching. It is not enough for faculty search committees to lower their qualifications for candidates who are persons of color. At the same time, they cannot come back to the faculty and say that "We have tried, but we have not found any"—they must have the evidence of what they have done and where they have looked for faculty.

In her discussion of the recruitment of Latino LIS faculty, Denice Adkins (2004) suggests that there are four specific barriers the field needs to overcome, particularly if recruiting from within the field, practicing librarians, and information professionals. They include isolation from the academy, the ethnocentrism within LIS education, financial concerns, and personal concerns. Faculty positions are hard to come by and they are difficult even without these particular barriers. East and Lam (1995) remind that these barriers are not exclusive to LIS but are prominent in higher education in general. The issue of recruiting more faculty of color is an issue that "has received increased attention and positive action," yet a "certain tension" still exists (201).

To try and remedy the barriers mentioned by Adkins (2004), there have been various initiatives to recruit a more diverse workforce, not only for the benefit of the profession but also to better serve increasingly diverse library clientele and communities. Programs such as the Spectrum Scholarship Program (ALA), Knowledge River (the University of Arizona's School of Information), and the Initiative to Recruit a Diverse Workforce (the Association of Research Libraries) have dedicated ample time and funding to recruiting aspiring librarians from racially diverse or underrepresented backgrounds (i.e., American Indian/Alaskan Native, Asian/Pacific Islander, black/African-American, and

Hispanic). These well-meaning initiatives have not gone unchallenged, and even after many years of consistent work, the field is still not as diverse as it should be. Often missing from these discussions and initiatives to diversify the library workforce is the importance of recruiting minority candidates to doctoral level programs, with the hope and intention that these candidates will eventually work in accredited LIS graduate programs (Cooke 2013b; Subramaniam and Jaeger 2010; Totten 200; 1977). While there is literature about recruiting librarians of color into the field, literature about minorities in doctoral programs (Achor and Morales 1990; Ellis 2001; Gardner 2008; Nettles 1990; Offerman 2011; Olson 1988; Pruitt and Isaac 1985; Turner, González, and Wood 2008), and literature about minorities in higher education as a whole (Antonio et al. 2004; Chesler and Crowfoot 1989; Denson and Chang 2009; Olneck 2000; Rankin and Reason 2005), there is a dearth of research explicitly about minority doctoral students in LIS education.

While the demographics of our country are shifting, those of the professions and the disciplines that support them remain essentially static. The dearth and attrition of minority students have, for a protracted period of time, held a prominent place in the literature of higher education; all disciplines face this challenge of struggling to attract and maintain diverse students (Manzo 1994; Meacham 2002; Pruitt and Isaac 1985). This problem is even more acute in LIS (Brown-Syed, Baker, and Wicks 2008; Franklin and Jaeger 2007; Reeling 1992). A corollary issue of diversity recruitment and retention in LIS education, typically addressed in relation to master's level degrees (Alire 2001; Barlow and Aversa 2006; Dewey and Keally 2008; Gollop 1999; Honma 2005; Jaeger, Bertot, and Franklin 2010; Neely and Peterson 2007; Stringer-Stanback 2008; Wheeler 2005; Winston 2010), is minority recruitment and retention in PhD programs, which deserves fresh and dedicated attention and study. The statistics, regularly compiled by ALISE (Albertson 2016, Table I-17), indicate that the LIS professoriate has been, and remains, sorely lacking in diversity.

This trend and its associated meaning for library education caused Dr. Betty J. Turock to sound the alarm. Turock (2003, 493) stated, "Overall, the involvement of people of color at the doctoral level can be fairly characterized as minimal. The need for immediate response is acute." The rates representing the demographic base in the doctoral faculty closely parallel those of minority librarians working in libraries. During her tenure as president of the ALA, Turock sought an immediate response to the imbalance between the population shifts in our nation and the lack of a concomitant shift in the composition of librarianship. In collaboration with then ALA Executive Director Elizabeth Martinez, Turock spurred the creation of the Spectrum Scholarship Program, a program designed to recruit and fund members of underrepresented minority populations to graduate programs in LIS. Because librarianship was accurately known and characterized as a primarily Caucasian and female field, Turock espoused the view that the field and the discipline must undergo transformation and that library services could become optimally responsive to their diverse clientele only if staff were equally diverse. She credits her friend and mentor E. J. Josey for being a major force in the creation of the Spectrum initiative. Expressing his frustration and "disgust" for the lack of diversity in the library discipline and field, Josey stated that "ALA only recruits one minority librarian per year and thinks that's progressive" (personal correspondence between

Josey and Turock, May 7, 1994). Determined to change this trend, Turock, in consultation with the ALA's ethnic affiliates, including the American Indian Library Association, the Asian Pacific American Librarians Association, the Black Caucus of the ALA, the Chinese American Librarians Association, and REFORMA (which promotes services to Latinos and the Spanish-speaking), made a prominent goal of her presidency that the association recruit and fund the education of at least 50 minority students annually to become librarians. And so Spectrum began. All members of the ALA did not uniformly welcome Turock's initiative, and she faced significant resistance from the members of the ALA whose support was needed to pass the Initiative. As Sandra Rios Balderrama (2000) observed, diversity inspires different reactions in different people, and instead of having difficult and revealing conversations, it is easier to stifle and ignore new ideas and initiatives like Spectrum. Turock's efforts in regard to Spectrum were about "advancing social justice and human rights within organizations and the profession" and wanting minority librarians and the population they serve to not only survive but also thrive. Turock has repeatedly pointed out that without a focus on diversity, "it is not clear that libraries will continue to support diverse populations, or understand their experiences, their needs, their languages, or their perspectives. And if we don't support them, how can we expect them to support us?" (personal correspondence, May 7, 2009). About Spectrum's long journey to acceptance, Elizabeth Martinez remembers:

> It was a grand idea that we developed when I was Executive Director of ALA. At that time, I was frustrated that, after hearing for 20 years how much diversity was a priority for ALA and the profession, there still were no national scholarships for librarians of color. The ALA Council struggled with accepting the proposal, and past president Betty Turock shamed them to vote yes. It was later embraced and supported by library schools and the profession. Today it is the largest and most prestigious ALA scholarship. (personal correspondence, May 20, 2009)

Out of these efforts emerged the Spectrum Doctoral Fellowship program, which has to date sponsored 18 individuals in their quests to earn doctoral degrees in LIS. The Spectrum Doctoral Fellowship program was preceded by programs specific to promoting doctoral candidates of color, such as Project Athena (a joint doctoral studies initiative between the University of Illinois, Urbana-Champaign, the University of North Carolina, Chapel Hill, the University of Washington and the Florida State University), and joined by numerous other initiatives funded by the Institute of Museum and Library Services (IMLS) and individual LIS graduate programs. Unfortunately, such doctoral initiatives did not have the longevity of their master's level counterparts, but they have made significant contributions by beginning to diversify the LIS professoriate.

Dr. Camila Alire (2001) lists the benefits of increased diversity in the field of librarianship and observes that people of color will: (1) recognize and root out obstacles to achieving diversity; (2) advocate for organizational culture in which change thrives and discrimination ends; (3) serve as mentors, leaders, and spokespersons; (4) and provide links to diverse service populations.

The importance of more representative professional and disciplinary populations is also clear if the operationalization of the virtuous circle within librarianship is to occur (Jaeger and Franklin 2007). Bonnici and Burnett (2005, 125)
show their support for the virtuous circle model when they say, "Doctoral fellows serve as the nucleus of energy for the continued recruitment of a diverse
doctoral population. Attrition through graduation will extend the diversity to
the LIS professoriate. Future generations of librarians are educated by the professoriate." Mark Winston (1998, 2001, 2010) has provided seminal research
on the recruitment and retention of people of color in the profession and the disciplines that support it. His early studies determined that common themes
emerge across the literature of the professions. One such commonality is that
what is known about the basis on which individuals have chosen their professional specialties provides a worthwhile basis for the development of recruitment strategies, since similarities exist between those currently employed in a
given profession and those who are likely candidates for recruitment into it
(Winston 2001). A model developed by Darden and Turock (2005, 341–343) that
builds on Winston's work suggests that people drawn to careers in librarianship
are facilitated or enabled by several factors, including work experience in libraries; targeted recruitment; membership in professional organizations;
conference attendance; having work accepted to publications; support of colleagues, family, and friends; and affirmative action.

Perhaps more interesting and telling are the barriers that these same librarians encounter. They include financial need; lack of role models and mentors;
insufficient access to and inclusion in networks; and affirmative action (when
used as a stigmatizer) (339–341). As important as the successes are, the barriers contain the information that can enable current programs to grow,
expand, and provide the impetus to begin new initiatives. Later research under-
taken by Winston (2008) makes the case that past studies indicate a "predispo-
sition to avoiding topics, such as race and racism, which is reflected in the use
of more benign terms, such as diversity." He focuses in his article on "diversity,
race and affirmative action and the relationship among them as a more
informed approach from which to address the continuing lack of diversity in
the profession" and by extension in the discipline and the professoriate (3).
The basic necessity to address communication about the difficult topics, as
described by Winston, and to take on his challenge for research that "goes
beyond what has been presented in the library literature" (4) lead the research
presented here to consider the broader context of the topics heretofore left
unaddressed and their relationship to how greater diversity can be fostered
within librarianship and in the professoriate in the future.

In a study of the Spectrum Doctoral Fellows, Cooke (2014b) investigated the
enablers and barriers (as put forth by Darden and Turock, 2005) experienced
by 10 minority doctoral students. In most ways, the enablers and barriers to
doctoral study experienced by these students are universal to all doctoral
students. The enablers identified include receiving funding and a stipend;
moving through their programs with a cohort; finding mentors; family and
community support; and having freedom to chart their own academic courses.
Perhaps the most interesting and telling results from the study are

the barriers that these same students encounter. They include lack of mentoring; lack of compatible faculty; loneliness and isolation; and lack of support. Fellows specifically mentioned that they felt their programs perceived them to be a "token," "cash cow," or "show pony." These perceptions of exclusionary treatment, in conjunction with preferential treatment toward students not of color, prompted comments such as "they don't know what to do with us," "I have skills they have yet to tap," and "I would pick a LIS program with more diverse faculty members and students," in addition to feelings of being pigeon-holed as students of color and having to constantly prove themselves as better because of their minority status. Some Fellows felt a general lack of understanding from other students and faculty in their programs and felt they were made to feel less-than because of special minority funding. They also experienced subtle and not so subtle comments indicating institutional racism (e.g., their admittance to the program was based solely on their minority scholarship) and a lack of confidence or awareness of what minority students are capable of (e.g., such candidates would certainly get jobs because they are diversity candidates), resulting in dissatisfaction with the doctoral experience. One student described their experience in this way: "This process has been an emotional roller coaster for me. I have felt every emotion from love and euphoria, to hatred and rage. I have loved being a PhD student in LIS and I have despised it." Despite such emotions and frustrations, most of the doctoral students interviewed for this study successfully graduated from their programs and are now LIS faculty members.

When asked to impart advice for future doctoral students of color, the responses were again universal and included cautions (1) to find a committed advisor (even before official enrollment in a program) and additional mentors early on in the process; (2) to be aware of the time and lifestyle commitments required by the program; (3) to be aware of the physical and emotional toll the program will introduce; (4) to attempt to be as debt-free as possible before enrolling (stipends rarely cover all expenses); (5) to get involved in research as soon as possible and be diligent about pursuing teaching experience; and (6) to select a program that fits professional and personal goals as well as personal needs and preferences (e.g., climate, scenery, and community characteristics). Experience has taught the Fellows other lessons, including being very careful about contracts and other issues involving funding; being assertive and learning how to say "no" and being judicious with time and energy (physical and mental); seeking and surrounding yourself with supporters and not naysayers; and, as one Fellow suggested, "kick the critics to the sidelines" and persevere through discouragement and frustration.

The experiences of these minority doctoral students concurred with and extended the work of Darden (2003), Darden and Turock (2005), and Winston (1998, 2001, 2008) by further pointing out the critical lack of diversity in the field of librarianship and extending recruitment theory by applying it to doctoral students who aspire to be faculty members in LIS graduate programs.

Specifically, the enablers and barriers described by the Spectrum Doctoral Fellows coincide with the enablers and barriers put forth by Darden (Darden and Turock 2005; Turock 2003); the factors that draw people to careers in librarianship are not surprisingly some of the same that draw library professionals to LIS doctoral study. Likewise, both populations experience similar barriers that can hamper or halt their progress and/or impact their desire to remain in their positions or programs. Results from the study, especially those in which words such as "token," "cash cow," and "show pony" were used, raise questions of institutional racism and potentially discriminatory treatment (whether intentional or not) of the Fellows. These findings coincide with Winston's (2008) challenge to address uncomfortable issues in LIS research, go beyond "what has been presented in the library literature" (4), and facilitate the continued discussion of topics that remain taboo or inflammatory within librarianship and its professoriate. Issues such as race, privilege, equity, and discrimination should not be invisible or "tiptoed around" (Honma 2005) or diluted with less threatening terms (Peterson 1995, 1996, 1999) in discussions about the future of the profession.

DIVERSITY AND SOCIAL JUSTICE THE LIS CURRICULA

Perhaps a partial result of not having enough faculty and instructors of color in LIS graduate programs, as of July 2015, there were 58 schools in the United States and Canada accredited by the ALA, and, according to the author's search of the websites, course catalogs, and registrar pages,[2] within those programs, there were approximately 68 courses related to diversity and social justice.

Within the curricula that house hundreds upon hundreds of courses, 68 is not a significant number and represents a significant gap in the conversations that take place and the education being provided in graduate programs and therefore in the preparation of aspiring information professionals.

Discussions in the literature about diversity in the LIS curricula, or the lack thereof, date back to at least 1973 (Chu 1995b, Summer, 5). There have been discussions about whether diversity is best served as a separate course(s), whether it should be infused across the curriculum, or if a mixture of both is warranted (Belay 1992; Cooke 2014a; Cooke 2016; Cooke and Minarik 2016; Cooke, Sweeney, and Noble 2016; Morris 2007). And how is this to be accomplished? Other discussions remind instructors and practitioners to be precise in the use of language. LIS educators Lorna Peterson (1996, 1999) and Christine Pawley (2006) encourage the use of direct talk. If an article or aspect of the curriculum is to discuss race, racism, privilege, or other potentially uncomfortable topics, those are the terms that should be used, instead of falling back to more comfortable and less controversial terms such as "multiculturalism" (see also Honma 2005). Both scholars suggest that multiculturalism is an easy way to dilute topics and ultimately avoid substantive changes that are so needed in the LIS profession and its education.

Courses dedicated to diversity and social justice can have several variables to consider, including their status (i.e., if it is a special topic or regularized course), their frequency, the currency of the content, and who is teaching the courses (i.e., core faculty, adjuncts, or advanced graduate students), but is it fair to assume that these topics are covered in a substantive, long-term, and hopefully

---

[2]These numbers depict modest improvement over the schools/courses reported by Foderingham-Brown in a 1993 article; at that time, there were 11 schools offering a total of 34 classes related to diversity and social justice.

meaningful way? When examining other courses within a curriculum, is there evidence that diversity and social justice are being discussed? Do the management, bibliographic instruction, and collection development courses incorporate issues of diversity in more than a cursory or tokenized way? Courses that are not dedicated to diversity or social justice can certainly cover such issues and concerns (i.e., a cataloging class discussing the work of Sanford Berman and debating the Library of Congress' continued use of the subject heading "illegal aliens"), but this can be harder to ascertain if access to a syllabus is not available. As with any other course offering, courses are dependent on faculty interest, expertise, and availability. Such courses are also taught by adjuncts and doctoral students; this scenario can cause some instability in course offerings as classes are abandoned or "fall off the books" when instructors resign, retire, or graduate. And, of course, if the student demand for these subject areas is not sufficient, the course will not run. But it is important to have these courses as viable options, particularly when they give students opportunity to think critically and allow them to prepare for the diversity that exists in the communities being served by LIS professionals. (See Chapter 6 for more discussion about diversifying the LIS curricula.)

Box 5.2   Diversifying the LIS Faculty

This column was published in *Library Journal* (BackTalk section) on September 25, 2013. http://lj.libraryjournal.com/2013/09/opinion/back talk/diversifying-the-lis-faculty-backtalk/. Reprinted here with permission.

Diversifying the LIS Faculty | BackTalk
By Nicole A. Cooke on September 25, 2013

LIS faculties need diversity: more so of gender, of ability, of thought, and of race and ethnicity. If we as a profession keep saying that we must recruit more minority students because this makes us better prepared to serve increasingly diverse patron populations, shouldn't we do the same at the faculty ranks?

Considering recent conversations, including those over editorials "The MLS and the Race Line" and "Diversity Never Happens" by former *LJ* editor in chief Michael Kelley, and my efforts to create a for-credit class about library services to diverse populations, I suggest an additional dimension to the LIS diversity recruitment agenda: strategic, ongoing, and purposeful recruitment of diverse candidates to the LIS professoriate.

A NUMBERS GAME

According to the latest Association of Library and Information Science Educators (ALISE) statistics, only 3.83 percent of full-time faculty members are Hispanic, compared to 16.7 percent of the total population (according to 2011 U.S. Census Bureau estimates); while African Americans comprise just 5.39 percent of full-time faculty, compared to 13.1 percent of the population. Another 15.33 percent of LIS full-time faculty are of Asian/Pacific Islander descent, compared to 5.2 percent of the population; and American Indian/ Alaska Natives comprise 0.84 percent of full-time faculty, compared to 1.2 percent of the population. Caucasians make up 74.61 percent of full-time faculty, compared with 63.4 percent of the population.

In an article in *Education Libraries*, Paul Jaeger and Renee Franklin propose that increased numbers of minorities in the LIS professoriate will shape and transform LIS graduate curricula and programs, which in turn will impact and inform the next generations of minority librarians, who will then adequately and appropriately serve the diverse communities that patronize libraries. One hopes the model of these minority librarians will inspire up-and-coming students to pursue librarianship as a career.

A VIRTUOUS CYCLE

Efforts along these lines already exist, such as the Spectrum Doctoral Fellowship from the American Library Association (ALA), an outgrowth of ALA's successful Spectrum Scholars Scholarship Program funded by the Institute of Museum and Library Services (IMLS). I was one of 12 inaugural fellows in the program, who began doctoral study in 2007 and 2008. Fellows were drawn from the four underrepresented ethnic populations (American Indian/Alaska Native, Black/African American, Hispanic/Latino, or Native Hawaiian/Other Pacific Islander). Most of the Fellows were librarians, and our interests ranged from distance education and information behavior to LIS education, technology, and critical studies to archives, academic librarianship, and medical librarianship. We fanned out to LIS schools nationwide, and so far three have graduated and are now tenure track assistant professors teaching in LIS graduate programs. In fall 2013, a new round of six librarians will begin PhD curricula.

This program is special because it aims to increase the ranks of the LIS professoriate with scholars from underrepresented populations. The focus is on teaching and research that will put minorities in front of LIS classrooms and facilitate the creation of research and publications for and about diverse populations.

RECRUITING FROM WITHIN

Where do we find good candidates to apply to doctoral study and ultimately join LIS faculties? Kelley suggested recruiting from the LIS workforce for master's programs. We should do the same for doctoral study. Concerted efforts should be made to recruit practicing librarians who are fired up by research and teaching and are looking for another dimension of librarianship and perhaps an alternative way to advance their careers. Where are the instruction and information literacy librarians, school and youth librarians, and catalogers who bring distinct expertise to the table? Practitioners' depth of experience enriches the classroom experience and can address real-world questions in ways that reflect an understanding of both theory and practice. Adjuncts should not be the only graduate school instructors who bring practical experience to the discussion. This is not to say that faculty life for diverse candidates does not have challenges. Diversity issues in LIS schools require care and deliberate attention to retention and inclusion issues.

> Our patrons are diverse and should have access to librarians who themselves represent diverse populations; similarly, to attract and retain excellent master's candidates from diverse backgrounds, there should be faculty members from similar backgrounds who share their needs and experiences. The better, and more inclusive, the graduate education experience for diverse candidates, the better prepared they will be to serve diverse patrons in their libraries.

STAFF DEVELOPMENT AND CONTINUING EDUCATION IN LIBRARIES

Librarians in all types of libraries wear many hats. Librarians of all kinds—academic, school, public, and special—are responsible for the acquisition and maintenance of comprehensive collections, both print and electronic; they are responsible for being well versed enough in these collections to answer questions and make recommendations; they are responsible for teaching their constituents how to reliably and effectively use the collections; they are responsible for marketing their collections and services; they are responsible for keeping the library on the radar of administrators and other stakeholders; they are responsible for participating in research; they are responsible for participating in national and international conversations about the value of libraries; and they are responsible for a host of other tasks, both small and large, mundane and crucial.

What is missing from many of the discussions in the literature is the necessity for librarians to be culturally competent. Some might suggest that this competency is implicit and automatically included in general training and educational offerings, but this chapter argues that it should be explicit in conversations about and planning of staff development and continuing education (henceforth, referred to as SD/CE) opportunities for librarians. Cultural competence is often not covered in LIS graduate programs and is often missing from professional conference programming (or conflated with broader and/or cursory talk about diversity or multiculturalism).

SD is thought of as training and learning that occurs within the library, specific to the employees of a particular library. CE is thought of as training and learning that occurs outside of the library and may be tailored to a specific topic or demographic, as opposed to being specific to a singular organization. The best practices, examples, and suggestions given in this chapter are fluid and sometimes interchangeable, in that they are applicable to both SD/CE offerings.

In addition to facilitating the development of LIS professionals as lifelong learners and keeping them abreast of new skills and trends in the field, SD/CE are key opportunities for librarians to learn about and aspire to cultural competence. Cultural competence, which was discussed at length in Chapter 2, is necessary for librarians not only in their dealings with patrons but also when dealing with peers and other library professionals. Being well versed in cultural competence can also facilitate librarians' satisfaction with their jobs and with the overall profession. Thornton (2000, 2001) posits that job satisfaction is very important and should be given more consideration; in addition to the core content and duties of a position, other factors such as opportunities to pursue research, fringe benefits, opportunities for advancement, and opportunities for professional development (2001, 149) are important in the long-term performance and retention of academic librarians, especially for African-American female librarians and other librarians of color. SD/CE require purposeful investments of time and resources, but they are crucial to the health and wellness of a librarian's career and to the "long-term future of libraries" (143). The promise of learning opportunities is an important component of the profession's ongoing conversations and strategy development for recruiting and retaining a racially diverse workforce.

Thornton's research also suggests that SD/CE can aid in lessening feelings of isolation; engaging in learning opportunities that not only facilitate scholarly productivity but also enable community development are psychologically beneficial, particularly if a home institution is lacking in "understanding, warmth, and empathy" (2001, 151). Damasco and Hodges (2012, 292) reported that 80 percent of the academic librarians in their research "felt professional development programs were either very important or important in terms of their development and progress toward tenure and promotion." They also concur with Thornton in their discussion of the job stressors of librarians. The authors state:

> When the findings in existing literature are synthesized, a complex picture of the work life of faculty of color emerges. Faculty of color more frequently find themselves burdened with teaching loads and service responsibilities that may detract from their research activity, research that may be undervalued by their colleagues. (282)

SD/CE, in their facilitation of community and development of new knowledge and skills, can provide library professionals with renewed focus, an external outlet, tactical and research skills, and the ability to connect and work with other professionals working in similar areas.

The Necessity for SD/CE

Everything in LIS is changing—the technology, the resources, the funding, and the populations being served. This change is constant and requires that librarians keep abreast in order to remain effective. SD/CE requires informal learning that occurs post-graduation and outside the classroom and SD/CE often requires varying levels of self-motivation and self-directed learning. Hurych (2002, 257) suggests that SD/CE are an essential obligation and part of a librarian's work life:

> Education for the contemporary professional no longer ends with the diploma, if it ever did. It has been recognized that continuing education strengthens not only knowledge and skills necessary for competent performance but also values and attitudes necessary for the service orientation of a profession.

Weingand concurs that SD/CE are essential and suggests that a formal degree, the master of library and information science (MLIS), is only the beginning of a librarian's education.

> The shelf life of a degree is approximately three years and declining. Maintaining competence and learning new skills must be at the top of every professional's "To Do" list. It is an ethical responsibility, to be sure, but also one that is pragmatic and critical for career success. . . . Continuing professional education is no longer an option, it is a requirement of professional practice. (Weingand 1999, 201)

Weingand goes on to define SD/CE as "education that takes place once professional qualification is achieved, with the intent of maintaining competence and/or learning new skills" (201).

Library professionals from underrepresented backgrounds as well as all library professionals who serve diverse populations should be culturally competent, and SD/CE are an important part of this process. Not every librarian will have had diversity-related content in their graduate programs, as may be the case with many library support staff; it becomes even more important that library staff engage in SD/CE, particularly opportunities that relate to issues of diversity and diverse populations. It can be difficult to find quality and culturally relevant SD/CE offerings, as such programs and workshops tend to focus on practical skills and work-related tasks (e.g., cataloging, programming, navigating social media). With this in mind, librarians should be prepared to craft their own personal and independent SD/CE agendas, agendas that are focused on diversity and related topics that will not only broaden their own perspectives and abilities but will also enable them to better serve the diverse patrons utilizing their services and collections.

The pursuit of an individual SD/CE agenda is referred to in the literature as a personal learning network (PLN); these networks can consist of an individual professional and his or her collected resources, and they can consist of multiple professionals working collaboratively to learn more about particular areas of interest (Cooke 2012, 2013a). Cooke states that PLNs are dynamic networks that "need not occur fact-to-face or in real time, nor does the learner have to personally know their knowledge collaborators. PLNs are often specifically devoted to professional learning and development, and are keenly applicable to the use of technology, which makes them as local or global in reach as the learner desires" (2012, 9). Additionally, PLNs are:

> customizable to an individual's work, research interests, and time constraints. They facilitate global learning collaboration opportunities that may not otherwise be feasible in times of financial difficulty. PLNs enable continuous and affordable professional development opportunities that will benefit librarians and their institutions. (Cooke 2013a, 111–112)

Why SD/CE Work: Learning Theory

A variety of learning theories are applicable to the learning that takes place during the SD/CE processes. To accommodate the various theories and situate professional development learning in the most holistic fashion, the work of theorist Knud Illeris is consulted. In his work, *The Three Dimensions of Learning*, Illeris (2002) positions learning at the intersection of internal and external cognitive, emotional, and social learning processes. Tapping into the fields of education, psychology, and management, Illeris posits that learning has two fundamental assumptions: (1) Learning involves two distinct processes: an internal psychological process in which new information is acquired and added to existing knowledge; and an external process where the individual's information acquisition is shaped and influenced by his or her interactions with his or her environment; (2) The learning that occurs during these internal and external processes encompasses three socially situated contexts: the cognitive domain of knowledge acquisition; psychological dimensions of emotion and motivation; and the social domains of communication and cooperation. If done well, professionals engaging in SD/CE will be employing cognitive, emotional, communication, and collaborations skills, as they reflect and interact with others.

Another primary component of the educational value of SD/CE is reflection. Reflection is a process by which learners critically and thoughtfully contemplate the content they are learning and applying to their lives and repertoires. Librarians will hopefully reflect not only on the new learning experience but also on their cumulative work. Ideally, the practice of reflection will develop LIS professionals as reflective practitioners, provide a sense of purpose to learning and promote awareness, self-empowerment, self-improvement, and emancipation. Reflection is facilitated by learning by doing and enhances problem-solving skills. Moon (2004, 75) indicates that there are several levels of reflection, including descriptive reflection (describing an event), dialogic reflection (stepping back from an event and contemplating the reasons for said event), and critical reflection (contemplating reasons for events in the "broader social, ethical, moral or historical contexts"). It is surmised that participation in culturally relevant and well-designed SD/CE opportunities will inspire dialogic, if not critical, reflection.

Models for SD

SD programs can be used to address specific organizational issues; however, SD or in-house training across libraries tends to address the same umbrella topics, because libraries have characteristics and problems in common despite having some individual features, services, location-based idiosyncrasies, and so on. In their book, *Staff Development: A Practical Guide*, a publication emanating from the ALA's Library Leadership and Management Association, Stewart, Washington-Hoagland, and Zsulya (2013) suggest that SD is useful for addressing the following internal organizational issues and concerns: the need to cross-train staff in different functional areas; orientation for new employees and orientation for employees in new positions; to introduce and reinforce core competencies; to introduce new hardware or software products; to improve or strengthen customer services skills; to encourage leadership skills and development; succession planning; to introduce and reinforce instructional design and teaching skills; ergonomics; to encourage coaching and facilitation skills; library marketing; and communication enhancement.

Jennerich (2006, 613) concurs and offers some of the benefits of SD, which include improvement of external and internal customer services; increased expectations and decreased anxiety among staff; improved group communication skills; acquisition of tools for tackling problems creatively; making library staff visible and valuable to the campus; invigorating the need for personal improvement; and instilling confidence throughout the organization.

The aforementioned programs, with their requisite benefits, are most likely singular events or perhaps a short series of events, which can be useful particularly if the staff members in attendance have the motivation to implement the new skills independently. Other examples in the literature suggest long-term SD programs such as journal clubs (Young and Vilelle 2011). A journal club consists of a group of staff reading the same article and coming together to discuss ideas. Such a group is ongoing, "generates a wealth of ideas for library improvement," facilitates opportunities to turn "research into practice" (133), allows participants to stay current on developments in librarianship, and encourages intraorganizational networking and faculty/administration dialog (135). While it is possible that such a group could build community and enhance group cohesion, long-term SD models such as this can be hard to sustain because of conflicting schedules, burnout, and the feeling that no real changes are being affected.

Other models of SD in the literature include librarians engaging in online webinars or other programs outside of their organizations. For example, WebJunction is an online learning hub produced by Online Computer Library Center, Inc. (OCLC) (www.oclc.org), the nonprofit membership computer library service and research organization. WebJunction describes itself as "the place where public library staff gather to build the knowledge, skills and support we need to power relevant, vibrant libraries" (2003). Offering a variety of workshops and courses on a wide range of topics, academic librarians also take advantage of WebJunction. Another online learning example is 23 Things (Blowers 2008). A self-paced course, librarians completed a series of 23 modules to learn about social media and Web 2.0 technologies. 23 Things was so popular when it came out of the Charlotte (North Carolina) Mecklenburg Library that it spawned conference workshops and saw wide adoption in libraries across the country. 23 Things was timely and the content was relevant.

Solutions for SD

SD is necessary for the health of a library; there are many benefits of this training, but there are also many instances when SD can be ineffective or even frustrating to participants. At the root of SD is the organizational culture of the library and administrative commitment. SD programs should have some alignment not only with the library's formal policies and strategic plans but also with the implicit rules, regulations, and interests of the organization. For example, if a library has particular interests in technology, then such workshops and their suggestions and recommendations may actually see the light of day, because that is what the administrators and power players wish to see at the library. If this same library has no real interest in information literacy, no amount of information literacy workshops will compel the management to institute new programming or services related to library instruction. This is where frustration can manifest; even if the librarians are interested in information literacy, it could be difficult to actually implement the ideas posited in a training session without administrative support or resources.

Shaughnessy (1988) details additional reasons why SD "frequently doesn't take" and why librarians engaging in SD often see no tangible changes in their organizations. The author suggests that many SD offerings employ instructional methods that do not promote hands-on learning or cater to the learning styles of adults. Similarly, the instructional style of the workshops/sessions/classes does not align with the learning goals of participants (10). Because of the misalignment between learning goals and pedagogy, many workshops often "typically fail to provide opportunities for self-assessment, opportunity to evaluate one's performance in a structured team environment" (11).

Another deficiency of current SD offerings is a lack of diverse content, not the least of which is cultural competence. None of the aforementioned articles, books, or online examples explicitly addresses diversity or cultural competence —that is a serious omission, particularly when many of these models and examples *could* discuss or incorporate issues of diversity.

This chapter suggests three solutions for SD: (1) bring in outside trainers and facilitators, or outsource SD to appropriate vendors; (2) prioritize diversity at the highest levels of organization; and (3) racialize the content of SD training (this will be discussed in the section *Solutions for CE*).

A potential solution for better aligning pedagogy with appropriate learning goals *and* the goals of the organization is to hire professional trainers who will come to the library and deliver the necessary content. Professional trainers have the skills and knowledge to teach adults in an effective manner. Similarly, libraries may consider sending their employees to off-site training, perhaps a local or regional library consortium that specializes in SD training. For example, a library with particular interests in digital preservation might send its librarians to workshops offered by LYRASIS (https://www.lyrasis.org/), which is a nonprofit membership organization of libraries, archives, museums, and cultural heritage organizations who create and manage digital content. Instead of recreating the wheel and developing in-house training sessions, librarians can easily participate in specialized SD trainings with content experts who also possess the necessary pedagogical skills.

Additionally, libraries can also employ diversity consultants to provide SD training. Consultants and experts who specialize in diversity can be found on college or university campuses (e.g., a staff member of a diversity resource center, diversity office, a cultural house; a faculty member; or an intergroup dialogue facilitator), or they could be brought in from a specialized diversity firm. There are many trainers who would be willing and able to provide SD programing on diversity and cultural competence to libraries and their staff.

Per the aforementioned Shaughnessy (1988) article, in order for issues of diversity to be important within an organization and to be included in SD offerings, it needs to be important to the leadership and organizational culture of a library. This is perhaps easier said than done if a library's leadership is unfamiliar or even disinterested in issues of diversity, but if they are active listeners and are receptive to staff opinions and input, it could be possible for others in the library to request SD that addresses diversity exclusively or incorporates it into other content areas. If efforts and requests to racialize SD content are unsuccessful, librarians still have many options for pursuing diversity and cultural competence on their own (to be discussed in the section *Solutions for CE*) and infuse it into their own professional practice.

Models for CE

CE programs or "updating activities" (Chan and Auster 2003) can have much more latitude than SD programs, offering programs on topics that could be considered more niche but still useful for the average library (i.e., using Drupal to build your library's website). But much like SD offerings, CE offerings tend to address the same general topics and often lack discussions of race, ethnicity, diversity, social justice, and the like. Cassner and Adams (2012) propose the following options for CE for academic librarians: attending conferences; joining professional organizations; serving on external committees; mentoring new librarians; attending online webinars; taking online courses; and reading blogs, columns, and professional journals. This list is a mix of face-to-face and online opportunities and features opportunities for both self-directed individuals and groups.

The authors in Smallwood, Harrod, and Gubnitskaia's (2013) anthology *Continuing Education for Librarians: Essays on Career Improvement through Classes, Workshops, Conferences and More* extend the CE possibilities for librarians by suggesting the following: pursuing advanced degrees and certifications; enrolling in massive open online courses (MOOCs); hosting a conference; traveling abroad; engaging with professional associations; teaching on campus; and mentoring LIS students. This list is perhaps more attune with scholarly and research demands placed on academic librarians (many of whom are tenure track and hold faculty rank); however, some of these suggestions require inordinate amounts of time and funds that many libraries do not have (i.e., pursuing a PhD or traveling abroad). These are also activities that are long-term and more individual and self-directed, as opposed to being completed in a few sessions in a group setting. Activities that encourage or revolve around research permit interdisciplinary study, which is also beneficial for academic librarians. For example, a librarian with liaison responsibilities to particular academic departments could have collaborative opportunities with those faculty members and be exposed to ideas and literature outside of LIS. The same can be said for librarians pursuing additional degrees, traveling abroad (i.e., being a Fulbright Scholar, http://www.cies.org), and those teaching outside of the library.

Flatley and Weber (2004) emphasize the importance of writing and publishing for librarians, whether that publishing occurs as a referred journal article, a web-based publication or blog, book chapter, encyclopedia article, bibliography, or as a book. Librarians have great expertise to offer and should be contributing to the literature. To this end, librarians should also be presenting their writing and research at conferences and in other venues (e.g., many librarians are now presenting at the popular South by Southwest Music, Film and Interactive Festivals [SXSW], [http://www.sxsw.com]).

A well-known CE opportunity for academic librarians is the Association of College and Research Libraries Immersion Program (http://www.ala.org/acrl/

immersion). Focused on information literacy instruction, its scope is limited and the experience is expensive in both time and money. Alumni of the program rightfully sing its praises, but it is an opportunity only available to a subset of the librarians who would benefit from the experience. To compensate for this, the Immersion Program has added some online components and shorter residency programs to complement its initial four- to five-day on-site immersive content model. Comparable immersive and residential CE opportunities (e.g., the Frye Leadership Institute, the Snowbird Leadership Institute, and the Aurora Leadership Institute) possess the same advantages and disadvantages as the Immersion Program.

Solutions for CE

Suggested solutions for CE included those discussed previously in *Solutions for SD*; however, additional structure and purpose can be applied to CE efforts because they are self-directed and occur over a greater length of time. CE efforts, particularly in regard to developing cultural competence, will benefit from a guided PLN and agenda. Developing a PLN requires commitment and focus to select the right content, content that is culturally relevant and relevant to the intellectual needs and experiences of librarians, as opposed to content designed explicitly to develop workplace skills. Developing such a PLN requires that LIS and CE discussions be racialized. Described and discussed in the literature of adult education, to take a racialized view of things, in this case CE readings and activities, is "to view it through the distinctive lens of a racial group's experience of the world, and to view that experience of membership as a positive constitutive element of a person's identity" (Brookfield 2003, 498–499). Racialism, which is not to be conflated with racism, "is the positive recognition of how his or her life world, positionality and sense of cultural identity comprise a set of pre-conscious filters and assumptions that frame how one's life is felt and lived" (499). To racialize CE content in this way is to strive toward cultural competence, which encourages librarians to empathize with the diverse patrons with whom they interact. Librarianship is a predominantly white and female profession, but the clientele served by the profession is distinctly diverse in terms of race, ethnicity, religion, sexual orientation, physical ability, socioeconomic status, and so on. Librarians cannot engage in one-size-fits-all service provision, instead they should strive to be aware, knowledgeable, and appreciative of other cultures. This empathy and understanding inform professional practice. Cultural competence can be learned and refined though CE activities.

This type of focused, diversity-based PLN and agenda are discussed in other disciplines as a paraversity. Goodman (2015) and Rolfe (2013) use the term "paraversity" to describe this phenomenon of creating a personal learning agenda that runs parallel to traditional or mainstream CE offerings. A "mental space of dissensus" and the "pursuit of difference," a paraversity seeks to disrupt the status quo and inject new ideas and alternative voices to the learning process (Goodman 2015, 638).

Perhaps among the easiest ways to create a paraversity devoted to cultural competence is to read—read the research in LIS and across disciplines. This can be accomplished, of course, by reading journal articles, but there are many good books, chapters, white papers, and conference proceedings that can be found on Google Scholar (https://scholar.google.com), Academia.edu (https://www.academia.edu), ResearchGate (http://www.researchgate.net), and Social Science Research Network (SSRN [http://ssrn.com/en/]).

Talking is another way to contribute to development of a personal learning agenda. Making use of social media and listservs are a great way to catch wind of new voices and opinions and learn about new researchers, conferences, and grassroots initiatives related to diversity and cultural competence (e.g., the #critlib hashtag on Twitter). There are many online communities of practice and think tanks that provide discussion spaces for academics and librarians (e.g., the National Center for Faculty Development and Diversity, http://www.facultydiversity.org/). Actual discussion, particularly with colleagues and scholars outside of LIS, is a sure way to learn new things. This author has learned an amazing amount from colleagues in social work, adult education, sociology, and educational psychology. Along these lines, attendance at conferences, especially international conferences and conferences outside of LIS, are not passé—networking is still a vital component to CE.

Finally, as has been mentioned, conducting research and collaborating with other scholars is a way to pursue a PLN and agenda (check out ScholarBridge [http://www.scholarbridge.com] if you are in need of collaborators), as is mentoring students and new professionals, and taking courses for credit. Again, the common denominators of these activities are interaction, commitment, and motivation.

> Professional education for librarians has to anticipate changes and developments in professional tasks, roles and expectations, both at the macro level of the profession as a whole and the micro level of different library specialties. Education programs must take account of standards set by national and international professional bodies, in addition to reflecting the realities of professional work in the sector. Program content should also be informed by research in the discipline, enabling the academy to influence professional thinking and practice, contributing to the development and positioning of the profession. (Corrall 2010, 567)

Librarians must take the lead in their own CE; if the existing SD/CE offerings are not sufficient or do not focus on diversity, cultural competence, or whatever other topic is of interest, then librarians can and should create their own opportunities or at least attempt to enhance what is currently available. Academic librarians owe it to their patrons, their colleagues, and themselves to constantly learn and improve their practice. In this instance, it is hoped that LIS professionals will recognize the need to become and remain culturally competent and will feel empowered to create and pursue their own PLNs and agendas to achieve this goal. It is achievable and so worthwhile.

CONCLUSION

As has been described, diversity is multifaceted and requires not only acquisition but also maintenance and management. Patricia Kreitz (2008) spells out steps for managing diversity in an organization. The steps are as follows: diversity must be a priority for its leadership and management; diversity should be part of the organization's vision and strategic plan; diversity should be linked to the organization's expectations for performance; members of the organization should be held accountable for implementing diversity and working with and within diversity plans, and this accountability should be able to be measured quantitatively and qualitatively; diversity should be considered long-term in regard to the recruitment and development of diverse leaders; diversity should be a family affair and should involve all members of an organization, regardless of rank or position; and the organization should be willing and able to provide the necessary training to achieve these diversity goals.

The management of diversity happens at many levels and requires work from individuals, groups, organizations, and from the profession at large. And much like mentoring, the management of diversity is dynamic and customizable, designed to suit the specific individuals and organizations involved. Managing is an ongoing and sometimes difficult undertaking but ultimately worthwhile and necessary for the health of the profession.

Regarding the recruitment and retention of diverse faculty and the diversification of the LIS curricula and the management of diversity in a general sense, this chapter will conclude with the words of another LIS educator, Clara Chu (1995a, Winter, 7), who stated, "LIS schools and the profession have much work to do in the future to strengthen our commitment to library and information science education in response to the needs of a culturally diverse society."

LESSON PLAN

Essential Readings:

Howland, Joan. "Beyond Recruitment: Retention and Promotion Strategies to Ensure Diversity and Success." *Library Administration and Management* 13, no. 1 (1999): 4–14.

Kreitz, Patricia A. "Best Practices for Managing Organizational Diversity." *The Journal of Academic Librarianship* 34, no. 2 (2008): 101–120.

St Lifer, Evan, and Corinne Nelson. "Unequal Opportunities: Race Does Matter." *Library Journal* 122, no. 18 (1997): 42–46.

Sue, Derald Wing, Christina M. Capodilupo, Gina C. Torino, Jennifer M. Bucceri, Aisha Holder, Kevin L. Nadal, and Marta Esquilin. "Racial Microaggressions in Everyday Life: Implications for Clinical Practice." *American Psychologist* 62, no. 4 (2007): 271–286.

Other Key Works:

Du Mont, Rosemary Ruhig. "Race in American Librarianship: Attitudes of the Library Profession." *Journal of Library History* 21, no. 3 (1986): 488–509.

Pawley, Christine. "Unequal Legacies: Race and Multiculturalism in the LIS Curriculum." *The Library Quarterly* 76, no. 2 (2006): 149–168.

Questions to Ask:

1. In another of his works, Derald Wing Sue talks about race and why it is so hard to talk about such issues openly and honestly and in a way that spurs change (Sue 2015). How can information professionals become more comfortable with hard conversations?

2. What mentoring and/or professional development opportunities would you most benefit from?

3. What topics of diversity would you like to see in the LIS curriculum?

REFERENCES

Achor, Shirley, and Aida Morales. 1990. "Chicanas Holding Doctoral Degrees: Social Reproduction and Cultural Ecological Approaches." *Anthropology and Education Quarterly* 21 (3): 269–287.

Acree, Eric Kofi, Sharon K. Epps, Yolanda Gilmore, and Charmaine Henriques. 2001. "Using Professional Development as a Retention Tool for Underrepresented Academic Librarians." *Journal of Library Administration* 33 (1–2): 45–61.

Adkins, Denice. 2004. "Latino Librarians on Becoming LIS Educators: An Exploratory Investigation of the Barriers In Recruiting Latino Faculty." *Journal of Education for Library and Information Science* 45 (2): 149–161.

Adkins, Denice, and Isabel Espinal. 2004. "The Diversity Mandate." *Library Journal* 129 (7): 52–54.

Alabi, Jaena. 2015. "Racial Microaggressions in Academic Libraries: Results of a Survey of Minority and Non-Minority Librarians." *The Journal of Academic Librarianship* 41 (1): 47–53.

Albertson, Dan, ed. 2016. "ALISE Library and Information Science Education Statistical Report 2015." Chicago: Association for Library and Information Science Education.

Alire, Camila A. 2001. "Diversity and Leadership: The Color of Leadership." *Journal of Library Administration* 32 (3–4): 99–114.

American Library Association. 2012a. "Diversity Counts." ALA Office for Research and Statistics and ALA Office for Diversity. Last modified September 28, 2012. http://www.ala.org/offices/diversity/diversitycounts/divcounts.

American Library Association. 2012b. American Library Association Releases New Data to Update "Diversity Counts" Report. ALA Office for Research and Statistics and ALA Office for Diversity. Last modified September 28, 2012. http://www.ala.org/news/2012/09/american-library-association-releases-new-data-update-diversity-counts-report.

American Library Association. "Immersion Program." Association of College and Research Libraries. Accessed March 1, 2016. http://www.ala.org/acrl/immersion.

Antonio, Anthony Lising, Mitchell J. Chang, Kenji Hakuta, David A. Kenny, Shana Levin, and Jeffrey F. Milem. 2004. "Effects of Racial Diversity on Complex Thinking in College Students." *Psychological Science* 15 (8): 507–510.

Attebury, Ramirose Ilene. 2010. "Perceptions of a Profession: Librarians and Stereotypes in Online Videos." Accessed March 1, 2016. http://www.webpages.uidaho.edu/~mbolin/attebury.htm.

Balderrama, Sandra Rios. 2000. "This Trend Called Diversity." *Library Trends* 49 (1): 194–214.

Barlow, Diane L., and Elizabeth Aversa. 2006. "Library Professionals for the 21st Century Academy." *Advances in Librarianship* 30: 327–364.

Belay, Getinet. 1992. "Conceptual Strategies for Operationalizing Multicultural Curricula." *Journal of Education for Library and Information Science* 33 (4): 295–306.

Bishop, Ann P., Bharat Mehra, Imani Bazzell, and Cynthia Smith. 2003. "Participatory Action Research and Digital Libraries: Reframing Evaluation." In *Digital Library Use: Social Practice in Design and Evaluation*, edited by Ann Peterson Bishop, Nancy A. Van House, and Barbara P. Buttenfield, 161–190. Boston: The MIT Press.

Bishop, Ann P., Tonyia J. Tidline, Susan Shoemaker, and Pamela Salela. 1999. "Public Libraries and Networked Information Services in Low-Income Communities." *Library and Information Science Research* 21 (3): 361–390.

Blowers, Helene. 2008. "Ten Tips about 23 Things." *School Library Journal* 54 (10): 53–57.

Boast, Robin. 2011. "Neocolonial Collaboration: Museum as Contact Zone Revisited." *Museum Anthropology* 34 (1): 56–70.

Bonnette, Ashley E. 2004. "Mentoring Minority Librarians up the Career Ladder." *Library Administration and Management* 18 (3): 134–139.

Bonnici, Laurie, and Kathleen Burnett. 2005. "A Web Model of Recruitment for LIS Doctoral Education: Weaving in Diversity." In *Unfinished Business: Race, Equity, and Diversity in Library and Information Science Education*, edited by Maurice Wheeler, 119–130. Lanham, MD: Scarecrow Press.

Brookfield, Stephen. 2003. "Racializing the Discourse of Adult Education." *Harvard Educational Review* 73 (4): 497-523.

Brown-Syed, Christopher, Lynda Baker, and Don A. Wicks. 2008. "Doctoral Recruitment Factors: Results of a Survey of Deans and Directors." *Journal of Education for Library and Information Science* 49 (2): 107–115.

Cassner, Mary, and Kate E. Adams. 2012. "Continuing Education for Distance Librarians." *Journal of Library and Information Services in Distance Learning* 6 (2): 117–128.

Chan, Donna C., and Ethel Auster. 2003. "Factors Contributing to the Professional Development of Reference Librarians." *Library and Information Science Research* 25 (3): 265–286.

Chesler, Mark, and James Crowfoot. 1989. "Racism in Higher Education: An Organizational Analysis." Ann Arbor: Center for Research on Social Organization, University of Michigan.

Chu, Clara M. 1995a. "Commitment to Multicultural Library and Information Science Education: Part 1—Current Status." *EMIE Bulletin* 12 (Winter, 2): 6–7.

Chu, Clara M. 1995b. "Commitment to Multicultural Library and Information Science Education: Part 2—A Model for Success." *EMIE Bulletin* 12 (Summer, 4): 4–11.

Chu, Clara M. 1999. "Transformative Information Services: Uprooting Race Politics." Speech, Black Caucus of the American Library Association Conference, Las Vegas, July 19–22.

Cooke, Nicole A. 2012. "Professional Development 2.0 for Librarians: Developing an Online Personal Learning Network (PLN)."*Library Hi Tech News* 29 (3): 1–9.

Cooke, Nicole A. 2013a. "Developing Your Personal Learning Network." In *Continuing Education for Librarians: Workshops, Conferences, College and Related Education*, edited by Carol Smallwood, Kerol Harrod, and Vera Gubnitskaia, 111–118. Jefferson, NC: McFarland & Company, Inc.

Cooke, Nicole A. 2013b. "Diversifying the LIS Faculty (BackTalk column)." *Library Journal* 138 (15): 34. http://lj.libraryjournal.com/2013/09/opinion/back-talk/diversifying-the-lis-faculty-backtalk/.

Cooke, Nicole A. 2014a. "Creating Opportunities for Empathy and Cultural Competence in the LIS Curriculum." *SRRT Newsletter* 187. http://libr.org/srrt/news/srrt187.php#9.

Cooke, Nicole A. 2014b. "The Spectrum Doctoral Fellowship Program: Enhancing the LIS Professoriate." *InterActions: UCLA Journal of Education and Information Studies* 10 (1). http://escholarship.org/uc/item/7vb7v4p8.

Cooke, Nicole A. 2016. "Counter-Storytelling in the LIS Curriculum." In *Perspectives on Libraries as Institutions of Human Rights and Social Justice*, edited by Ursula Gorham, Natalie Greene Taylor, and Paul T. Jaeger, 331–348. Bingley, UK: Emerald Group Publishing Limited.

Cooke, Nicole A., and Minarik, Joseph P. 2016. "Linking LIS Graduate Study and Social Justice Education: Preparing Students for Critically Conscious Practice." In *Progressive Community Action: Critical Theory and Social Justice in Library and Information Science*, edited by B. Mehra and K. Rioux, 181–214. Sacramento, CA: Library Juice Press.

Cooke, Nicole A., Miriam E. Sweeney, and Safiya U. Noble. 2016. "Social Justice as Topic and Tool: An Attempt to Transform A LIS Curriculum and Culture." *The Library Quarterly: Information, Community, Policy* 86 (1): 107–124.

Corrall, Sheila. 2010. "Educating the Academic Librarian as a Blended Professional: A Review and Case Study." *Library Management* 31 (8/9): 567–593.

Damasco, Ione T., and Dracine Hodges. 2012. "Tenure and Promotion Experiences of Academic Librarians of Color." *College and Research Libraries* 73 (3): 279–301.

Darden, Barbara S. 2003. "Career Paths of African American Women Academic Library Administrators." (Unpublished doctoral dissertation). New Brunswick, NJ: Rutgers University.

Darden, Barbara S., and B. Turock. 2005. "Career Patterns of African American Women Academic Library Administrators." *Advances in Library Administration and Organization* 22 (1): 315–360.

Denson, Nida, and Mitchell J. Chang. 2009. "Racial Diversity Matters: The Impact of Diversity-Related Student Engagement and Institutional Context." *American Educational Research Journal* 46 (2): 322–353.

Dewey, Barbara I., and Jillian Keally. 2008. "Recruiting for Diversity: Strategies for 21st Century Research Librarianship." *Library Hi Tech* 26 (4): 622–629.

East, Dennis, and Errol Lam. 1995. "In Search of Multiculturalism in the Library Science Curriculum." *Journal of Education for Library and Information Science* 36 (3): 199–216.

Echavarria, Tami, and Andrew B. Wertheimer. 1997. "Surveying the Role of Ethnic-American Library Associations." *Library Trends* 46 (2): 49.

Ellis, Evelynn M. 2001. "The Impact of Race and Gender on Graduate School Socialization, Satisfaction with Doctoral Study, and Commitment to Degree Completion." *Western Journal of Black Studies* 25 (1): 30–45.

Flatley, Robert K., and Michael A. Weber. 2004. "Perspectives on Professional Development Opportunities for New Academic Librarians." *The Journal of Academic Librarianship* 30 (6): 488–492.

Franklin, Renee E., and Paul T. Jaeger. 2007. "A Decade of Doctorates: An Examination of Dissertations Written by African American Women in Library and Information Studies, 1993–2003." *Journal of Education for Library and Information Science* 48 (3): 187–201.

Gardner, Susan K. 2008. "Fitting the Mold of Graduate School: A Qualitative Study of Socialization in Doctoral Education." *Innovative Higher Education* 33 (2): 125–138.

Gilliland, Anne. 2011. "Neutrality, Social Justice and the Obligations of Archival Educators and Education in the Twenty-first Century." *Archival Science* 11 (3–4): 193–209.

Gollop, Claudia J. 1999. "Library and Information Science Education: Preparing Librarians for a Multicultural Society." *College and Research Libraries* 60 (4): 385–395.

Goodman, Benny. 2015. "The Academic in the University of Excellence: The Need to Construct the 'Paraversity' Using the Web." *Nurse Education Today* 35 (5): 638–640.

Hollis, Deborah. 1996. "On the Ambiguous Side: Experience in a Predominantly White and Female Profession." In *In Our Own Voices: The Changing Face of Librarianship*, edited by Teresa Y. Neely and Khafre K. Abif, 139–154. Lanham, MD: Scarecrow.

Honma, Todd. 2005. "Trippin' over the Color Line: The Invisibility of Race in Library and Information Studies." *InterActions: UCLA Journal of Education and Information Studies* 1 (2).

Howland, Joan. 1999. "Beyond Recruitment: Retention and Promotion Strategies to Ensure Diversity and Success." *Library Administration and Management* 13 (1): 4–14.

Hurych, Jitka. 2002. "Continuing Professional Education as an Ethical Issue." In *Continuing Professional Education for the Information Society: The Fifth World Conference of Continuing Professional Education for the Library and Information Science Professions*, 256–263. The Hague, Netherlands: International Federation of Library Associations and Institutions.

Illeris, Knud. 2002. *The Three Dimensions of Learning*. Denmark: Roskilde University Press.

Jaeger, Paul T., John Carlo Bertot, and Renee E. Franklin. 2010. "Diversity, Inclusion, and Underrepresented Populations in LIS Research." *The Library Quarterly* 80 (2): 175–181.

Jaeger, Paul T., and Renee E. Franklin. 2007. "The Virtuous Circle: Increasing Diversity in LIS Faculties to Create More Inclusive Library Services and Outreach." *Education Libraries* 30 (1): 20–26.

Jennerich, Elaine Z. 2006. "The Long-Term View of Library Staff Development the Positive Effects on a Large Organization." *College and Research Libraries News* 67 (10): 612–614.

Jimerson, Randall C. 2006. "Embracing the Power of Archives." *American Archivist* 69 (1): 19–32.

Josey, E. J. 1993. "The Challenges of Cultural Diversity in the Recruitment of Faculty and Students from Diverse Backgrounds." *Journal of Education for Library and Information Science* 34 (4): 302–311.

Josey, E. J. 1994. "The State of Diversity." *The Reference Librarian* 21 (45–46): 5–11.

Josey, E. J., and Ismail Abdullahi. 2002. "Why Diversity in American Libraries." *Library Management* 23 (1/2): 10–16.

Kim, Kyung-Sun, and Sei-Ching Joanna Sin. 2006. "Recruiting and Retaining Students of Color in LIS Programs: Perspectives of Library and Information Professionals." *Journal of Education for Library and Information Science* 47 (2): 81–95.

Kim, Kyung-Sun, and Sei-Ching Joanna Sin. 2008. "Increasing Ethnic Diversity in LIS: Strategies Suggested by Librarians of Color." *The Library Quarterly: Information, Community, Policy* 78 (2): 153–177.

Kreitz, Patricia A. 2008. "Best Practices for Managing Organizational Diversity." *The Journal of Academic Librarianship* 34 (2): 101–120.

Lance, Keith Curry. 2005. "Racial and Ethnic Diversity of US Library Workers." *American Libraries* 36 (5): 41–43.

Lonetree, Amy. 2006. "Missed Opportunities: Reflections on the NMAI." *The American Indian Quarterly* 30 (3): 632–645.

Manley, Will. 2007. "Move Over, Marian." *American Libraries* 38 (6): 152.

Manzo, Kathleen Kennedy. 1994. "Flaws in Fellowships: Institutional Support Essential to Boosting Number of African American Doctoral Students." *Diverse Issues in Higher Education* 11 (10): 46–52.

McCook, Kathleen de la Pena, and Kate Lippincott. 1997. "Library Schools and Diversity: Who Makes the Grade?" *Library Journal* 122 (7): 30–32.

Meacham, Jack. 2002. "Our Doctoral Programs Are Failing Our Undergraduate Students." *Liberal Education* 88 (3): 22–28.

Moon, Jennifer A. 2004. *Reflection in Learning and Professional Development: Theory and Practice.* New York: Routledge.

Morris, Vanessa J. "A Seat at the Table: Seeking Culturally Competent Pedagogy in Librarian Education." Paper presented at the annual meeting for the Association of Library and Information Science Education, Seattle, WA, January 15–18, 2007. Accessed April 1, 2016. http://www.pages.drexel.edu/~gdc27/final/documents/seatatthetable.pdf.

Neely, Teresa Y., and Lorna Peterson. 2007. "Achieving Racial and Ethnic Diversity among Academic and Research Librarians: The Recruitment, Retention, and Advancement of Librarians of Color—A White Paper." *College and Research Libraries News* 68 (9): 562–565.

Nettles, Michael T. 1990. "Success in Doctoral Programs: Experiences of Minority and White Students." *American Journal of Education* 98 (4): 494–522.

"OCLC WebJunction." 2003. http://www.webjunction.org.

Offerman, Michael. 2011. "Profile of the Nontraditional Doctoral Degree Student." *New Directions for Adult and Continuing Education* 2011 (129): 21–30.

Olneck, Michael. 2000. "Can Multicultural Education Change What Counts as Cultural Capital?" *American Educational Research Journal* 37 (2): 317–348.

Olson, Carol. 1988. "Recruiting and Retaining Minority Graduate Students: A Systems Perspective." *The Journal of Negro Education* 57 (1): 31–42.

Olson, Hope A. 1998. "Mapping beyond Dewey's Boundaries: Constructing Classificatory Space for Marginalized Knowledge Domains." *Library Trends* 47 (2): 233–254.

Olson, Hope A. 2001. "The Power to Name: Representation in Library Catalogs." *Signs* 26 (3): 639–668.

Patterson, Lotsee. 2000. "History and Status of Native Americans in Librarianship." *Library Trends* 49 (1): 182–193.

Pawley, Christine. 2006. "Unequal Legacies: Race and Multiculturalism in the LIS Curriculum." *The Library Quarterly: Information, Community, Policy* 76 (2): 149–168.

Peresie, Michelle, and L. B. Alexander. 2005. "Librarian Stereotypes in Young Adult Literature." *Young Adult Library Services* 4 (1): 24–31.

Peterson, Lorna. 1995. "Multiculturalism: Affirmative or Negative Action?" *Library Journal* 120 (12): 30–31, 33.

Peterson, Lorna. 1996. "Alternative Perspectives in Library and Information Science: Issues of Race." *Journal of Education for Library and Information Science* 37 (2): 163–174.

Peterson, Lorna. 1999. "The Definition of Diversity: Two Views. A More Specific Definition." *Journal of Library Administration* 27 (1–2): 17–26.

Poulin, Eric. 2008. "A Whole New World of Freaks and Geeks: Libraries and Librarians on YouTube." *Libres* 18 (2). http://libres-ejournal.info/568/.

Pruitt, Anne S., and Paul D. Isaac. 1985. "Discrimination in Recruitment, Admission, and Retention of Minority Graduate Students." *The Journal of Negro Education* 54 (4): 526–536.

Radford, Marie L., and Gary P. Radford. 1997. "Power, Knowledge, and Fear: Feminism, Foucault, and The Stereotype of the Female Librarian." *The Library Quarterly: Information, Community, Policy* 67 (3): 250–266.

Radford, Marie L., and Gary P. Radford. 2003. "Librarians and Party Girls: Cultural Studies and Meaning of the Librarian." *The Library Quarterly: Information, Community* 73 (1): 54–69.

Randall, Ann. 1988. "Minority Recruitment in Librarianship." In *Librarians for the New Millennium*, edited by William E. Moen and Kathleen M. Heim, 11–25. Chicago: American Library Association, Office for Library and Personnel Resources.

Rankin, Susan R., and Robert Dean Reason. 2005. "Differing Perceptions: How Students of Color and White Students Perceive Campus Climate for Underrepresented Groups." *Journal of College Student Development* 46 (1): 43–61.

Reeling, Patricia G. 1992. "Doctorate Recipients in Library Science: How They Compare with Doctorate Recipients in Other Disciplines." *Journal of Education for Library and Information Science* 33 (4): 311–329.

Roberson, Loriann, and Carol T. Kulik. 2007. "Stereotype Threat at Work." *The Academy of Management Perspectives* 21 (2): 24–40.

Rolfe, Gary. 2013. *The University in Dissent: Scholarship in the Corporate University.* New York: Routledge.

Sampson, Zora F. 1999. "The Role of Civility in Diverse Relations." *Journal of Library Administration* 27 (1–2): 93–110.

Shaffer, Christopher, and Olga Casey. 2012. "Behind the Glasses and beneath the Bun: Portrayals of Librarians in Popular Cinema and a Guide for Developing a Collection." *Collection Building* 32 (2): 39–45.

Shaughnessy, Thomas W. 1988. "Staff Development in Libraries: Why It Frequently Doesn't Take." *Journal of Library Administration* 9 (2): 5–12.

Smallwood, Carol, Kerol Harrod, and Vera Gubnitskaia, eds. 2013. *Continuing Education for Librarians: Essays on Career Improvement through Classes, Workshops, Conferences and More.* Jefferson, NC: McFarland.

Stewart, Andrea Wigbels, Carlette Washington-Hoagland, and Carol T. Zsulya. 2013. *Staff Development: A Practical Guide* (4th Edition). Chicago: American Library Association.

St. Lifer, Evan, and Corinne Nelson. 1997. "Unequal Opportunities: Race Does Matter." *Library Journal* 122 (18): 42–46.

Stringer-Stanback, Kynita. 2008. "Recruitment, Retention and Diversity in Libraries and Higher Education: Why Doing the Right Thing Is Easier Said than Done." *North Carolina Libraries* 66 (1): 25–27.

Subramaniam, Mega M., and Paul T. Jaeger. 2010. "Modeling Inclusive Practice? Attracting Diverse Faculty and Future Faculty to the Information Workforce." *Library Trends* 59 (1): 109–127.

Sue, Derald Wing. 2015. *Race Talk and the Conspiracy of Silence: Understanding and Facilitating Difficult Dialogues on Race.* Hoboken, NJ: John Wiley and Sons.

Sue, Derald Wing, Christina M. Capodilupo, Gina C. Torino, Jennifer M. Bucceri, Aisha Holder, Kevin L. Nadal, and Marta Esquilin. 2007. "Racial Microaggressions in Everyday Life: Implications for Clinical Practice." *American Psychologist* 62 (4): 271–286.

Thornton, Joyce K. 2000. "Job Satisfaction of Librarians of African Descent Employed in ARL Academic Libraries." *College and Research Libraries* 61 (3): 217–232.

Thornton, Joyce K. 2001. "African American Female Librarians: A Study of Job Satisfaction." *Journal of Library Administration* 33 (1–2): 141–164.

Totten, Herman L. 1977. "A Survey and Evaluation of Minority Programs in Selected Graduate Library Schools." *Journal of Education for Librarianship* 18 (1): 18–34.

Totten, Herman L. 2000. "Ethnic Diversity in Library Schools: Completing the Education Cycle." *Texas Library Journal* 76 (1): 16–19.

Turner, Caroline Sotello Viernes, Juan Carlos González, and J. Luke Wood. 2008. "Faculty of Color in Academe: What 20 Years of Literature Tells Us." *Journal of Diversity in Higher Education* 1 (3): 139–168.

Turock, Betty J. 2003. "Developing Diverse Professional Leaders." *New Library World* 104 (11/12): 491–498.

Weingand, Darlene E. 1999. "Describing the Elephant: What Is Continuing Professional Education?" *IFLA Journal* 26 (3):198–202.

Wheeler, Maurice B. 2005. *Unfinished Business: Race, Equity, and Diversity in Library and Information Science Education.* Lanham, MD: Scarecrow Press.

Winston, Mark. 1998. "The Role of Recruitment in Achieving Goals Related to Diversity." *College and Research Libraries* 59 (3): 240–247.

Winston, Mark D. 2001. "Recruitment Theory: Identification of Those Who Are Likely to Be Successful as Leaders." *Journal of Library Administration* 32 (3–4): 19–35.

Winston, Mark. 2010. "Managing Diversity." *Library Leadership and Management* 24 (3): 58–63.

Young, Philip, and Luke Vilelle. 2011. "The Prevalence and Practices of Academic Library Journal Clubs." *The Journal of Academic Librarianship* 37 (2): 130–136.

Chapter 6

Becoming New Storytellers: Counter-Storytelling in LIS

As a graduate student in library and information science (LIS), I noticed the lack of courses in diversity and social justice, and I noticed a lack of diverse faculty members in the front of my classes. These two deficits are not mutually exclusive, as I really believe that the call to teach and research in this area can be answered by anyone with sufficient desire and empathy. My goal as a practitioner in LIS was to diversify the field, working with various professional organizations to recruit outstanding diverse candidates to LIS graduate programs. Now, several years later, on the other side of the table, as a faculty member teaching in a graduate LIS program, I realize that the dearth of classes in diversity and social justice in LIS is more acute than I realized and is very much tied to the lack of diversity at the faculty ranks. And while I have the academic knowledge, personal passion, and administrative support to create new classes in my curriculum to address this gap, it is hard work innovating curriculum and teaching in these areas. It is hard work teaching about racism, social justice, and other topics, especially in LIS, which is characteristically known as a white and female field, and it is even harder to teach these topics when I am typically the only person of color in the classroom. My experiences thus far have been twofold: teaching classes related to diversity and social justice have, without question, been my most rewarding experiences, and these are the classes where I can actually see and hear the differences in my students' rhetoric and writing at the end of the semester. On the other side of that coin, teaching these classes is the hardest and most exhausting work I do as a teacher. However, at the end of the day, I believe that I am working toward changing the story of LIS education (Cooke 2013, 2014a, 2014b; Cooke, Sweeney, and Noble 2016).

Teaching such courses is an act of counter-storytelling and allows future information professionals the opportunity to hear and know "the stories of those people whose experiences are not often told" (Solorzano and Yosso 2002, 32). Delgado (1989, 2415) posited that counter-stories "quicken and engage the conscience," and, as a result, they can elucidate falsely held beliefs and

113

assumptions, enable listeners to acquire new information and empathy, and help redefine the status quo. Information professionals are serving increasingly diverse populations and need to be aware of and empathic toward communities different from theirs. Specifically, this chapter briefly discusses LIS and its curricula through the Storytelling Project (STP) framework developed (Bell 2009; Bell and Roberts 2010). STP theorizes that there are four types of stories: stock (public, ubiquitous stories), concealed (stories depicting struggle that are not mainstream), resistance (stories of overcoming and survival), and emerging/ transforming stories (new stories that build on the previous three types of stories and consequently challenge the status quo) (Bell and Roberts 2010, 2309–2313). This story typology forms a counter-storytelling matrix "in which stories about race and racism can be openly shared, respectfully heard, and critically discussed and analyzed" (2307).

Another part of the counter-storytelling effort to be examined in this chapter is the difficulty that can accompany instructors from diverse backgrounds teaching nondiverse students about racism, social justice, and other emotionally charged, but ever so important, topics. This part of the narrative draws upon the work of Delpit (1986, 1988, 2006) and Tatum (1992, 1994) who have classically written about this same dilemma as manifested in K-12 classrooms. In addition to describing the challenges of being a teacher of color, particularly one who teaches issues of culture and social justice, these authors recommend pedagogies for teaching these subjects. Tatum (1992, 18) encourages setting up the classroom in such a way that the "power of self-generated knowledge" is made central. In this way, students are allowed to claim and share their own experiences, in effect "pivoting the center" of the educational process (Mayberry and Rose 1999, 30). In a curriculum and field known for its hands-on and practical nature, this type of learning and education is invaluable and moves us toward the reimagining of LIS education where faculty are more diverse than not, and the curriculum is wholly inclusive and representative of the communities our students will serve. (See Chapter 5 for a brief discussion on the status of diversity coursework in the LIS curricula.)

COUNTER-STORYTELLING

The aforementioned definition of counter-stories states that such stories buck the status quo and challenge the long held collective stories of a hegemonic society, which tacitly maintain the narratives and normative behaviors of dominant groups. Counter-storytelling affords diverse voices and experiences a platform (Delgado 1989; Solorzano and Yosso 2002). Harris, Carney, and Fine (2000, 6) concur by stating that counter-stories are new narratives that seek to "interrupt, contradict, expose, challenge or deny" dominant discourses. Dominant discourses or narratives can be particularly entrenched and implicit; narratives "are not static, single or unchanging," which can render them hard to challenge and counteract (7). Narratives, which do not have to be inherently bad or harmful, can be multilayered and complex, incorporating cultural elements and "deeply raced, classed and gendered versions of reality" (7). These dominant narratives are repeated, mirrored and ultimately become the norms by which a society operates; narratives are "labeled as common sense and therefore become invisible in everyday life and academic productions" (8).

Counter-storytelling is drawn from Critical Race Theory, which originated in the legal literature and examines the intersections of race, law, and power (Bell 1980; Crenshaw 1988; Delgado 1989; Harris 1993). Since originating in the legal domain, counter-storytelling had been applied to other disciplines, including education (DeCuir and Dixson 2004; Ladson-Billings 1998; Ladson-Billings and Tate 1995; Solorzano and Yosso 2001, 2002; Yosso 2006), sociology (Yosso and Solorzano 2005), and LIS, and, in recent years, it has been used in numerous articles by faculty of color in the academy struggling with experiences of racism and microaggressions within higher education (Cooke 2014c; Garrison-Wade et al. 2012; Griffin, Ward, and Phillips 2014; Levin et al. 2013; Rodriguez and Boahene 2012; Tuitt et al. 2009; Verjee 2013). Within LIS, the application of counter-storytelling has been applied to youth services and its related literature, collection development, and to the school library setting (Hughes-Hassell 2013; Kumasi 2011; Kurz 2012; Williams 2004). This author argues that counter-storytelling has wider implications in LIS, one application being to the LIS curriculum (Cooke 2014a, 2013).

> Counter-stories demand that the reader or listener begin to question dominant frames. Counter-stories have the complexity of lived experience at their heart—they resist simplistic understanding in favor of complicated, morally ambiguous and sometimes messy analyses of privilege and domination. (Harris, Carney, and Fine 2000, 9)

The field of LIS is rich albeit with some warts and many dominant narratives that require challenge and correction. What better place to reveal and create counter-stories than in the LIS classroom?

Ultimately, counter-storytelling and having a diverse and representative curriculum are social justice issues, because it is about access. As Foderingham-Brown (1993, 143) states, "All library school students should be able, through library school curriculums, to learn how an ethnic group's history, language, culture, race and socioeconomic conditions influence their information needs." As the notion of the virtuous circle implies (Jaeger et al. 2015; Jaeger and Franklin 2007), in order to best serve diverse communities, the field needs more diverse information professionals; and, in order to have more diverse information professionals, the field needs more diverse faculty. The field also needs more diverse curricula because "graduate library schools that address diversity issues in their curriculums will also attract more minority students who will prefer a curriculum that is relevant to their needs" (Foderingham-Brown 1993, 143). Morris (2007, 10–11) concurs by stating, "Because the profession is basically white and female, it behooves library schools to ensure that students are taught competencies that create librarians that are culturally aware of their own social and cultural privilege as well as aware of the social and cultural realities of the underprivileged." At its heart, LIS is a service profession, matching people with information and resources; LIS education must prepare aspiring professionals to work with and in all types of communities and environments.

COUNTER-STORYTELLING IN THE LIS CLASSROOM: THE STORYTELLING PROJECT MODEL

As Honma (2005), Pawley (2006), Peterson (1995, 1996, 1999), and many other LIS educators and authors have stated, there is a dearth of acknowledgment and implementation when it comes to diversity, social justice, race, racism, and related topics, not only in the literature but also in the field at large and in the LIS classroom. This dearth of awareness and understanding impacts how information professionals effectively and empathetically serve and interact with their communities and stakeholders. A socially just library workforce can improve and enrich the communities they serve. The challenging question remains as to how the narrative of the field can be changed. A potential framework is the Storytelling Project Model by Bell (2009, 107) that focuses on addressing "race, racism, and social justice through arts-based storytelling." Bell's curriculum focuses on K-12 education and the hands-on participation of her students, but it is nonetheless applicable to the LIS curriculum, particularly her focus on the types of stories told and created in the classroom.

Stories are powerful and dynamic vehicles, and they comprise our individual and collective narratives, which in turn "make visible and tangible" knowledge that is implicit and taken for granted (Bell and Roberts 2010, 2301) and informs how we learn about the world; this is particularly true when it comes to stories related to race and stereotypes. Stories are also very contextual. Bell states, "While in a way it is my voice telling my individual story, that story comes out of a context that shapes the kind of stories I tell. This also applies to the kinds of stories that I can hear" (2009, 109).

Bell's model consists of four types of stories: (1) stock stories, (2) concealed stories, (3) resistance stories, and (4) emerging/transforming stories. Stock stories are the same as the aforementioned dominant narratives, and concealed, resistance, and emerging/transforming stories are three types of counter-stories (Bell's model expands the notion of counter-stories as put forth by Critical Race Theory).

Stock Stories

Stock stories (also known as ubiquitous stories) are "the normalizing or hegemonic stories that support things as they are. They are promoted in mainstream ideas, institutions, and media that rationalize and reinforce the racial status quo" (Bell, Desai, and Irani 2013, 16). Stock stories are "vocalized through individual stories, but also echo and redound and resound through broad cultural stories that collectively assert what is right and proper and true and normal in the broader society" (Bell 2009, 111–112).

When thinking about the LIS profession, a common stock story is that it is an amiable field full of older white women, most of whom wear sensible cardigans, shoes, glasses, and pearls around their necks. Stock stories can indeed contain truth—white women dominate the field. But beyond that, the common (mis)conception of what a librarian is ventures into the realm of stereotypes. Stereotypes are erroneous and can actually do damage. The field of LIS is unequal in representation, but there are many men, people of color, and young white women who comprise the ranks. This is still often unknown to the general public, which is a consistent problem as the field tries to recruit and retain candidates from diverse backgrounds and extol its virtues to the public.

Concealed Stories

Concealed stories, direct responses to stock stories, are stories that are not mainstream and depict some form of struggle or disagreement with the common knowledge promoted by stock stories. They are stories about overcoming and survival.

> Underneath the stock stories are numerous, teeming stories that talk back to the stock stories, that challenge them, that speak otherwise. Even though we in the mainstream do not hear these stories, that does not mean they are not being told and heard in subterranean communities or in communities that are not invited into the center. Given their special vantage point, concealed stories can teach us much about stock stories. (Bell 2009, 112)

A concealed story that depicts some of the diversity that exists within the field is the "This is what a librarian looks like" campaign. A series of portraits taken at 2013 and 2014 American Library Association conferences was popular on social media and attempted to depict librarians of all stripes.

Other concealed stories, those that do not fare as well on social media, are those that feature people of color leaving the field because they have faced racism and discrimination. The field not only has a recruitment problem but also a retention problem. A concealed story of female librarians being sexually harassed at professional conferences made headlines in 2014–2015. When these women discussed their opinions and experiences on social media against an alleged perpetrator, they were subsequently sued and faced additional harassment (and even threats of violence) from others who suggested they were lying or even worthy of the sexual misconduct they attempted to expose. Such concealed stories push back against the stock story that LIS is a happy lily-white field and, in the process, reveal that the profession has no shortage of problems and issues to discuss.

Resistance Stories

Resistance stories are those that when they are revealed, the listener may think or even exclaim, "I had no idea!" or perhaps, "how can that be?" Like concealed stories, they buck against stock stories, but they also highlight great injustices.

> Such stories call into question the ahistorical and individualized representations of reality that are so popular in our talk-show, personality-saturated media. They connect us to the broader patterns in our history

that persist into and shape the present, reminding us that things can be otherwise. (Bell, Desai, and Irani 2013, 17)

These stories "are not taught in history books but rather exist within communities to be drawn upon and learned from" (Bell 2009, 113), and they demonstrate that the effects of collective history are far-reaching and can be hard to reconcile.

For example, the LIS field has a long history of segregation (Fultz 2006); libraries have been credited with accepting and socializing immigrants to the United States, but that history also includes denying access and information to people of color. This segregation was very much a product of the country's history, but libraries were not exempt from egregious practices, and this history should not be excluded when new librarians learn about the field. Another example of resistance stories can be found in how the field classifies information and therefore grants access to information. Specifically, information about minority cultures and lesbian, gay, bisexual, trans, and queer (LGBTQ) communities is often buried or so obfuscated that it is rendered useless to those seeking said information. Historically, there are vast differences in how information is entered into catalogs and how that same information is actually described by its creators (Adler 2009; Drabinski 2013). These discrepancies keep entire histories out of classrooms and out of the hands of the public. These stories are particularly important because they bring to the forefront marginalized communities, whose "stories are a way of bearing witness to struggle and survival in a racist system" (Bell and Roberts 2010, 2305).

Emerging/Transforming Stories

"Concealed and resistance stories are excavated to reveal new knowledge, and emerging / transforming stories are (re)constructed knowledge built on concealed and resistance stories" (Bell and Roberts 2010, 2302). These stories come to be by extrapolating and learning from concealed and resistance stories; emerging/transforming stories are a product of reflection and new intentions and have the possibility of replacing existing stock stories. These are the stories that especially need to be in LIS classrooms and should be replacing outdated and false stereotypes and tropes about librarians. A great example of an emerging/transforming story is the Ferguson (Missouri) Public Library (Marsh 2015). When uprisings occurred over the death of an unarmed teenager, the library became a beacon for the community, remaining open when all other business and schools were closed. The Ferguson Library and its director went viral on social media and made the rounds on news outlets; the public was amazed at this library and seemed to newly discover the commitment libraries have to their communities. A similar situation occurred in Baltimore, Maryland, after the apprehension and subsequent death of a suspect in police custody; when the uprisings began, the Pennsylvania Avenue Branch of the city of Baltimore's Enoch Pratt Free Library was lauded for remaining open and serving as key resource for the community in crisis (Peet 2015). These libraries and their staff were complemented for engaging in radical hospitality, but this level of service and commitment and the notion of engagement between the library and its community are not new, but, to the general public, these concepts and ethics of service were not well known. How can aspiring librarians be taught to be resilient social justice advocates in their organizations? This is the type of emerging/transforming story that should be in the LIS curriculum.

Other stories that deserve more attention and should be norm when people think of libraries include libraries that employ social workers and public health workers and the work that libraries are doing to support the incarcerated (Morris 2013) and juveniles in detention centers (Austin 2012). Libraries proactively send materials and personnel to facilities to work with this underserved population, and they provide a wide assortment of services and resources to the former inmates trying to restart their lives in their communities.

THE NEW STORYTELLERS

In the LIS Classroom

Ultimately, Bell's model is about "creating a community in which stories about race and racism can be openly shared, respectfully heard, and critically discussed and analyzed" (Bell and Roberts 2010, 2307). An additional counter-story, perhaps a fifth element to add to Bell's (2009) model is that of the *new storytellers*. In addition to the social workers, prison librarians, and others embodying emerging/transforming stories in libraries every day, there are faculty members and instructors in LIS graduate programs who are working diligently to incorporate new stories into the classroom and employing new pedagogical strategies to create the spaces necessary to discuss race, racism, social justice, and other necessary and difficult issues.

Teaching courses related to diversity and social justice are vital to providing counter-stories to the traditional LIS curriculum and profession, but they can be challenging and delicate propositions for both white instructors and instructors who themselves are members of minority or marginalized groups (see Box 6.1). Delpit (1988, 282) writes of the silenced voices of educators of color, who in many classrooms in predominantly white institutions, violate the "culture of power" that is the status quo. Delpit continues by stating, "The rules of the culture of power are a reflection of the rules of the culture who have power. ... Those with power are frequently least aware of—or least willing to acknowledge—its existence" (282). This is a significant dynamic that bears more attention and research into the lack of faculty of color in graduate LIS programs (Cooke 2013, 2014b) and in higher education in general. This dynamic can complicate but certainly does not prevent the telling and creation of new stories in the curriculum.

Another significant dynamic is the content itself; sensitive and/or "taboo" topics such as racism and privilege can create "cognitive dissonance" as students begin to digest and understand the differences between their lives and experiences and that of other groups (Tatum 1994, 464). Tatum (1992, 1) states, "The inclusion of race-related content in college courses often generates emotional responses in students that range from guilt and shame to anger and despair. The discomfort associated with these emotions can lead students to resist the learning process." This dissonance can be overcome, but if not addressed with care, instructors can find themselves teaching in "environments of resistance" (Bell et al. 1999), because students who are unused to such confronting ideas and "whose practices and perspectives are being challenged by critical discussions of power relations may react with discomfort and hostility" (25). To this end, hooks (1994) wrote extensively about the necessity to incorporate engaged pedagogy in the classroom (no matter the subject). Based on the work of Paulo Freire, hooks's philosophy is the opposite of the banking method of education and knowledge; rather she advocates for encouraging and modeling critical and independent thinking in such a way that classrooms are places of "promise and possibility" (4) and not boring places where only the instructors' authority, opinions, and knowledge matter. "There must be an ongoing recognition that everyone influences the classroom dynamic, that everyone contributes. These contributions are resources. Used constructively, they enhance the capacity of any class to create an open learning community" (8).

Courses and instructors that seek to integrate and diversify LIS curricula should strive to create a learning space that features engaged pedagogy and should focus on developing the cultural responsiveness of their LIS students, who will in turn become culturally responsive LIS professionals.

Box 6.1   Fatigue, Burnout, and Maintaining Your Voice in the Profession

Doing the work to advance social justice and diversity is hard, whether you are on the front lines in your library, whether you are out organizing your community, or whether you are in the position to educate others. Getting into librarianship is unfortunately not the most difficult challenge new librarians may face; staying in the profession (retention) can be just as difficult an endeavor, particularly in spaces that are not hospitable to people of color and/or diverse perspectives and sensibilities. When I teach diversity and social justice courses in my graduate LIS program, I talk often with students about the realities of the field, some of which include discrimination and systematic racism, and the question always emerges: How do we keep going? Or, how do we keep from burning out? The short answer, in my opinion, is you cannot prevent burnout or fatigue. I think the answer lies in how we respond to these episodes, which can be accompanied by depression, anger, and a host of other physical and emotional responses. As a popular adage tells us, it is not how many times we are knocked down, what is important is how many times we get up. With that in mind, how are we prepared to get back up when the work becomes difficult or overwhelming?

Below is a personal account of burnout and subsequent critical self-reflection, detailing how I got back up from a particularly difficult episode. This episode occurred once I began working as a professor, but I have certainly had similar episodes as a practicing librarian. It is my fervent hope that this reflection might inspire others to keep doing the important work of infusing diversity and social justice into the LIS profession and make these sensibilities a priority.

After having worked so very hard as a practicing professional, in that time earning a second master's degree and a doctorate, I found myself at a highly ranked and respected table as a tenure track assistant professors, at a Research 1 institution, the top in my field. And amazingly enough, this magnificent table has consistently served up some rather complicated dishes and at times made me question whether I arrived to the right house for dinner. Certainly some of the discomfort at the table can be attributed to entering a new institution and joining a new faculty as an assistant professor, the new kid. However, it became clear that part of the problem was the fact that I am a fairly young African American female in a larger academic environment that is not entirely used to, or appreciative of, faculty members who exist outside of the status quo (i.e., white males). I am living with multiple marginalities and seemingly don't fit with the traditional imagery associated with the ivory tower of academe. Defying the expectation of being an older white, straight male in the front of the classroom elicited double takes from both other faculty and students.

After my first full year at the table, I had the pleasure of hearing Dr. Todd Honma speak at a conference where he discussed the status of race and racism in the field of library and information science (LIS). Despite years of talk and various well-meaning and successful recruitment initiatives, the field still has a long way to go in regards to integrating, retaining, promoting, and celebrating librarians of color. And clearly this applies to faculty of color in LIS schools and departments. Honma's talk was both humbling and validating; but what was most striking was Honma's suggestion that "maybe we don't even want to be at this table" (Honma 2012), meaning that maybe we don't want to be, or even belong, in this field. The remark was sobering and devastating, and provided me with serious food for thought. After experiencing a year of consistent microaggressions (from the unsolicited and continued insistence that I am "so articulate and well spoken"; to being challenged by white students not used to and uncomfortable with the first African American professor in their academic careers; to calling me by the name of another African American colleague; to being subject to a physical attempt at intimidation designed to figuratively put me in my place, I was beginning to wilt, chafe and become uncomfortable in my new environment.

I thought: Maybe I don't want to be at this table?

After a year of consistent microaggressions and microinsults, I began to feel as though I didn't fit into this environment and perhaps was even unwanted by some. It became clear that remaining and being academically productive in this environment was going to be a consistent challenge and require extra work on my part. Another realization was that I was going to HAVE to get my voice back, if only to leave the institution and regain my physical and mental well-being.

No, I don't want to be at this table.

After internalizing comments and experiences I realized that I no longer wanted to participate or speak at meetings or engage with people outside of a small and trusted group of established allies. I simply wanted to teach my classes and do my research and I wanted to be left alone as I contemplated the idea that I had made a mistake by coming into academia. I was losing my voice. And in many ways, I began to lose my good health. No stranger to stress and stress related illness, my symptoms of anxiety and exhaustion were becoming chronic and manifesting themselves in new and not-so-welcome ways. I was physically and emotionally spent after my first year in the academy. Despite knowing myself to be a competent scholar and an award-winning practitioner, I began to consider whether or not the academy was the right environment for me. Do I have what it takes to survive and thrive is this environment? By speaking up would I become known as a "rabble rouser"? Would I have to change myself and/or lose my voice to be able to remain in this environment?

Should I cut my losses, push back and give back my seat at the table?

In an effort to re-center myself and understand what was happening, and to ensure that I wasn't just being naïve, sensitive, or simply in over my head, I started reaching out to my still small academic network (many peers and mentors from my doctoral work, and new peers in similar predicaments) and I started reading and researching, networking and building connections with people I haven't met but who have shared their comparable stories. While the literature did not disappoint, in the sense that I saw myself over and over again in the accounts of minority faculty, it did emphasize that in academia the more things change, the more they stay the same. Minority faculty members are still marginalized and face additional challenges in the academy. However, I was and am in good company. There are many brilliant women and men of color surviving and making strides in the academy, and their stories provide much needed strength and validation. These accounts in the literature are necessary to combat the "crisis of representation" experienced by faculty of color (Ellis and Bochner 2000, 733).

Microaggressions, Invisibility and Hyper-Visibility

I realized early on that what I was experiencing could be categorized as microaggressions, which Pierce et al., define as "subtle, stunning, often automatic, and non-verbal exchanges which are 'put downs' of blacks by offenders" (1977, 66). Davis concurs by stating that microaggressions are "stunning, automatic acts of disregard that stem from unconscious attitudes of white superiority and constitute a verification of black inferiority" (1989, 1576). Microaggressions emerge from the literature and phenomenon of racism, which Marable defines as, "a system of ignorance, exploitation, and power used to oppress African Americans, Latinos, Asians, Pacific Americans, American Indians and other people on the basis of ethnicity, culture, mannerisms, and color" (1992, 5).

Certainly I had experienced these behaviors and comments before, but not so consistently and not in such a subtle and nuanced way (which is an element that makes these comments even more offensive and damaging). The facts that I was in a brand new environment, in a new job, in a new part of the country, in an entirely new world made the microaggressions much more acute. It is because of Sue et al. (2007) that I came to understand how pervasive and complicated microaggressions are; they are part of the structural and institutional racism that is so tightly woven into the fabrics of organizations (those of higher education, business, etc.). Understanding microaggressions provided a framework for understanding and coping with my own situations, better negotiating the stories appearing in the literature, and provided a language for conveying my concerns to others.

The nuances of microaggressions provide insight in the phenomena of invisibility and hyper-visibility; the stereotyping and assumptions that come along with microaggressions serve to make their targets invisible in some instances and super or hyper-visible in others. For example, it is easy to ignore a minority faculty member in a meeting, but when a "diverse perspective" or "diversity representative" are needed, said faculty member is put on the spot and asked to represent an entire race, ethnic or minority group (i.e., the disabled, LGBTQ, etc.). Alfred (2001, 121) states, "Although Black women are rendered invisible by virtue of their female-ness and their Blackness, successful Black women are rendered highly visible by their institutions." Invisibility can include being left out of social occasions, being passed over for promotions and other professional opportunities, and generally being made to feel like an outsider. Hyper-visibility can result in extra service work (because the committees and organizations need a diverse perspective) and can also result in minority faculty becoming a beacon for any and all students of color, even for those outside of their discipline. This extra work is often uncredited and is done for the good of the order. But this extra work can be draining and ultimately takes time from the things that count for tenure and promotion.

Pollak and Niemann (1998) also discuss hyper-visibility, instead referring to the phenomenon as "distinctiveness" (954). Krusemark (2012) and Phelps (1995) concur. Phelps specifically talks about the curse of being "special"; minority faculty members are often the only ones in their departments. This not unique status can result in faculty being put on a pedestal and being sought out for particular areas of expertise, but more often results in undue service, isolation, and the other negative qualities that come with hyper-visibility.

Tokenism and Double Consciousness

In her research in the business world, Kanter (1977) discusses the notion of women being tokens, as exceptions to the rule in a male-dominated environment. Her assessment was based on the idea that based solely on the number of women employed in corporations, women were "numerical minorities" in the workforce (206–242). Kanter's discussion of *Numbers: Minorities and Majorities* provides an excellent background on the phenomenon of being different in a larger group or context.

Kanter characterizes tokens as: Being pressured to conform and be exceptional; becoming invisible and unnoticeable; feeling lonely and excluded from the larger group(s); having limited social capital; being stereotyped and/or discriminated against; and, having higher levels of personal stress (206–209). While not explicitly talking about women of color or academia, these characteristics of a token are wholly applicable to the life of minority in the academic environment. Kanter's conclusion is that anyone who is "rare and scarce" (207) in a given environment can have these feelings. The characteristics of tokens discussed by Kanter appear often in the literature, typically about minorities in various environments and professions—minority faculty, minority students, minority executives and managers, minority teachers, minority librarians, minority social workers, minority lawyers, minorities in science and technology, and the like.

Niemann (1999) writes specifically about the tokenism faced by minority women in academia. As a Latina woman her experiences resonate as she describes overcoming numerous obstacles even before entering the academy. After defying cultural and gender roles that discouraged the advanced education of independent women, women of color faced institutional racism and socioeconomic barriers while pursing education. Tokenism is not unrelated to the concept of double consciousness, which was first discussed by W.E.B. DuBois in 1897. The basic concept of DuBois's double consciousness is that you cannot remove your primary identity, but instead you assume a second (or perhaps multiple) identity, one crafted and assumed to better fit in and hopefully not be so prone to stereotyping, racism, or other abuse.

Women of color in the academy (as well as men of color, as well as LGBT faculty and others in the minority) routinely assume dual roles and personas in an attempt to assimilate and gain credibility in the dominant culture of academia. Alfred (2001) concurs by stating that double consciousness is "the process by which women of color internalize their location within and their interactions with White-dominated institutional cultures" (114). Creating and maintaining a double consciousness can be a challenging and exhausting mental and physical endeavor.

Maintaining My Voice

Audre Lorde said "It is not difference which immobilizes us, but silence. And there are so many silences to be broken" (1984, 44). And Harley (2008) states that the "survival of African American women in the academy is contingent upon many variables, but none as important as their own self-worth, self-reliance, and generating support networks inside and outside the university setting" (33).

I do not have to relinquish my seat at the table; I have to resituate myself at the table and make myself heard.

The statements by Lorde and Harley emphasized to me that my continued presence at the table was up to me; the microaggressions and varying levels of racism and hostility will not change or go away. What have to change are my reactions and responses to them, and whether or not I choose to internalize the remarks, actions and the pain they cause.

I deserve to be at the table and I need to stay at the table. How do I make this happen?

Harley devotes a great deal of discussion to the idea of coping. Specifically she discusses: singing our own praises (don't wait for anyone else to do so); recognizing our own limitations; maintaining mental, physical and spiritual health; and, recognizing our institutional culture (2008, 33).

Reclaiming and maintaining the voice I was losing would take not only learning to cope in this new environment, but it would take a great deal of internal and external work. It would take introspection and reflection, and talking often and candidly with others in my network. This process also meant soliciting and listening to lots of stories. It's easy to gather facts and statistics on the lack of minorities in the academy, or the retention rates of African American females in a given discipline; it's the stories that imbue strength and reason that matter. Reading, networking, and seeking out mentors have facilitated this story gathering.

In order to expand my internal and external support networks, my networking efforts became systematic as I sought out women in my same situation, women who are still students, and women who have retired. I needed the sympathy, empathy, wisdom, and ideas for strategies and self-care. I needed physical and mental safe spaces in order to have the "freedom to think out loud" (Fries-Britt and Kelly 2005, 238) and have the ability to be vulnerable with like-minded friends and colleagues. Ward says "the safe space serves as a prime location for the Black woman to resist objectification as the Other" (1995, 153). I also joined a writing group with other women of color at my institution and I joined an accountability group through a national faculty development program; these have been profound and powerful experiences as they are safe spaces, which are also productive for my writing and scholarship. It is through the writing group and the accountability group that I discovered my professional counter-spaces. Counter-spaces are sites where "deficit notions of people of color can be challenged and where a positive collegiate racial climate can be established and maintained" (Solórzano, Ceja, and Yosso 2000, 70). I have come to rely on these counter-spaces and I sincerely value my colleagues' insight and camaraderie. I have also sought out new mentors, from among my peers and with more senior colleagues, in addition to maintaining connections with existing mentors. Mentoring relationships have been particularly helpful because many of my mentors have had similar experiences and are proof positive of survival, and where there have been missteps or ill consequences in their lives, it is magnanimous of them to share their wisdom, strategies, and hindsight with me. I envision my mentors and peers as enabling me to sure up my foundation, giving me the tools and fortitude to move forward though the tenure track process.

Final Thoughts

While a painful experience, it has been cathartic to use the literature and my networks (both near and far, those I know and those I don't know personally) to explore, process, and navigate my way through the beginning years of the tenure track process. I am relearning the importance of story and self-care. This process has also brought me to a new research area (or rather a rebirth and extension of diversity work I began as a student) and exposed me to new theories and schools of thought. But most importantly, this process has renewed my commitment to succeed in this space even at the expense of forgoing a space in the community. It's OK not to change the world, it's OK to step back, and it's OK to put myself first. I will preserve myself and work towards making incremental changes in the lives of my students and in my profession. Those are good and attainable goals.

Maybe instead of pushing back from the table, I will just occasionally lean back in my seat.

So I remain at the table—I, and those before me, have worked too hard to earn this seat. However, I'm now at the table with revised intentions and goals. And perhaps I will even occasionally and temporarily excuse myself from the table from time to time in order to regroup, reconstitute, and renew. But I will not give up the seat and I will perform well while at this table.

I'm staying at the table.

Excerpted from: Cooke, Nicole A. "Pushing Back from the Table: Fighting to Maintain My Voice as a Pre-Tenure Minority Female in the White Academy." *Polymath: An Interdisciplinary Arts and Sciences Journal* 4, no. 2 (2014): 39–49.

In the Community and in Libraries

Similarly, I would suggest that librarians and library professionals aspire to be new storytellers in the field, on the ground, behind the services points, and in the community. Chapter 2 discussed the importance of critical self-reflection and being culturally competent, but let us extend those notions and think about what they look like in day-to-day praxis. Library professionals need to "critically reflect on their own racial and cultural identities and to recognize how these identities coexist with the cultural compositions of their students" (Howard 2003, 196). Appropriate pedagogy can help us frame our cultural competence and self-reflection and put these new skills and self-knowledge into action. Specifically, this section will focus on culturally responsive pedagogy (CRP) and culturally sustaining pedagogy (CSP) as a way to enhance our desired role as a new storyteller.

Andragogy and Feminist Pedagogy

Before launching into a discussion of CRP and CSP, a mention of two other key pedagogies relevant to LIS is warranted, as they help create the foundation for a critically reflective and culturally competent LIS practice. While pursuing a degree in adult education in attempt to improve my library instruction abilities (Cooke 2010), I was introduced to the concept of andragogy, which in the adult education field is most associated with Malcolm Knowles (1968, 1980, 1984, 1996). Andragogy, which is pedagogy-specific to adult learners, has a number of tenets that emphasize the idea that adults learn differently than children and have different needs and requirements in the classroom (or library). They include the ideas that adults must want to learn; adults will learn only what they feel is relevant; adults learn by doing; adults' learning focuses on realistic problem solving; adults' experience greatly affects their learning; adults learn well in informal environments; and adults want someone to facilitate their learning, as opposed to someone dictating information to them. These precepts mesh well with the notion of feminist pedagogy and the aforementioned engaged pedagogy.

Feminist pedagogy was specifically addressed in LIS (as it pertains to library instruction) by Maria Accardi (2013), and that work was clearly built upon the work of scholars in the field of education, including Shauna Butterwick and Jan Selman (2003); Darlene Clover (2002); Patricia Hill Collins (1986, 2002); bell hooks (1989, 1994); Patti Lather (1995, 2001), and Libby Tisdell (1993, 2001), all of whom built upon Paulo Freire's concepts of critical theory and critical consciousness (1973, 2000). Accardi provides a succinct description of feminist pedagogy by suggesting that teachers who subscribe to this framework envision the classroom as a collaborative, democratic, and transformative space, and they aspire to raise the consciousness of their students while exhibiting a clear and sincere interest in their well-being (ethics of care). Perhaps, most important, and where feminist pedagogy dovetails most closely with andragogy, is the value that feminist pedagogues place on the personal, lived experiences of their learners and their assumption that these experiences contribute to the learning process. Andragogy and feminist pedagogy are typically written about in regard to teacher education and classroom learning but are, of course, applicable to all of the services and programs provided by librarians and libraries. Add to this our discussions about cultural competence and critical self-reflection, and we can transition into the concepts of CRP and CSP as a way of practice in the LIS profession.

CRP and CSP

Moving from being culturally competent to engaging in CRP (also seen in the literature as culturally relevant pedagogy) (Ladson-Billings 1995b) is a seemingly natural progression but one that requires purposeful application. To become culturally responsive, teachers and librarians need to engage in honest, critical reflection that challenges them to see how their positionality and intersectionality influence their students in both positive and negative ways. Educator and author Parker Palmer said, "We teach who we are," and, as such, we need to concern ourselves more with *who* we are teaching, and their needs, and not as much with *what* we want to teach. Palmer ([1998] 2010, 2) maintains the following:

> Teaching, like any truly human activity, emerges from one's inwardness, for better or worse. As I teach, I project the condition of my soul onto my students, my subject, and our way of being together. The entanglements I experience in the classroom are often no more or less than the convolutions of my inner life. Viewed from this angle, teaching holds a mirror of the soul. If I am willing to look in that mirror and not run from what I see, I have a chance to gain self-knowledge and knowing myself is as crucial to good teaching as knowing my students and my subject. ... In fact, knowing my students and my subject depends heavily on self-knowledge. When I do not know myself, I cannot know who my students

are. I will see them through a glass darkly, in the shadows of my own unexamined life—and when I cannot see them clearly, I cannot teach them well.

Palmer presents a salient argument for why librarians and other educators need to reflect and revisit their personal pedagogies; specifically, we should be moving toward CRP and CSP as individual librarians and as larger organizations that provide and promote information and knowledge.

CRP has been discussed at length in the education literature. Many scholars have described this pedagogy as one that effectively meets the academic and social needs of diverse students (Gay [2000] 2010; Howard 2001; Ladson-Billings 1994; Shade, Kelly, and Oberg 1997). Specifically, Gay ([2000] 2010, 29) stresses that CRP uses:

> the cultural knowledge, prior experiences, frames of reference, and performance styles of ethnically diverse students to make learning more relevant to and effective [for students]. ... It teaches to and through strengths of these students. It is culturally validating and affirming.

Ladson-Billings, considered the pioneer of this line of inquiry, states:

> I have defined culturally relevant teaching as a pedagogy of opposition not unlike critical pedagogy but specifically committed to collective, not merely individual, empowerment. Culturally relevant pedagogy rests on three criteria or propositions: (a) students must experience academic success; (b) students must develop and/or maintain cultural competence; and (c) students must develop a critical consciousness through which they challenge the status quo of the current social order. (Ladson-Billings 1995a, 159)

The move toward CRP requires cultural competence plus continuous application. Librarians need to become well versed in and comfortable with issues of race, ethnicity, and culture and be cognizant of how these issues affect how the library works and provides services to diverse populations. On a more granular level, librarians "must be able to construct pedagogical practices that have relevance and meaning to students' social and cultural realities" (Howard 2003, 195).

Much of what we know about becoming culturally competent applies to CRP; practitioners, be they teachers or librarians, should be knowledgeable and celebratory of other cultures, be caring and empathetic, and be critically self-reflective (Rychly and Graves 2012). Culturally responsive practitioners should engage with students, address race and other difficult issues, and be cognizant of the long-term futures of said students. Additionally, these pedagogues should understand the dynamic relationships between identity, culture, and learning; they should be aware of how socioeconomic status influences the learning process; they should have high expectations of their learners; they should provide information that creates bridges between school and the homes and communities of their learners; and they should understand the importance of the community to the lifelong learning process (Ryan 2002, 8). Is this enough? Is CRP enough?

Scholar Django Paris (2012; Paris and Alim 2014) believes that a culturally responsive practice is good, but it is indeed not enough. The suggestion is that pedagogy and practice should be sustaining and not just responsive. Just as cultural humility extends the concept of cultural competence (Chapter 2), CSP extends the practice of CRP. CSP asks practitioners to take their pedagogy further and specifically consider the multiple cultural and linguistic identities of learners, minimize the cultural loss that can occur in the learning process, and resist the "White middle-class norms of knowing and being that continue to dominate notions of educational achievement" in our society (Paris and Alim 2014, 85). Cultural identities and language are not fixed or static, and practitioners should be looking for and understand the fluidity of cultures that enter our libraries and respective learning environments. Indeed, practitioners should be fully aware of and anticipate the ever-changing subcultures that develop within and between larger cultures and communities (Dancu 2014). The works done by librarians and educators should be long-lasting and have impact beyond the classroom. When describing their ideal pedagogy and practice, Paris and Alim (2014, 86) say:

> In our work here we are committed to envisioning and enacting pedagogies that are not filtered through a lens of contempt and pity (e.g., the "achievement gap") but, rather, are centered on contending in complex ways with the rich and innovative linguistic, literate, and cultural practices of Indigenous American, African American, Latina/o, Asian American, Pacific Islander, and other youth and communities of color.

Absorbing this information about CRP and CSP and turning it into a full-fledged practice in the LIS profession, a practice that is not solely related to classroom instruction is not presented as a quick fix or a suggested framework that will magically transform librarians or their organizations. Rather, developing a holistic and sustaining professional practice is hard work, but it is something that is attainable, and this is a challenge I present to you as we conclude this text. Most of the information in this book is meant to help you develop such a practice. Think back to the discussions of community analysis and the importance of building relationships with the diverse communities served by our libraries (Chapter 2). Think back to the definition of stereotype threat (Chapter 4); having an environment that promotes or condones stereotype threat means that the library and the librarians within the organization are not engaging in a culturally competent, responsive, or sustaining practice. Developing a sustaining practice is multifaceted and begins with individual work; then, organizations need to move toward a larger institutional practice that has its values and commitments to diversity and social justice reflected in their collections, vision and mission statements, policies, and assessment plans. Another dimension to be considered is the physical space. Space should be redefined and re-created to reflect an organization's commitment to diversity and inclusion (i.e., is there signage in multiple language? Is the space physically accommodating to persons with disabilities? See Chapter 4 for more examples). Hughes-Hassell and Hitson (n.d.) have developed a Culturally Responsive Library Walk that can help librarians and their organizations thoughtfully analyze and reconsider physical spaces to determine if they are barrier-free (literally and figuratively) and if they coincide with their espoused commitment to diversity. Other resources, such as Syracuse University's Project Enable: Expanding Nondiscriminatory Access by Librarians Everywhere (n.d.) can also help libraries participate in culturally sustaining practice. Additionally, libraries should invest in training and professional collections for staff that will emphasize diversity awareness and skill building (please see Chapter 5 for more discussion of continuing and professional development).

CONCLUSION

Training culturally sustaining and socially responsible LIS professionals is imperative, and it requires a blended approach that extends across curricula, professional practice, and research. While pursuing graduate degrees in LIS, it is hoped that students will learn the basics necessary for competent, inclusive, and caring professional practice. This is increasingly important as librarians face ever-diverse patron demographics and an increasingly complicated society that influences, shapes, and colors their organization's services and resources. In an often-eclectic collection of graduate courses, students should have an opportunity (if not multiple opportunities) to learn about the harder, sensitive, or more personal topics that may permeate their professional environments, such as race, class, sexuality, and gender. If it is expected that the next generations of information professionals will work with diverse populations, they should be equipped to deal with these populations and be able to deal with them in a respectful, compassionate, and unbiased manner. Likewise, if LIS hopes to further diversify the profession and tell new stories about faculty and student recruitment and retention, prioritization of these skills, values, epistemologies, and pedagogies must be woven into the fabric of LIS culture.

Teaching and creating counter-stories in LIS classrooms allow students to become engaged and reflect on themselves and others and hopefully result in personal growth and a transformation of thinking. Such students will be better prepared and more successful in their roles as information professionals. Recasting the stories and empowering new storytellers for the profession function as an important framework for fostering the critical, inclusive, and culturally competent professional engagement that is so desperately needed in LIS programs and in the profession at large.

LESSON PLAN

Essential Readings:

Accardi, Maria T. *Feminist Pedagogy for Library Instruction.* Duluth, MN: Library Juice Press, 2013.

Ladson-Billings, Gloria. "Toward a Theory of Culturally Relevant Pedagogy." *American Educational Research Journal* 32, no. 3 (1995): 465–491.

Paris, Django. "Culturally Sustaining Pedagogy: A Needed Change in Stance, Terminology, and Practice." *Educational Researcher* 41, no. 3 (2012): 93–97.

Williams, Bronwyn T. "The Truth in the Tale: Race and 'Counterstorytelling' in the Classroom." *Journal of Adolescent and Adult Literacy* 48, no. 2 (2004): 164–169.

Other Key Works:

Cooke, Nicole A. "Becoming an Andragogical Librarian: Using Library Instruction as a Tool to Combat Library Anxiety and Empower Adult Learners." *New Review of Academic Librarianship* 16, no. 2 (2010): 208–227.

Delpit, Lisa. "The Silenced Dialogue: Power and Pedagogy in Educating Other People's Children." *Harvard Educational Review* 58, no. 3 (1988): 280–299.

Questions to Ask:

1. What stock and concealed stories does your library tell?

2. What resistance or transforming stories does your library tell? If your library does not tell these stories, what are the other examples that come to mind?

3. What are you prepared to do in order to become a new storyteller? What does that progression or journey look like, and what will you have to do to maintain this level of critical culturally sustaining practice?

REFERENCES

Accardi, Maria T. 2013. *Feminist Pedagogy for Library Instruction*. Duluth, MN: Library Juice Press.

Adler, Melissa. 2009. "Transcending Library Catalogs: A Comparative Study of Controlled Terms in Library of Congress Subject Headings and User-Generated Tags in LibraryThing for Transgender Books." *Journal of Web Librarianship* 3 (4): 309–331.

Alfred, Mary V. 2001. "Expanding Theories of Career Development: Adding the Voices of African American Women in the White Academy." *Adult Education Quarterly* 51 (2): 108–127.

Austin, Jeanie. 2012. "Critical Issues in Juvenile Detention Center Libraries." *The Journal of Research on Libraries and Young Adults*. Accessed March 2, 2016. http://www.yalsa.ala.org/jrlya/2012/07/critical-issues-in-juvenile-detention-center-libraries/.

Bell, Derrick A., Jr. 1980. "Brown v. Board of Education and the Interest-Convergence Dilemma." *Harvard Law Review* 93 (5): 518–533.

Bell, Lee Anne. 2009. "The Story of The Storytelling Project: An Arts-Based Race and Social Justice Curriculum." *Storytelling, Self, Society* 5 (2): 107–118.

Bell, Lee Anne, Dipti Desai, and Kayhan Irani. 2013. "Storytelling for Social Justice." In *Culturally Relevant Arts Education for Social Justice: A Way Out of No Way*, edited by Mary Stone Hanley, George W. Noblit, Gilda L. Shepard, and Tom Barone, 15–24. New York: Routledge.

Bell, Lee Anne, and Rosemarie A. Roberts. 2010. "The Storytelling Project Model: A Theoretical Framework for Critical Examination of Racism through the Arts." *Teachers College Record* 112 (9): 2295–2319.

Bell, Sandra, Marina Morrow, Evangelia Tastsoglou, Maralee Mayberry, and Ellen Cronan Rose. 1999. "Teaching in Environments of Resistance: Toward a Critical, Feminist, and Antiracist Pedagogy." In *Meeting the Challenge: Innovative Feminist Pedagogies in Action*, edited by Maralee Mayberry and Ellen Cronan Rose, 23–46, New York: Routledge.

Butterwick, Shauna, and Jan Selman. 2003. "Deep Listening in a Feminist Popular Theatre Project: Upsetting the Position of Audience in Participatory Education." *Adult Education Quarterly* 54 (1): 7–22.

Clover, Darlene E. 2002. "Toward Transformative Learning." In *Expanding the Boundaries of Transformative Learning*, edited by Edmund O'Sullivan, Amish Morrell, and Mary Ann O'Connor, 159–172. New York: Palgrave Macmillan US.

Collins, Patricia Hill. 1986. "The Emerging Theory and Pedagogy of Black Women's Studies." *Gender Issues* 6 (1): 3–17.

Collins, Patricia Hill. 2002. *Black Feminist Thought: Knowledge, Consciousness, and the Politics of Empowerment.* New York: Routledge.

Cooke, Nicole A. 2010. "Becoming an Andragogical Librarian: Using Library Instruction as a Tool to Combat Library Anxiety and Empower Adult Learners." *New Review of Academic Librarianship* 16 (2): 208–227.

Cooke, Nicole A. 2013. "Diversifying the LIS Faculty (BackTalk column)." *Library Journal*, September 25: 34. http://lj.libraryjournal.com/2013/09/opinion/backtalk/diversifying-the-lis-faculty-backtalk/.

Cooke, Nicole A. 2014a. "Creating Opportunities for Empathy and Cultural Competence in the LIS Curriculum." *SRRT Newsletter* 187. http://libr.org/srrt/news/srrt187.php#9.

Cooke, Nicole A. 2014b. "The Spectrum Doctoral Fellowship Program: Enhancing the LIS Professoriate." *InterActions: UCLA Journal of Education and Information Studies* 10 (1). http://escholarship.org/uc/item/7vb7v4p8.

Cooke, Nicole A. 2014c. "Pushing Back from the Table: Fighting to Maintain My Voice as a Pre-Tenure Minority Female in the White Academy." *Polymath: An Interdisciplinary Arts and Sciences Journal* 4 (2): 39–49.

Cooke, Nicole A., Miriam E. Sweeney, and Safiya Umoja Noble. 2016. "Social Justice as Topic and Tool: An Attempt to Transform an LIS Curriculum and Culture." *The Library Quarterly* 86 (1): 107–124.

Crenshaw, Kimberlé Williams. 1988. "Race, Reform, and Retrenchment: Transformation and Legitimation in Antidiscrimination Law." *Harvard Law Review* 101 (7): 1331–1387.

Dancu, Toni. 2014. "Culturally Sustaining Pedagogy: Expanding Culturally Responsive Theory and Practice: An ISE Research Brief Discussing Paris' 'Culturally Sustaining Pedagogy: A Needed Change in Stance, Terminology, and Practice.'" *Accessed March 1, 2016.* http://relatingresearchtopractice.org/article/328.

Davis, Peggy C. 1989. "Law as Microaggression." *The Yale Law Journal* 98 (8): 1559–1577.

DeCuir, Jessica T., and Adrienne D. Dixson. 2004. "'So When It Comes Out, They Aren't That Surprised That It Is There': Using Critical Race Theory as a Tool of Analysis of Race and Racism in Education." *Educational Researcher* 33 (5): 26–31.

Delgado, Richard. 1989. "Storytelling for Oppositionists and Others: A Plea for Narrative." *Michigan Law Review* 87 (8): 2411–2441.

Delpit, Lisa D. 1986. "Skills and Other Dilemmas of a Progressive Black Educator." *Harvard Educational Review* 56 (4): 379–386.

Delpit, Lisa D. 1988. "The Silenced Dialogue: Power and Pedagogy in Educating Other People's Children." *Harvard Educational Review* 58 (3): 280–299.

Delpit, Lisa D. 2006. *Other People's Children: Cultural Conflict in the Classroom.* New York: The New Press.

Drabinski, Emily. 2013. "Queering the Catalog: Queer Theory and the Politics of Correction." *The Library Quarterly* 83 (2): 94–111.

Ellis, Carolyn S., and Arthur Bochner. 2000. "Autoethnography, Personal Narrative, Reflexivity: Researcher As Subject." In *The Handbook of Qualitative Research* (2nd Edition), edited by Norman K. Denzin and Yvonna S. Lincoln, 733–768. Thousand Oaks, CA: Sage.

Foderingham-Brown, Monica. 1993. "Education for Multicultural Librarianship: The State of the Art and Recommendations for the Future." *The Acquisitions Librarian* 5 (9–10): 131–148.

Freire, Paulo. 1973. *Education for Critical Consciousness.* Vol. 1. New York: Bloomsbury Publishing.

Freire, Paulo. 2000. *Pedagogy of the Oppressed.* New York: Bloomsbury Publishing.

Fries-Britt, Sharon, and Bridget Turner Kelly. 2005. "Retaining Each Other: Narratives of Two African American Women in the Academy." *The Urban Review* 37 (3): 221–242.

Fultz, Michael. 2006. "Black Public Libraries in the South in the Era of De Jure Segregation." *Libraries and the Cultural Record* 41 (3): 337–359.

Garrison-Wade, Dorothy F., Gregory A. Diggs, Diane Estrada, and Rene Galindo. 2012. "Lift Every Voice and Sing: Faculty of Color Face the Challenges of the Tenure Track." *The Urban Review* 44 (1): 90–112.

Gay, Geneva. (2000) 2010. *Culturally Responsive Teaching: Theory, Research, and Practice.* New York: Teachers College Press.

Griffin, Rachel Alicia, LaCharles Ward, and Amanda R. Phillips. 2014. "Still Flies in Buttermilk: Black Male Faculty, Critical Race Theory, and Composite Counterstorytelling." *International Journal of Qualitative Studies in Education* 27 (10): 1354–1375.

Harley, Debra A. 2008. "Maids of Academe: African American Women Faculty at Predominately White Institutions." *Journal of African American Studies* 12 (1): 19–36.

Harris, Cheryl I. 1993. "Whiteness as Property." *Harvard Law Review* 106 (8): 1707–1791.

Harris, Anita, Sarah Carney, and Michelle Fine. 2000. "Counter Work: Theorising the Politics of Counter Stories." *International Journal of Critical Psychology* 4 (2): 6–18.

Honma, Todd. 2005. "Trippin' over the Color Line: The Invisibility of Race in Library and Information Studies." *InterActions: UCLA Journal of Education and Information Studies* 1 (2). Accessed September 18, 2016. https://escholarship.org/uc/item/4nj0w1mp.

Honma, Todd. 2012. "In Visibility: Race and Libraries." Proceedings from the American Library Association, Annual Conference. Chicago, IL.

hooks, bell. 1989. *Talking Back: Thinking Feminist, Thinking Black.* Boston: South End Press.

hooks, bell. 1994. *Teaching to Transgress: Education as the Practice of Freedom.* New York: Routledge.

Howard, Tyrone C. 2001. "Powerful Pedagogy for African American Students: A Case of Four Teachers." *Urban Education* 36 (2): 179–202.

Howard, Tyrone C. 2003. "Culturally Relevant Pedagogy: Ingredients for Critical Teacher Reflection." *Theory into Practice* 42 (3): 195–202.

Hughes-Hassell, Sandra. 2013. "Multicultural Young Adult Literature as a Form of Counter-Storytelling." *The Library Quarterly* 83 (3): 212–228.

Hughes-Hassell, Sandra, and Amanda Hitson. n.d. "Culturally Responsive Library Walk." Libraries, Literacy, and African American Male Youth. Accessed April 1, 2016. http://librariesliteracyandaamaleyouth.weebly.com/uploads/7/9/2/7/7927688/culturally_responsive_library_walk_with_examples.pdf.

Jaeger, Paul T., Nicole A. Cooke, Cecilia Feltis, Michelle Hamiel, Fiona Jardine, and Katie Shilton. 2015. "The Virtuous Circle Revisited: Injecting Diversity, Inclusion, Rights, Justice, and Equity into LIS from Education to Advocacy." *The Library Quarterly* 85 (2): 150–171.

Jaeger, Paul T., and Renee E. Franklin. 2007. "The Virtuous Circle: Increasing Diversity in LIS Faculties to Create More Inclusive Library Services and Outreach." *Education Libraries* 30 (1): 20–26.

Kanter, Rosabeth Moss. 1977. *Men and Women of the Corporation.* New York: Basic Books.

Knowles, Malcolm Shepherd. 1968. "Andragogy, Not Pedagogy." *Adult Leadership* 16 (10): 350–352.

Knowles, Malcolm Shepherd. 1980. *The Modern Practice of Adult Education: From Pedagogy to Andragogy.* Englewood Cliffs, NJ: Prentice Hall/Cambridge.

Knowles, Malcolm Shepherd. 1984. *Andragogy in Action.* San Francisco, CA: Jossey-Bass.

Knowles, Malcolm Shepherd. 1996. *Andragogy: An Emerging Technology for Adult Learning.* London: Routledge.

Krusemark, Stephanie. 2012. "The Campus as Stage: A Qualitative Study of the Hypervisibility and Invisibility of African American Female Identity in the Built Campus Environment." *Journal of Research on Women and Gender* 3 (1): 25–51.

Kumasi, Kafi D. 2011. "Critical Race Theory and Education: Mapping a Legacy of Activism and Scholarship." In *Beyond Critique: Exploring Critical Social Theories and Education*, edited by Bradley A. U. Levinson, 196–219. Boulder, CO: Paradigm.

Kurz, Robin F. 2012. "Missing Faces, Beautiful Places: The Lack of Diversity in South Carolina Picture Book Award Nominees." *New Review of Children's Literature and Librarianship* 18 (2): 128–145.

Ladson-Billings, Gloria. 1994. *The Dreamkeepers: Successful Teachers of African American Students.* San Francisco, CA: Jossey-Bass.

Ladson-Billings, Gloria. 1995a. "But That's Just Good Teaching! The Case for Culturally Relevant Pedagogy." *Theory into Practice* 34 (3): 159–165.

Ladson-Billings, Gloria. 1995b. "Toward a Theory of Culturally Relevant Pedagogy." *American Educational Research Journal* 32 (3): 465–491.

Ladson-Billings, Gloria. 1998. "Just What Is Critical Race Theory and What's It Doing in a Nice Field like Education?" *International Journal of Qualitative Studies in Education* 11 (1): 7–24.

Ladson-Billings, Gloria, and William Tate IV. 1995. "Toward a Critical Race Theory of Education." *Teachers College Record* 97 (1): 47–68.

Lather, Patti. 1995. "Post-Critical Pedagogies: A Feminist Reading." *Postmodernism, Postcolonialism and Pedagogy*: 167–186.

Lather, Patti. 2001. "Ten Years Later, Yet Again: Critical Pedagogy and Its Complicities." *Feminist Engagements: Reading, Resisting, and Revisioning Male Theorists in Education and Cultural Studies*: 183–195.

Levin, John S., Laurencia Walker, Zachary Haberler, and Adam Jackson-Boothby. 2013. "The Divided Self: The Double Consciousness of Faculty of Color in Community Colleges." *Community College Review*: 311–329.

Lorde, Audre. 1984. "Sister Outsider. Freedom." Freedom, CA: Crossing Press.

Marable, Manning. 1992. *Black America: Multicultural Democracy in the Age of Clarence Thomas, David Duke and the LA Uprisings.* Westfield, NJ: Open Media.

Marsh, Don. 2015. " Ferguson Library Director Looks for New Ways to Serve Community." *St. Louis on the Air.* April 1. Accessed March 1, 2016. http://news.stlpublicradio.org/post/ferguson-library-director-looks-new-ways-serve-community.

Mayberry, Maralee, and Ellen Cronan Rose. 1999. *Meeting the Challenge: Innovative Feminist Pedagogies in Action.* New York: Psychology Press.

Morris, Jen. 2013. "Free to Learn: Helping Ex-Offenders with Reentry." *Public Library Quarterly* 32 (2): 119–123.

Morris, Vanessa J. "A Seat at the Table: Seeking Culturally Competent Pedagogy in Librarian Education." Paper presented at the Association of Library and Information Educators Conference, Seattle, WA. 2007.

Niemann, Yolanda Flores. 1999. "The Making of a Token: A Case Study of Stereotype Threat, Stigma, Racism, and Tokenism in Academe." *Frontiers: A Journal of Women Studies* 20 (1): 111–134.

Palmer, Parker J. (1998) 2010. *The Courage to Teach: Exploring the Inner Landscape of a Teacher's Life.* San Francisco: John Wiley and Sons.

Paris, Django. 2012. "Culturally Sustaining Pedagogy: A Needed Change in Stance, Terminology, and Practice." *Educational Researcher* 41 (3): 93–97.

Paris, Django, and H. Samy Alim. 2014. "What Are We Seeking to Sustain through Culturally Sustaining Pedagogy? A Loving Critique Forward." *Harvard Educational Review* 84 (1): 85–100.

Pawley, Christine. 2006. "Unequal Legacies: Race and Multiculturalism in the LIS Curriculum." *The Library Quarterly* 76 (2): 149–168.

Peet, Lisa. 2015. "Baltimore's Enoch Pratt Free Library Provides Haven in Troubled Times." *Library Journal*, May 5. Accessed March 1, 2016. http://lj.library journal.com/2015/05/public-services/baltimores-enoch-pratt-free-library-provides-haven-in-troubled-times/#_.

Peterson, Lorna. 1995. "Multiculturalism: Affirmative or Negative Action?" *Library Journal* 120 (12): 30.

Peterson, Lorna. 1996. "Alternative Perspectives in Library and Information Science: Issues of Race." *Journal of Education for Library and Information Science* 37 (2): 163–174.

Peterson, Lorna. 1999. "The Definition of Diversity: Two Views. A More Specific Definition." *Journal of Library Administration* 27 (1–2): 17–26.

Phelps, Rosemary E. 1995. "What's in a Number? Implications for African American Female Faculty at Predominantly White Colleges and Universities." *Innovative Higher Education* 19 (4): 255–268.

Pierce, Chester M., Jean V. Carew, Diane Pierce-Gonzalez, and Deborah Wills. 1977. "An Experiment in Racism TV Commercials." *Education and Urban Society* 10 (1): 61–87.

Pollak, Kathryn I., and Yolanda Flores Niemann. 1998. "Black and White Tokens in Academia: A Difference of Chronic Versus Acute Distinctiveness." *Journal of Applied Social Psychology* 28 (11): 954–972.

"Project Enable: Expanding Nondiscriminatory Access by Librarians Everywhere." n.d. Center for Digital Literacy (CDL), the School of Information Studies (iSchool@Syracuse), and the Burton Blatt Institute (BBI) at Syracuse University. Accessed April 1, 2016. http://projectenable.syr.edu.

Rodriguez, Dalia, and Afua Boahene. 2012. "The Politics of Rage Empowering Women of Color in the Academy." *Cultural Studies Critical Methodologies* 12 (5): 450–458.

Ryan, Ann Marie. 2002. "Core Elements of Preparing Teachers for Culturally Relevant Practice." Big City Teacher Preparation Initiative. Chicago, IL: University of Illinois at Chicago Department of History. Accessed March 1, 2016. http://eric.ed.gov/?id=ED467795.

Rychly, Laura, and Emily Graves. 2012. "Teacher Characteristics for Culturally Responsive Pedagogy." *Multicultural Perspectives* 14 (1): 44–49.

Shade, Barbara J., Cynthia A. Kelly, and Mary Oberg. 1997. *Creating Culturally Responsive Classrooms.* Washington, DC: American Psychological Association.

Solorzano, Daniel, Miguel Ceja, and Tara Yosso. 2000. "Critical Race Theory, Racial Microaggressions, and Campus Racial Climate: The Experiences of African American College Students." *Journal of Negro Education* 69 (1–2): 60–73.

Solorzano, Daniel G., and Tara J. Yosso. 2001. "Critical Race and Latcrit Theory and Method: Counter-Storytelling." *International Journal of Qualitative Studies in Education* 14 (4): 471–495.

Solorzano, Daniel G., and Tara J. Yosso. 2002. "Critical Race Methodology: Counter-Storytelling as an Analytical Framework for Education Research." *Qualitative Inquiry* 8 (1): 23–44.

Sue, Derald Wing, Christina M. Capodilupo, Gina C. Torino, Jennifer M. Bucceri, Aisha Holder, Kevin L. Nadal, and Marta Esquilin. 2007. "Racial Microaggressions in Everyday Life: Implications for Clinical Practice." *American Psychologist* 62 (4): 271–286.

Tatum, Beverly. 1992. "Talking about Race, Learning about Racism: The Application of Racial Identity Development Theory in the Classroom." *Harvard Educational Review* 62 (1): 1–25.

Tatum, Beverly. 1994. "Teaching White Students about Racism: The Search for White Allies and the Restoration of Hope." *Teachers College Record* 95 (4): 462–476.

Tisdell, Elizabeth J. 1993. "Feminism and Adult Learning: Power, Pedagogy, and Praxis." *New Directions for Adult and Continuing Education* 1993 (57): 91–103.

Tisdell, Elizabeth J. 2001. "Feminist Perspectives on Adult Education: Constantly Shifting Identities in Constantly Changing Times." In *Making Space: Merging Theory and Practice in Adult Education*, edited by Vanessa Sheared and Peggy A. Sissel, 271–285. Westport, CT: Bergin and Garvey.

Tuitt, Frank, Michele Hanna, Lisa M. Martinez, Maria del Carmen Salazar, and Rachel Griffin. 2009, Fall. "Teaching in the Line of Fire: Faculty Of Color in the Academy." *Thought and Action*: 65–74.

Verjee, Begum. 2013. "Counter-Storytelling: The Experiences of Women of Colour in Higher Education." *Atlantis: Critical Studies in Gender, Culture and Social Justice* 36 (1): 22–32.

Williams, Bronwyn T. 2004. "The Truth in the Tale: Race and "Counterstorytelling" in the Classroom." *Journal of Adolescent and Adult Literacy* 48 (2): 164–169.

Yosso, Tara Joy. 2006. *Critical Race Counterstories along the Chicana/Chicano Educational Pipeline.* New York: Routledge.

Yosso, Tara J., and Daniel Solorzano. 2005. "Conceptualizing a Critical Race Theory in Sociology." In *The Blackwell Companion to Social Inequalities*, edited by Mary Romero and Eric Margolis, 117–146. Malden, MA: Blackwell Publishing.

1

Sample Syllabus

This is the 2015 Syllabus for the *Information Services to Diverse Populations* course at the School of Information Sciences at the University of Illinois, Urbana-Champaign. This class was created by the author and first offered in 2013.

LIS 547—INFORMATION SERVICES FOR DIVERSE POPULATIONS

Fall 2015
Class Meeting: Tuesdays, 10 am–12 pm
Instructor: Dr. Nicole Cooke

Course Description

Given the increasing diversity of information users in society, information professionals need to learn more about specific groups in order to provide appropriate services. This course is designed to prepare future information professionals to develop and provide inclusive services to underrepresented populations and to analyze and evaluate services to ensure equality of access to information in a range of institutional settings. Through readings, discussions, guest lectures, and site visits, students will explore diversity issues that impact information services and develop skills for planning, implementing, and evaluating programs and services for addressing these issues. Specific diversity issues include race and ethnicity; education; language; literacy; disability; gender and sexual orientation; social class; national origin; physical, psychological, and learning ability; and age.

Expected Learning Outcomes

This is a subject related to all areas of librarianship. The increased ethnic diversity of the United States and the increase in relations between people of different cultures and countries affect collection development, technical services, reference services, library instructions, library programming, staffing, and all other aspects of library services. This topic is important, regardless of which aspect of librarianship students concentrate on or what type of libraries students work in. Public, academic, and school libraries have all developed approaches that can be useful in other settings. This course will complement information conveyed in other courses, and it will describe problems and challenges unique to serving diverse populations and some possible solutions.

LIS 547 is designed to introduce students to the theoretical and practical aspects of serving diverse populations through all aspects of librarianship. The following will be addressed:

- Philosophical aspects of diversity in institutional settings
- Developing cultural competencies
- Diversity issues in the acquisition, cataloging, and classification of materials and diversity issues in reference work, library instruction, and other library programs
- Recruiting, hiring, and mentoring diverse staff
- History of services to specific groups

Instructional Method

This is a seminar class and will incorporate a mixture of lectures, discussions, in-class exercises, and student presentations. Students are expected to attend classes regularly and actively lead and engage in class discussions. Student participation is vital to the learning process and the exchange of ideas.

Classroom Environment

As a graduate seminar, the classroom environment should be professional and respectful. Discussions should be based on course readings and critical thinking. Issues of policy can involve strongly held beliefs and current political controversies. Remember, your classmates may have different perspectives on issues than you, but they still deserve your respect.

Academic Integrity and Ethics

Please review and reflect on the academic integrity policy of the University of Illinois, http://admin.illinois.edu/policy/code/article1_part4_1-401.html, to which we subscribe. By turning in materials for review in LIS 547, you certify that all work presented is your own and has been done by you independently or as a member of a designated group for group assignments.

If, in the course of your writing, you use the words or ideas of another writer, proper acknowledgment must be given (using MLA, APA, or another standard style). Not to do so is to commit plagiarism, a form of academic dishonesty. If you are not absolutely clear on what constitutes plagiarism and how to cite sources appropriately, now is the time to learn. Please ask me! Or plan to visit the university's Writing Center—http://www.cws.illinois.edu/.

They provide a wealth of resources, including individual appointments and assistance.

Please be aware that the consequences for plagiarism or other forms of academic dishonesty will be severe. Students who violate university standards of academic integrity are subject to disciplinary action, including a reduced grade, failure in the course, and suspension or dismissal from the university. Violations will be dealt with swiftly and will be addressed with the utmost seriousness.

Statement of Inclusion

http://www.inclusiveillinois.illinois.edu/supporting_docs/Inclusive%20Illinois%20Diversity%20Statement.pdf

As the state's premier public university, the core mission of the University of Illinois at Urbana-Champaign is to serve the interests of the diverse people of the state of Illinois and beyond. The institution thus values inclusion and a pluralistic learning and research environment, one in which we respect the varied perspectives and lived experiences of a diverse community and global workforce. We support diversity of worldviews, histories, and cultural knowledge across a range of social groups, including race, ethnicity, gender identity, sexual orientation, abilities, economic class, religion, and their intersections.

Disability Statement

From the Graduate College website

To obtain disability-related academic adjustments and/or auxiliary aids, students with disabilities must contact the course instructor and the Disability Resources and Educational Services (DRES) as soon as possible. To contact DRES, you may visit 1207 S. Oak St., Champaign, call 333-4603 (V/TTY), or email a message to disability@uiuc.edu.

Required Text

Grover, R. J., R. C. Greer, and J. Agada. 2010. *Assessing Information Needs: Managing Transformative Library Services*. Santa Barbara, CA: Libraries Unlimited.

- All texts are on reserve at the Main Library.
- Additional readings will be available on reserve at the library through the University Library's Online Journals, Newspapers and Databases tool (http://openurl.library.uiuc.edu/sfxlcl3/az) or the open web (as indicated).

Student Agreement

Attendance in this class signifies that the student has agreed to abide by and adhere to the policies and regulations specified earlier. It is understood that the instructor may adapt or change this syllabus and the assignments contained within it according to circumstances that may arise during the course of the class.

CALENDAR AND CLASS READINGS

This schedule indicates reading assignments and due dates for assignments. Readings are chapters from the course texts and various articles unless otherwise indicated. *Changes or adjustments in readings and/or activities may be made.* Any changes or adjustments will be announced in class and the syllabus will be updated to reflect the changes.

TOPICS	READINGS
Week 1	***Read and be prepared to discuss***
• Class Introductions and Course Overview	• Peterson, L. "The Definition of Diversity: Two Views. A More Specific Definition." *Journal of Library Administration* 27, no. 1–2 (1999): 17–26.
• Introduction to Diversity, Inclusion and Information Services	• Halvorson-Bourgeois, B., L. Zipse, and C. Haynes. "Educating Culturally Competent Clinicians: Using Multiple Perspectives to Review Curriculum Content." *SIG 10 Perspectives on Issues in Higher Education* 16, no. 2 (2013): 51–62.
Week 2	***Read and be prepared to discuss***
• LIS and Inclusion	• Honma, T. "Trippin' over the Color Line: The Invisibility of Race in Library and Information Studies." *InterActions: UCLA Journal of Education and Information Studies* 1, no. 2 (2005). http://escholarship.org/uc/item/4nj0w1mp.
	• Adkins, D., and I. Espinal. "The Diversity Mandate." *Library Journal* 45, no. 2 (2004): 149–161.
• Becoming Culturally Competent	• El Turk, G. "Diversity and Cultural Competency." *Colorado Libraries* 29, no. 4 (2003, Winter): 5–7.
	• Overall, P. M. "Cultural Competence: A Conceptual Framework for Library and Information Science Professionals." *Library Quarterly* 79, no. 2 (2009): 175–204.
	Useful but not required:
	• Agosto, D. E. "Bridging the Culture Gap: Ten Steps toward a More Multicultural Youth Library." *Journal of Youth Services in Libraries* 14, no. 3 (2001, Spring): 38–41.

TOPICS	READINGS
	• "Diversity Standards: Cultural Competency for Academic Libraries," American Library Association, May 4, 2012, accessed August 7, 2015, http://www.ala.org/ala/mgrps/divs/acrl/standards/diversity_draft.pdf.
	• Jaeger, P. T., J. C. Bertot, and R. E. Franklin. Diversity, Inclusion, and Underrepresented Populations in LIS Research." *Library Quarterly* 80, no. 2 (2010): 175–181.
	• Kennan, M. A., A. Lloyd, A. Qayyum, and K. Thompson. "Settling In: The Relationship between Information and Social Inclusion."*Australian Academic and Research Libraries* 42, no. 3 (2011): 191–210.
	• Kumasi, K., and R. F. Hill. "Examining the Hidden Ideologies within Cultural Competence Discourses among Library and Information Science Students: Implications for School Library Pedagogy." *School Libraries Worldwide* 19, no. 1 (2013, March): 128–139. http://digitalcommons.wayne.edu/slisfrp/94/.
	• Press, N. O., and M. Diggs-Hobson. "Providing Health Information to Community Members Where They Are: Characteristics of the Culturally Competent Librarian." *Library Trends* 53, no. 3 (2005): 398–410.
Week 3	***Read and be prepared to discuss***
• Services to Underrepresented Populations	• Hall, T. D. "Race and Place: A Personal Account of Unequal Access." *American Libraries* 38, no. 2 (2007): 30–33.
	• Malone, C. K. "Toward a Multicultural American Public Library History." *Libraries and Culture* 35, no. 1 (2000): 77–87.
• Contexts of Inclusive Services	• Buddy, J. W., and M. C. Williams. "A Dream Deferred: School Libraries and Segregation." *American Libraries* 36, no. 2 (2005): 33–35.
	• Prasad, P. "Reference Services to Senior Groups in the San Antonio Public Library." *The Reference Librarian* 50, no. 1 (2009): 99–108.
	Useful but not required: (examples of context)
	• "Library Instruction for Diverse Populations Bibliography," American Library Association, September 29, 2006, accessed August 7, 2015, http://www.ala.org/acrl/aboutacrl/directoryofleadership/sections/is/iswebsite/projpubs/diversebib.
	• "Resources," The Association of Specialized and Cooperative Library Agencies, December 4, 2006, accessed August 7, 2015, http://www.ala.org/ascla/asclaissues/issues.
	• Van Sant, W. "Librarians Now Add Social Work to Their Resumes." *Tampa Bay Times*, June 8, 2009, accessed August 7, 2015, http://www.tampabay.com/news/humaninterest/librarians-now-add-social-work-to-their-resumes/1008244.

(*continued*)

TOPICS	READINGS
	• Westbrook, L. "Understanding Crisis Information Needs in Context: The Case of Intimate Partner Violence Survivors." *Library Quarterly* 78, no. 3 (2008): 237–261.
	• White, K. L., and A. J. Gilliland. "Promoting Reflexivity and Inclusivity in Archival Education, Research, and Practice."*Library Quarterly* 80, no. 3 (2010): 231–248.
Week 4	***Read and be prepared to discuss***
• Community Analysis	• Japzon, A. C., and H. Gong. "A Neighborhood Analysis of Public Library Use in New York City." *Library Quarterly* 75, no. 4 (2005): 446–463.
	• Futterman, M. "Finding the Underserved: Close Examination Using Market Segmentation Can Reveal Useful Surprises about the People Your Library Is Leaving Behind." *Library Journal* 2008, October 15, Access date September 18, 2016. http://lj.library journal.com/2008/10/managing-libraries/finding -the-underserved/#.
• Cultural Humility	• Ortega, R. M., and K. C. Faller. "Training Child Welfare Workers from an Intersectional Cultural Humility Perspective: A Paradigm Shift." *Child Welfare* 90, no. 5 (2011): 27.
	• Tervalon, M., and J. Murray-Garcia. "Cultural Humility versus Cultural Competence: A Critical Distinction in Defining Physician Training Outcomes in Multicultural Education." *Journal of Health Care for the Poor and Underserved* 9, no. 2 (1998): 117–125.
Week 5	***Read and be prepared to discuss***
• Race, Ethnicity, and National Origin	• Du Mont, R. R. "Race in American Librarianship." *Journal of Library History* 21, no. 3 (1986): 488–509.
	• Fultz, M. "Black Public Libraries in the South in the Era of De Jure Segregation." *Libraries and the Cultural Record* 41, no. 3 (2006): 337–359.
• Diversity and Technology	• Brock, A. "From the Blackhand Side: Twitter as a Cultural Conversation." *Journal of Broadcasting and Electronic Media* 56, no. 4 (2012): 529–549.
	Useful but not required:
	• Adkins, D., and L. Hussey. "The Library Lives of Latino College Students." *The Library Quarterly* 76, no. 4 (2006): 456–480.
	• Burke, S. "The Use of Public Libraries by Native Americans." *The Library Quarterly* 77, no. 4 (2007): 429–461.
	• Chu, C. M. "Literacy Practices of Linguistic Minorities: SociolingusiticIssues and Implications for Literacy Services." *The Library Quarterly* 69, no. 3 (1999): 339–359.
	• Hand, S. "Transmitting Whiteness: Librarians, Children, and Race, 1900–1930s." *Progressive Librarian* 38/39 (2009): 34–63.

TOPICS	READINGS
	• Hughes-Hassell, S., and E. J. Cox. "Inside Board Books: Representations of People of Color." *Library Quarterly* 80, no. 3 (2010): 211–230.
	• Krebs, A. B. "Native America's Twenty-First-Century Right to Know." *Archival Science* 12, no. 2 (2012): 173–190.
Week 6	**Read and be prepared to discuss**
• Collection Develop-ment of Diverse Materials	• Hughes-Hassell, S. "Multicultural Young Adult Literature as a Form of Counter-Storytelling." *The Library Quarterly* 83, no. 3 (2013): 212–228.
	• Kurz, R. F. "Missing Faces, Beautiful Places: The Lack of Diversity in South Carolina Picture Book Award Nominees." *New Review of Children's Literature and Librarianship* 18, no. 2 (2012): 128–145.
	• Maloney, M. M. "Cultivating Community, Promoting Inclusivity: Collections as Fulcrum for Targeted Outreach." *New Library World* 113, no. 5/6 (2012): 281–289.
• Incarceration Ι Services to Prison or Detention Facilities	• We Need Diverse Books Campaign. Access date: September 16, 2016, http://weneeddiversebooks.org.
	• Payne, W., and M. J. Sabath. "Trends in the Use of Information Management Technology in Prison Libraries." *Behavioral and Social Sciences Librarian* 26, no. 2 (2007): 1–10.
	• Shirley, G. L. "Correctional Libraries, Library Stan-dards, and Diversity." *Journal of Correctional Educa-tion* 54, no. 2 (2003): 70–74.
	Useful but not required:
	• Alexander, L. B., & S. Miselis. "Barriers to GLBTQ Collection Development and Strategies for Overcoming Them." *Young Adult Library Services* 5, no. 3 (2007): 43–49.
	• Bernis, M. "You Work Where? Prison Librarian—an Inside Job with Outsize Benefits. *Library Journal* 136, no. 7 (2011): 108.
	• Dowling, B. "The Accidental Prison Librarian: An Interview with Avi Steinberg." *Public Libraries*, May 7, 2013, accessed August 7, 2015, http://publi clibrariesonline.org/2013/05/the-accidental -librarian-an-interview-with-avi-steinberg/.
	• Meyers, Christopher. "The Apartheid of Children's Literature." *The New York Times*, March 15, 2014, accessed August 7, 2015, http://www.nytimes .com/2014/03/16/opinion/sunday/the-apartheid -of-childrens-literature.html.
	• Meyers, Walter Dean. "Where Are the People of Color in Children's Books?" *The New York Times*, March 15, 2014, accessed August 7, 2015, http://www.nytimes .com/2014/03/16/opinion/sunday/where-are-the -people-of-color-in-childrens-books.html?smid =fb-share&_r=5.

(*continued*)

TOPICS	READINGS
	• Vogel, B. "Bailing out Prison Libraries." *Library Journal* 122, no. 19 (1997): 35–37.

Week 7 | **Read and be prepared to discuss**

• Services to Veterans and the Mentally Ill
    • Berk, J. "Mental Health Training in Public Libraries." *Public Libraries Online*, January 5, 2015, accessed August 7, 2015, http://publiclibrariesonline.org/2015/01/mental-health-training-in-public-libraries/.
    • Mills, C. P., E. B. Paladino, and J. C. Klentzin. "Student Veterans and the Academic Library." *Reference Services Review* 43, no. 2 (2015): 262–279.

• Political, Social, and Technological Divides
    • Josey, E. J. "Diversity: Social and Political Barriers." *Journal of Library Administration* 27, no. ½(1999): 191–201.
    • Kinney, B. "The Internet, Public Libraries, and the Digital Divide." *Public Library Quarterly* 29, no. 2 (2010): 104–161.

Useful but not required:

• Hoppenfeld, J., T. Wyckoff, J. A. J. Henson, J. N. Mayotte, and H. P. Kirkwood Jr. "Librarians and the Entrepreneurship Bootcamp for Veterans: Helping Disabled Veterans with Business Research." *Journal of Business and Finance Librarianship* 18, no. 4 (2013): 293–308.
• Maxey-Harris, C. "Multicultural E-resources: An Exploratory Study of Resources Held by ARL Libraries." *Behavioral and Social Sciences Librarian* 29, no. 1 (2010): 65–80.

Week 8 | **Read and be prepared to discuss**

• Archives and Diversity
    • Mason, K. M. "Fostering Diversity in Archival Collections: The Iowa Women's Archives." *Collection Management* 27, no. 2 (2003): 23–31.
    • O'Neal, J. R. " 'The Right to Know': Decolonizing Native American Archives." *Journal of Western Archives* 6, no. 1 (2015): 2. http://digitalcommons.usu.edu/westernarchives/vol6/iss1/2/.

• Comics, Graphic Novels, Zines, and Urban Fiction
    • Guerra, S. F. "Using Urban Fiction to Engage At-Risk and Incarcerated Youths in Literacy Instruction." *Journal of Adolescent and Adult Literacy* 55, no. 5 (2012): 385–394.
    • Upson, M., and C. M. Hall. "Comic Book Guy in the Classroom: The Educational Power and Potential of Graphic Storytelling in Library Instruction." *Kansas Library Association College and University Libraries Section Proceedings* 3, no. 11 (2013): 28–38. (Google Scholar).

Useful but not required:

• Caswell, M. "Khmer Rouge Archives: Accountability, Truth, and Memory in Cambodia." *Archival Science* 10, no. 1 (2010): 25–44.

TOPICS	READINGS
	• "Graphic Novel Depicts John Lewis' 'March' toward Justice," 2013, accessed August 7, 2015, http://www .npr.org/blogs/codeswitch/2013/08/31/21688 4526/graphic-novel-depicts-john-lewis-march -toward-justice. • Street Literature Blog, accessed August 7, 2015, http://www.streetliterature.com/.
Week 9 • Outreach • Migration and Immigration	***Read and be prepared to discuss*** • Elton, C. I. "Breaking down Invisible Barriers: Using Bookmobiles to Facilitate Library Outreach in Urban and Suburban Communities," 2015, accessed August 7, 2015, http://ir.uiowa.edu/ bsides/40/. • Audunson, R., S. Essmat, and S. Aabo. "Public Libraries: A Meeting Place for Immigrant Women?" *Library and Information Science Research* 33, no. 3 (2011): 220–227. • Martin, J. A., K. M. Reaume, E. M. Reeves, and R. D. Wright. "Relationship Building with Students and Instructors of ESL: Bridging the Gap for Library Instruction and Services." *Reference Services Review* 40, no. 3 (2012): 352–367. ***Useful but not required:*** • Becvar, K. M., and R. Srinivasan. "Indigenous Knowledge and Culturally-Responsive Methods in Information Research." *The Library Quarterly* 79, no. 4 (2009): 421–441. • Fisher, K. E., E. Marcoux, L. S. Miller, A. Sánchez, and E. R. Cunningham. "Information Behaviour of Migrant Hispanic Farm Workers and Their Families in the Pacific Northwest." *Information Research* 10, no. 1 (2004), accessed April 27, 2009, http:// informationr.net/ir/10-1/paper199.html. • van der Linden, K., J. Bartlett, and J. Beheshti. "New Immigrants' Perceptions and Awareness of Public Library Services." *Canadian Journal of Information and Library Sciences* 38, no. 2 (2014): 65–79.
Week 10 • Disability and Age/ Services to the Blind and Handicapped • Information Poverty and Socioeconomic Status	***Read and be prepared to discuss*** • Lazar, J., and P. T. Jaeger. "Reducing Barriers to Online Access for People with Disabilities." *Issues in Science and Technology* 27, no. 2 (2011): 68–82. • Xie, B., and P. T. Jaeger. "Computer Training Programs for Older Adults at the Public Library." *Public Libraries* 47, no. 5 (2008): 42–49. • Gehner, J. "Libraries, Low-Income People, and Social Exclusion." *Public Library Quarterly* 29, no. 1 (2010): 39–47. • Nyquist, E. B. "Poverty, Prejudice, and the Public Library." *Library Quarterly* 38, no. 1 (1968): 78–89.

(continued)

TOPICS	READINGS
	Useful but not required:
	• CNN. "Hard Economic Times: A Boon for Public Libraries. *CNN.com*, 2009, accessed August 7, 2015, http://www.cnn.com/2009/US/02/28/ recession.libraries/index.html.
	• Haider J., and David Bawden. "Conceptions of 'Information Poverty' in LIS: A Discourse Analysis." *Journal of Documentation* 63, no. 4 007): 534–557.
	• Hersberger, J. "Are the Economically Poor Information Poor? Does the Digital Divide Affect the Homeless and Information Access?"*Canadian Journal of Information and Library Science* 27, no. 3 (2002): 45–63.
Week 11	**Read and be prepared to discuss**
• LIS Microaggressions	• Alabi, J. "Racial Microaggressions in Academic Libraries: Results of a Survey of Minority and Non-Minority Librarians." *The Journal of Academic Librarianship* 41, no. 1 (2015): 47–53.
	• LIS Microaggressions Blog, accessed August 7, 2015, http://lismicroaggressions.tumblr.com.
• Diversity Hiring/ Librarian Stereotypes	• "Diversity Counts" Report (ALA), accessed August 7, 2015, http://www.ala.org/offices/diversity/ diversitycounts/divcounts.
	• Excerpt from Pagowsky, N., and M. Rigby. *The Librarian Stereotype: Deconstructing Perceptions of Information Work.* Chicago: ACRL, 2014.
Week 12	**Read and be prepared to discuss**
• Social Work and Libraries	• Cathcart, R. "Librarian or Social Worker: Time to Look at the Blurring Line?" *Reference Librarian* 49, no. 1 (2008): 87–91.
	• Luo, L., D. Estreicher, P. A. Lee, C. Thomas, and G. Thomas. "Social Workers in the Library: An Innovative Approach to Address Library Patrons' Social Service Needs." *Qualitative and Quantitative Methods in Libraries (QQML)* 1 (2012): 73–82, accessed August 7, 2015, http://www.qqml.net/papers/ July_Issue/8QQML_Journal_2012_Luo_Estreicher _Lee_Thomas_Thomas_1_73-82.pdf.
• Services to the Hungry, Homeless, and Impoverished	• Hersberger, J. "The Homeless and Information Needs and Services." *Reference and User Services Quarterly* 44, no. 3 (2005): 199–202.
	• Wollam, K., and B. Wessel. "Recognizing and Effectively Managing Mental Illness in the Library." *Colorado Libraries* 29, no. 4 (2003): 17–20.
	Useful but not required:
	• Hanley, R. "Library Edgy over Order to Tolerate Homeless." *The New York Times*, May 29, 1991, accessed August 7, 2015, http://www.nytimes.com/ 1991/05/29/nyregion/library-edgy-over-order-to- tolerate-homeless.html.

TOPICS	READINGS
	• Stern, H. "Aimless and Homeless, He Wins Fortune in Court: Lawsuit: Library Who Banned Him, Police Who Harassed Him, Wish They Hadn't—To Tune of $250,000." *Los Angeles Times*, March 22, 1992, accessed August 7, 2015, http://articles.latimes.com/1992-03-22/news/mn-7262_1_police-harassment.

Week 13

Read and be prepared to discuss

- Diversity and School Libraries

- Agosto, D. E. "Bridging the Cultural Gap: Ten Steps toward a More Multicultural Youth Library." *Journal of Youth Services in Libraries* 14, no. 3 (2001): 38–41.
- Lafferty, K. E. "What Are You Reading?" How School Libraries Can Promote Racial Diversity in Multicultural Literature." *Multicultural Perspectives* 16, no. 4 (2014): 203–209.

- Evaluation and Assessment of Services for Diverse Users

- Love, J. B. "The Assessment of Diversity Initiatives in Academic Libraries." *Journal of Library Administration* 33, no. 1–2 (2001): 73–103.
- Mehra, B., and R. Davis. "A Strategic Diversity Manifesto for Public Libraries in the 21st Century." *New Library World* 116, no. 1/2 (2015): 15–36.

Week 14

Read and be prepared to discuss

- Sexual Orientation and Gender Identity

- Curry, A. "If I Ask, Will They Answer? Evaluating Public Library Reference Service to Gay and Lesbian Youth." *Reference and User Services Quarterly* 45, no. 2 (2005): 65–75.
- Greenblatt, E. "Lesbian, Gay, Bisexual, Transgender Library Users: Overcoming the Myths." *Colorado Libraries* 29, no. 4 (2003): 21–25.

- Course Wrap Up

Useful but not required:

- Alexander, L. B., and S. Miselis. "Barriers to GLBTQ Collection Development and Strategies for Overcoming Them." *Young Adult Library Services* 11, no. 3/4 (2007): 43–49.
- Maack, M. N. "Gender, Culture, and the Transformation of American Librarianship, 1890–1920." *Libraries and Culture* 33, no. 1 (1998): 51–61.
- Mehra, B., and D. Braquet. "Library and Information Science Professionals as Community Action Researchers in an Academic Setting: Top Ten Directions to Further Institutional Change for People of Diverse Sexual Orientations and Gender Identities. *Library Trends* 56, no. 2 (2007): 542–565.
- Pruitt, J. "Gay Men's Book Clubs versus Wisconsin's Public Libraries: Political Perceptions in the Absence of Dialogue." *Library Quarterly* 80, no. 2 (2010): 121–141.

Sample Assignments and Exercises

ARTICLES IN A FLASH SESSION

This exercise is useful for diversifying class discussions and enables learners to find articles of interest to them. These sessions can be broadly or narrowly defined—students can find articles generally related to diversity, or they can identify articles on a particular diversity topic (i.e., library services to the incarcerated).

The instructor will determine time limits and other parameters for the readings and brief presentations (i.e., scholarly articles, article length).

Students will select an appropriate article and be prepared to briefly talk about it in class (two to five minutes).

Students proceed in a round robin session, summarizing their articles and describing how they relate to class content. Q&A can follow each student presentation or can occur once everyone has presented.

SELF-DIRECTED READINGS

As a class, we will cover a core curriculum with common readings. As an individual student, you will be responsible for identifying and reading additional articles, book chapters, or other resources that best fit your experience, personal needs, and career goals.

Select one *research* article or *book chapter** (NOT an article on the weekly reading list but an article you found in the literature) and write a 400–500 word response paper to the article. *No newspaper or magazine articles.

These summaries will be due throughout the semester, dates TBA.

Writing about Articles

For each article, provide (in this order):

1. A complete citation;
2. A two-paragraph summary (i.e., what is the article about?); and
3. A two-paragraph response (e.g., what did you think about the author's argument? How did the article relate to other course readings or discussions? Would you recommend this article? How might you implement the ideas in this article?). Your summary should be 400–500 words in length.

Although it can be tempting to write more than four paragraphs about an article you really like (or to write very long paragraphs), stick to the four-paragraph limit. Librarians need to write clearly and succinctly—this is a good opportunity to practice editing for both clarity and brevity.

It is a good idea to use these papers as the basis for your class discussions/contributions.

PODCAST/VIDEO REVIEW

There is a wealth of information on the Internet related to diversity. Find a video or podcast (aim for a talk or lecture—something substantive) related to diversity and information services, and write a summary about what you viewed/listened to. I will provide a list of potential podcasts, but check out TED talks and other similar venues for content. If you are unsure, please consult with Dr. Cooke before you watch/write/submit.

Writing about Your Podcast or Video

Provide (in this order):

- The title and URL;
- A two-paragraph summary (i.e., what is the talk about?); and
- A two-paragraph response (e.g., what did you think about the author's argument? How did the talk relate to other course readings or discussions? Would you recommend this talk? How might you implement the ideas in this article?). Your summary should be 400–500 words in length.

Although it can be tempting to write more than four paragraphs about a talk you really like (or to write very long paragraphs), stick to the four-paragraph limit. Librarians need to write clearly and succinctly—this is a good opportunity to practice editing for both clarity and brevity.

SYSTEMATIC BIBLIOGRAPHY

You will produce a systematic bibliography based upon the work of Dr. Marcia J. Bates. The goal of this assignment is to increase your understanding of the literature in the area of diversity and information services, with attention to one narrower subject area therein. Read the article "Rigorous Systematic Bibliography" (Bates 1976) to learn the fundamentals of an excellent scholarly bibliography.

Your tasks are to:

1. Select your topic—one of the content areas we are covering this semester.

2. Conduct a literature search utilizing the major periodical indexes of library and information studies (LIS). Focus mainly on the academic journal literature in LIS; sources from across the social sciences may be included if appropriate.

3. Follow Bates's guidelines of domain, selection principles, bibliographic units, information fields, and organization.

4. Your bibliography should contain a 400–500 word *introduction* that explicitly addresses Bates's approach as applied to your work and *10–15 (minimum) ANNOTATED REFERENCES*. Be certain to focus on contemporary publications (within the past decade). Your annotations should be comprised of scholarly articles (book chapters are acceptable).

5. The grade for the assignment will be based upon the accurate implementation of the rigorous systematic bibliography format; the identification of relevant sources from within LIS and other social sciences, if appropriate; and the quality and accuracy of the annotations.

Bates, M. J. "Rigorous Systematic Bibliography." *Reference Quarterly* 16, no. 1 (1976): 7–26.

DISCUSSION LEADERSHIP

Each student will lead/co-lead a discussion that addresses one of the content areas. A good discussion leader may provide some background on the readings we are doing and contextualize them as well as be ready to promote critical discussion by having probes for the class. The discussion leaders may split their responsibilities any way they see fit; however, each student will be evaluated both individually and as a group.

Procedure

Select your topic from one of the content areas we are covering this semester.

Before Your Presentation

From the articles you find and use for preparation, select one document that you would like the class to read, and send a PDF or link to the professor one week before your presentation date.

Prepare an "executive summary" of your presentation points, with a selected bibliography, to distribute to your colleagues. The summary should be one page (full page, single spaced), and your bibliography should not exceed two pages (APA or MLA formatting).

Creating Your Presentation

You will likely begin your presentation by introducing yourselves, then your user group, then discussing the research literature, elaborating on your findings and your own interpretations, and concluding with a discussion of the practical implications of your research (i.e., how is this going to help us serve these users better). If you think it will make for a more interesting presentation, you might also organize it thematically by introducing relevant questions and findings and elaborating on how they are manifest in the scholarly literature and your group's research.

Be creative about your delivery of the content so your presentation is interesting and stimulating. Remember, "presentation" ≠ "lecture" or at least not a straightforward talking-head style lecture. You might also include an experiential component either as active participants or as engaged spectators and discussants. The nature and purpose of your experiential component is up to you, as is its positioning in the structure of your presentation, but it might do any of the following:

1. Engage your colleagues' attention and demonstrate the relevance of your research;
2. Encourage your classmates to put themselves in the shoes of the user group you have studied;
3. Enable them to understand some of the constraints members of your user group face in their personal and/or professional lives; and
4. Allow them to apply your insights in an imaginary setting.

Feel free to exercise your creativity, and take risks in designing your presentation.

You are encouraged to incorporate media and other sources of information; but the most important thing for you is to help your classmates understand, assimilate, and critique the assigned readings.

Each discussion group will be prepared to lead the class for 40 minutes plus additional time for Q&A.

DIVERSIFYING WIKIPEDIA

[Inspired by an assignment created by Dr. Miriam Sweeney (SLIS, University of Alabama)]

We all know that Wikipedia is a popular and often consulted resource. But how representative is it when it pertains to LIS and diversity? You are going to contribute to the Wikipedia corpus by selecting a topic related to *LIS and diversity* that is *not already present on the site.*

In the spirit of exploring the landscape of LIS, this assignment encourages you to investigate an area of LIS and diversity that is not covered in the course. You are free to select any person, place, collection, and the like, provided it *relates to diversity AND LIS.*

Your Wikipedia entry will be graded on how thoroughly it addresses the following criteria:

1. Provides a thorough overview of the topic, including background, current status, points of contention, or controversy
2. Provides resources for anyone who wants to know more about the topic (agencies and institutions, government resources, web resources, scholarly articles, news media, etc.)
3. Provides a list of references used for the site content (APA or MLA formatted)
4. Makes use of media resources (YouTube, podcasts, etc.) in a way that advances interaction with or understanding of the topic
5. Presents the information in an organized, accessible way

3-2-1 SUMMARIES

Select one *RESEARCH* article from the week's reading list (or if you are feeling ambitious, select a relevant article not listed on the syllabus), and write a short two-page response paper to the article. For your summary you will:

Requirement 1: Read an article, then choose and describe the *three* most important aspects (concepts, issues, factual information, etc.) of the reading, justifying your choices.

Requirement 2: Identify *two* aspects of the reading you do not understand, and briefly discuss why these confusing aspects interfered with your general understanding of the reading. Although you may identify more than two confusing elements, you must put them in priority order and limit yourself to the two most important ones.

Requirement 3: Pose *one* question to the text's author, the answer to which should go beyond the reading content and does not reflect the areas of confusion in requirement 2.

It is a good idea to use these papers as the basis for your class discussions/contributions.

LIBRARY SITE VISIT

Visit a library of your choice, a library that serves a diverse population in which you are interested. Prepare a one-page summary of your visit, and be prepared to give a 10-minute presentation in class. Please bring a flyer/advertisement/pamphlet/pathfinder, and the like from the library you visited to share with the class.

Sample questions/considerations include:

1. Introduce the library you visited and the diverse population they serve.
2. Do they serve that population well? If so, how?
3. Could their services/resources for this population be improved? If so, how?
4. How did what you encountered in this library influence your role as a future information professional?

MOCK GRANT PROPOSAL

You will be writing a (MOCK) grant proposal designed to serve your chosen diverse/underserved population (population to be cleared by the professor). Your grant will be set on the foundation of a community analysis and will be modeled on the format/structure of Institute of Museum and Library Services (IMLS) grants: https://www.imls.gov/grants. You may choose which IMLS grant to apply for as long as it will accommodate your user group.

Go through the IMLS guidelines carefully (including length and formatting), and prepare your grant as if you were actually going to submit to IMLS (who knows?! Maybe someday you will!). Also consult https://www.imls.gov/grants/apply-grant/sample-applications.

You will also be submitting a brief annotated bibliography (minimum of 8–10 sources) about your diverse/underserved population. This will inform your needs assessment/ community analysis.

DIVERSITY RESEARCH REVIEW

The Library Instruction Round Table (of the American Library Association) annually comes up with a list of the year's Top 20 articles written about library instruction: http://www.ala.org/lirt/top-twenty.

For this class, we will be coming up with a list of the *Top 10 list of DIVERSITY* related articles. As a group, students will act as a "jury," and the list will be compiled as a class resource.

The jury process will consist of two stages:

1. EACH JURY MEMBER will search (widely and deeply) for scholarly articles (*no* newspaper or magazine articles) related to diversity and/or diverse/multicultural/marginalized/underserved populations written in the last year, and determine which of the articles you would include on a Top 10 list. Your Top 10 list should include complete and properly formatted citations, a score for each article, and a brief annotation/rationale for each article's inclusion on the list.

2. The jury will compare their articles, and score sheets determine which of the articles as a group will make the final cut (the articles with the highest scores). This final list will include citations and the accompanying annotations. The jury would be advised to select a Chair(s) who will act as a potential mediator, your spokesperson, and will compile the one-page jury report that details your process.

Rubric for Selection of Diversity Top 10 Articles

You will use the following scoring guidelines:
(You may use fractions in your scoring, i.e., awarding a score of 3.25, 3.5, or 3.75.)

4 Strongly Recommended (Best)

This is a high-quality, well-written article that brings new knowledge to the field of library instruction. The article has unique and timely content, and it offers new insights for those involved in instruction.

3 Recommended (Very Good)

This article is well written and thoughtful. It might be of interest to someone who is new to library instruction, but it might be less interesting to someone more experienced in the field. Perhaps the topic has been discussed at great length in the past, and this article adds a little to the discussion.

2 Good Article (Good)

This is a good article, but it may not be appropriate for the Top 10 list. This article is not in-depth and does not contribute much to the literature on instruction.

1 Not Recommended

I would not recommend this article to be included in the Top 10 list. It falls short of what I would expect from articles in the Top 10 list.

Uncertain

I really am not sure how to rate this article. I would like to hear the opinions of others on the committee.

LIGHTNING TALKS

Diversity is a wide-ranging course of study with important implications for libraries. This assignment asks that you delve deeper into an area of diversity (one covered in class or another that you have discovered on your own) and focus specifically on how you feel it relates to services in libraries (feel free to tailor your topic to the type of library in which you aspire to work). You will need to clear your topic with your instructor before you begin.

You will deliver a *10-minute lightning talk* (think TED talk)—this will require a PowerPoint (or other type of media) presentation (specific directions on how to prepare/give a lightning talk will be discussed in class). Also, take a look at these resources:

1. How to Give a Great Ignite Talk: http://scottberkun.com/2009/how-to-give-a-great-ignite-talk/
2. So, You Want to Give a Lightning Talk? https://barriebyron.word press.com/2013/02/17/so-you-want-to-give-a-lightning-talk/

Your goals for giving a lightning talk include:

1. Creating a presentation that clearly and accurately describes your topic and makes a compelling argument as to how said topic is/should be incorporated into library services, sources, and practice;
2. Clear and appropriate use of presentation/media;
3. Evidence that the talk/presentation has been informed by the literature and class resources; and
4. Adherence to time limits!

ADVOCACY ESSAY

An advocacy essay is a specific and brief paper designed to gain support from your readers, encouraging them to support your specific cause or user group. This essay combines your thorough knowledge of an issue or user group (acquired through research), facts that can be easily recognized and referenced by your reader, and a healthy dose of emotional appeal.

For example, you are a (outreach/special collections, etc.) librarian and you want your library to earmark funds and personnel for a new initiative that will focus on resources for the (Latino/veteran/senior citizen) community. In order to secure buy-in from the powers that be, you will have 10 minutes to present to your department chair/director/dean/board of trustees, etc. and tell them why they should fund your project. You will also provide them a copy of your essay!

Once you have done a good amount of reading and research on your diverse population and have come up with an idea for a service or initiative, check the following site for ideas on how to compose your essay.

How to Write an Advocacy Essay: http://www.ehow.com/how_7779714 _write-advocacy-essay.html

MARKETING PLAN

The best resources, programs, and initiatives are rendered useless if the community is not aware of them and does not take advantage of them. Coming up with a great idea and getting support for it is only the beginning of the process. Programs and resources have to be effectively marketed to targeted communities.

Select your diverse population of interest, come up with a great idea to serve this community, and then devise a marketing plan—how will you market this great idea to this community?

For background, consult the following resources:

1. Effective Marketing Is No Accident: http://booksblog.infotoday .com/2013/04/effective-marketing-is-no-accident/
2. Marketing @ Your Library (ALA): Simple Steps That Will Help You Create @ Your Library Campaign: https://www.ala.org/ala/pio/ campaign/prtools/marketing_wkbk.pdf

And then take a look at the following resources for information about how to write up your plan:

1. How to Write a Marketing Plan: http://www.infotoday.com/mls/ jun99/how-to.htm
2. Library Marketing Plan Workbook: http://www.nmstatelibrary.org/ docs/development/planning/Marketing_Plan_Workbook.pdf

COMMUNITY ANALYSIS

Based on readings from the text—Grover, Robert, Roger C. Greer, and John Agada. *Assessing Information Needs: Managing Transformative Library Services.* Santa Barbara, CA: ABC-CLIO, 2010—you will be conducting a community analysis on the diverse community of your choice. Focus on your community of choice, and you may even limit your community by geography or other refining factors.

Consult these resources for additional information:

1. *Community and Library Services Analysis Tools (WebJunction):* http:// www.webjunction.org/documents/webjunction/Community_and _Library_Services_Analysis_Tools.html
2. IMLS Data Analysis Tools: http://www.imls.gov/research/data_analysis _tools.aspx
3. Library of Michigan, Community Analysis Resources: http://www .michigan.gov/libraryofmichigan/0,2351,7-160-18668_54901_18688 -52763—,00.html
4. Community Analysis and Needs Assessment (IFLA): http://www .ifla.org/files/assets/library-services-to-multicultural-populations/ publications/ifla-unesco-multicultural-library-manifesto_community -analysis.pdf

LONG-FORM BOOK REVIEW

[Adapted from an assignment created by Dr. Robin Kurz (SLIM, Emporia State University)]

For this assignment, I will provide a list of primarily nonfiction, biographical, and autobiographical books related to the topics covered in the class. Students will select a book on a "first-come-first-served" basis.

Students will then:

1. Read their selected books;
2. Complete further outside reading/research as needed; and
3. Write a long-form book review (1,500–1,800 words).

This style of review combines a narrative, descriptive, and analytical style to persuade readers to read the book. Through a close reading of the text, the reviewer tells the "story" of the book, identifying important passages that give deeper meaning to the thesis, as well as quoting from the text to provide factual authenticity, rather than opinion. Developing a coherent argument in favor of the book—not offering mere judgment—gives readers reasons why they should read the book itself. Although there is no investigative reporting or first-hand knowledge of the subject, these reviews are deeply researched. The books are chosen for complexity, relevance, value, and style.

—Description from
http://bookscover2cover.com/2014/06/longform/

For an example, please consult the course web page.

Detailed Instructions

1. Select a book you have not already read.
2. Please do not read any reviews of the book you select. It will just make it much more difficult to write your review.
3. On the Google form linked through the course web page, sign up for one of the titles listed.
4. Read the book, taking notes along the way.
5. Consult the following for more information:
   a. The UNC Writing Center: http://writingcenter.unc.edu/handouts/book-reviews/;
   b. The "Writing Book Reviews" pdf posted on the course webpage.
6. When you are ready to write, please consult the course writing guidelines detailed in the syllabus.
7. Name your file "Lastname Firstname Review" and save it often!

Professional Organizations, Conferences, and Initiatives Related to Diversity

These organizations focus in some way on diversity, culture, or social justice and are comprised of and/or serve professional librarians who engage in services to diverse populations.

American Indian Library Association (ALIA). American Library Association (ALA). http://ailanet.org

Asian Pacific American Librarians Association (APALA). ALA. http://www.apalaweb.org

Association of Specialized and Cooperative Library Agencies (ASCLA). ALA. http://www.ala.org/ascla/

ASCLA Library Services to the Incarcerated and Detained. Supports ALA members who serve patrons of any age who are held in jail, prison, detention or immigration facility. http://connect.ala.org/node/155875

ASCLA Library Services for Youth in Custody Interest Group. The purpose of this interest group is to advocate, promote, and improve library services for youth who have been detained in correctional facilities of various kinds. http://connect.ala.org/node/159343

Association of Tribal Archives, Libraries, and Museums (ATALM). http://www.atalm.org/

Black Caucus of the American Library Association. ALA. http://bcala.org.

Chinese American Librarians Association (CALA). ALA. http://www.cala-web.org

Ethnic and Multicultural Information Exchange Round Table (EMIERT). ALA. http://www.ala.org/emiert/

Gay, Lesbian, Bisexual, and Transgender Round Table (GLBTRT). ALA. http://www.ala.org/glbtrt/

Initiative to Recruit a Diverse Workforce. Association of Research Libraries. http://www.arl.org/leadership-recruitment/diversity-recruitment/initiative-to-recruit-a-diverse-workforce-irdw

Joint Conference of Librarians of Color (JCLC). The conference is sponsored by the five associations of ethnic librarians. http://jclc-conference.org

Lesbian, Gay, Bisexual, Transgender and Queer/Questioning Users Special Interest Group. International Federation of Library Associations and Institutions (IFLA). http://www.ifla.org/lgbtq

Library Services to Multicultural Populations Section. International Federation of Library Associations and Institutions (IFLA). http://www.ifla.org/mcultp

Library Services to People with Special Needs Section. International Federation of Library Associations and Institutions (IFLA). http://www.ifla.org/lsn

National Diversity in Libraries Conference. Association of Research Librarieshttp://ndlc.info.

Office for Diversity, Literacy, and Outreach Services. ALA. http://www.ala.org/offices/diversity

Progressive Librarians Guild (PLG). http://www.progressivelibrariansguild.org.

REFORMA, The National Association to Promote Library & Information Services to Latinos and the Spanish Speaking. ALA. http://www.reforma.org/

Social Responsibilities Round Table. ALA. http://www.libr.org/srrt/about.html

Spectrum Scholarship Program. Office for Diversity, Literacy, and Outreach Services. ALA. http://www.ala.org/offices/diversity/spectrum

Urban Libraries Council. http://www.urbanlibraries.org

Urban Libraries Unite. http://urbanlibrariansunite.org

Index

About the Author

NICOLE A. COOKE is an assistant professor at the School of Information Sciences at the University of Illinois, Urbana-Champaign, and a faculty affiliate at the school's Center for Digital Inclusion. She holds an MEd in adult education from Penn State and an MLS and a PhD in communication, information, and library studies from Rutgers University, where she was one of the first 12 ALA Spectrum Doctoral Fellows. She was named a "Mover and Shaker" by *Library Journal* in 2007 and was the 2016 recipient of the ALA's Equality Award.

Her research and teaching interests include human information behavior (particularly in the online context), critical cultural information studies, and diversity and social justice in librarianship (with an emphasis on infusing them into LIS education and pedagogy).

Her work has appeared in *Journal of the Association for Information Science and Technology (JASIST)*, *The Library Quarterly*, *Advances in Librarianship* series (Emerald), *InterActions: UCLA Journal of Education and Information*, *Polymath: An Interdisciplinary Arts and Sciences Journal*, *Library and Information Science Research*, *Information Research*, *New Review of Academic Librarianship*, and *The Library and Book Trade Almanac 2013*. Cooke has also coauthored *Instructional Strategies and Techniques for Information Professionals* (Chandos Press, 2012) and coedited *Teaching for Justice—Implementing Social Justice in the LIS Classroom* (Library Juice Press, 2017). Cooke is professionally active in several professional organizations, including ALA, ALISE, and ASIS&T.

Made in the USA
Monee, IL
21 January 2021